"Until the Christian world begins to read its own sources with the contemplative mind that is offered here, I see little hope for its in depth renewal. The argumentative mind that has dominated so much of our recent past has not served history well. Vincent Pizzuto is offering us both inspiration and very readable scholarship here. This is the Great Tradition!"

—Fr. Richard Rohr, OFM
Center for Action and Contemplation
Albuquerque, New Mexico

"Denizens of the land of silence owe a debt of gratitude to Vincent Pizzuto for the gift of this book. Clearly written and based on solid scholarship, grounded in Scripture itself, the author clarifies the simplest of truths: to become a contemplative is quite simply a matter of becoming fully normal. Paradoxically our becoming natural involves a lifetime of loves soul-sifting. As Meister Eckhart puts it: 'The eye with which I see God is the same eye with which God sees me.' One seeing, one loving, one knowing."

—Martin Laird, OSA
Professor of Early Christian Studies
Villanova University

"A magnificent, nutritious book of spiritual counsel, both visionary and compassionate! *Contemplating Christ* patiently trains us to rethink familiar texts, feelings, and attitudes by recovering the grandeur of the cosmic Christ from the Gospels, the hymn of Colossians 1, and the teachers of ancient Christianity. This work of mystagogy grasps anew the 'transgressive' power of the Incarnation that 'has made mystics of us all,' and offers practical ways to live into our wondrous 'divinized' identity after baptism. At the same time, it performs microsurgery upon our spiritual practices and predilections (its rethinking of asceticism and of demonic power is particularly fine). Like an ancient painting restored, vivid colors burst anew from the countercultural beauty of the Gospel. A feast for the spirit!"

—Michael Cameron
Professor of Historical Theology
University of Portland
Author of *Christ Meets Me Everywhere: Augustine's Early Figurative Exegesis*

Contemplating Christ

The Gospels and the Interior Life

Vincent Pizzuto

LITURGICAL PRESS
Collegeville, Minnesota

www.litpress.org

Cover design by Monica Bokinskie.
Cover art: "White Pine," mixed media on wood, by Jennifer Williams. Used with permission.

Library of Congress Cataloging-in-Publication Data

Names: Pizzuto, Vincent, author.
Title: Contemplating Christ : the Gospels and the interior life / by Vincent Pizzuto.
Description: Collegeville, Minnesota : Liturgical Press, 2018.
Identifiers: LCCN 2018005338 (print) | LCCN 2017048253 (ebook) | ISBN 9780814647295 (ebook) | ISBN 9780814647059
Subjects: LCSH: Mysticism. | Contemplation.
Classification: LCC BV5082.3 (print) | LCC BV5082.3 .P59 2018 (ebook) | DDC 248.3/4—dc23
LC record available at https://lccn.loc.gov/2018005338

To

Forrest

who loves to fetch sticks

"My dog is better than I am,

because he loves and does not judge."

~ Abba Xanthios, *Sayings of the Desert Fathers*

Contents

Acknowledgments ix

Introduction xiii

Chapter One
Words Made Flesh: *Scripture and the Interior Life* 1

Chapter Two
O! Happy Fault: *Salvation History and the Interior Life* 35

Chapter Three
Exile Interrupted: *Incarnation and the Interior Life* 65

Chapter Four
We Are Legion: *Asceticism and the Interior Life* 93

Chapter Five
Becoming Prayer: *Discipleship and the Interior Life* 136

Appendix
Mum's the Word: *The Origins of Christian Mysticism* 175

Glossary 183

Notes 189

Index 207

Acknowledgments

Behind the publication of every book there is a community of collaborators, supporters, and contributors, both past and present, who has helped bring it to fruition. I am grateful to all of my mentors and colleagues, who have formed me as a priest and theologian, and who have influenced in big and small ways the reflections throughout these pages. From Leuven, Belgium, to the University of San Francisco, to the Diocese of California—all of these institutions are filled with people who have shaped me, encouraged me, and supported me, and I will always be grateful.

Many thanks to Liturgical Press, especially to Hans Christoffersen, for your kindness, professionalism, and encouragement from the outset. You have been wonderful. And to Jennifer Williams, whose stunning and mystical landscape, *White Pine*, I am privileged to own and delighted to share—as it now graces the cover of this book.

Among those who have been present with me throughout the writing of this book, there are some whose outstanding dedication, support, and sacrifices I cannot fail to mention. First among them is Rose Levinson, who believed in this project even before I did, and whose love and friendship encouraged me to persist. To my dear friend Rev. Rachel Rivers, for your careful reading of my manuscript and your heartfelt engagement with me as you reflected thoughtfully and honestly on each of my chapters. This book is better because of you. To Monica Doblado, Lisa da Silva, Walter Tanner, Ann and John McChesney-Young, for your thoughtful critique. To John, especially, for the countless hours you have dedicated to assisting me with obscure translations and proper citations. Thank you for trying to hunt down the most famous things Meister Eckhart *never* said, and for doing so with humor, patience, and infinite kindness. And to Dominic Scheuring, my former student and research assistant at the University of San Francisco, who in the early stages of my writing helped invaluably in my research.

To my contemplative Christian community, New Skellig, whom I founded in 2006, and who has sustained me in the contemplative life ever since—*Beannaim Chriost ionat!* As we have grown over the years, your love, guidance, patience, and deep-down capacity to embody Christ in the world has remained a source of faith and joy for me.

To St. Columba's Episcopal Church and Retreat House in Inverness, California, for whom I serve as vicar—thank you for your encouragement and your patience as I have completed this work. I am hopeful that this book and the contemplative ministry we are building together will sustain one another in new and surprising ways in that uncanny "spiritual vortex" we call "St. Columba's."

Love and gratitude to my parents, whom I could always count on for completely biased, uncritical, and ever faithful encouragement (and who, if they could, would proudly hang this book on their refrigerator—even if hardly to understand a word of it).

And of course to my partner Fernando who did the laundry . . . and the chores . . . and the errands. Who for hours and days lived on the other side of a closed door so I would have what I most needed to complete this project: silence and solitude. Who, not so long ago, on a trek together through Cappadocia conceived the title *Contemplating Christ*, and whose love, support, and encouragement is written lavishly—even if secretly—on every page. As always and ever, you alone know the rest.

And finally, although he could never understand, I will be forever grateful to our little rescue pup Forrest whom I loved from the first. Forrest, who has taught me more about being in the present moment than any human teacher ever has, who in his silence has taught me the language of "being," who knows what it means to eat and snuggle and play with abandon, and whose utter simplicity is a virtue for which I will always strive. It is to him that I dedicate this little volume, that for as long as he lives, and for even longer after, all who take up this book might whisper his name in honor of the little sacrament who "rescued" me.

Introduction

The incarnation has made mystics of us all. What if we read the gospels as if that were true? This book is an attempt to do just that.

As an Episcopal priest and college professor, I have made a pastoral commitment to share insights from the Christian intellectual tradition with the broader church and society, especially from my own passionate interest in biblical studies and contemplative spirituality. Despite an abundance of accessible literature in both, most people in our churches today remain completely unaware of the modern methods of interpretation that inform our understanding of the Scriptures, and have no idea that there is an ancient and integral contemplative tradition within Christianity. As a result, whether teaching or preaching from the tradition, I am often confronted with the same question, "Why have we never heard this before?" Mixed with excitement and regret, questions like this betray a hunger for a more thoughtful interpretation of the Bible and a deeper intimacy with the beauty of Christian faith.

In response, I simply point to what is most beautiful and central to Christian faith: *the incarnate Christ*. In doing so, it is my hope that those who seek to live a contemplative life in the world today will be given a deeper appreciation of the Scriptures and the distinctive heritage of the Christian mystical tradition. Too many are still unaware of the treasure trove of resources available to them. Centuries of witnesses, beginning with Scripture itself, up through the present day, convey the spiritual wisdom of those who have given their lives over to contemplating Christ in a commitment to meditative prayer, asceticism, and a radical fidelity to love.

Much of the popular literature that has surfaced in the areas of Scripture and spirituality over the past several decades is insightful, though at times oversimplified, no doubt in order to be made more accessible to a lay readership. I am attempting to walk something of a thin line in this presentation of the same. On the one hand, I wish to minimize as far as possible the depth of insight that is inevitably lost when a long and complex tradition is too readily simplified for the sake of accessibility. On the other hand, I have written this book not primarily for the academic community but for the broader Christian church, and more specifically for those who long, even vaguely, for a more sustained commitment to a kind of contemplative interiority for which there is so little support or even awareness in many of our churches today. Perhaps something of the reader's spiritual life may be rekindled (or dare I hope, set ablaze!) not by this book, but by the beauty of the Christian contemplative life that they discover through it.

However, if we are to read biblical texts with a view to the interior life, writing to a broad readership presents a unique challenge. There is a vast amount of scholarship in both disciplines to which I cannot presume all will have had equal exposure. I have attempted to address this in two distinct ways in order to increase the reader's theological understanding of biblical interpretation and CONTEMPLATION in service of deepening their meditative practices.

First, in anticipation of certain theological terms with which some readers may not be familiar, all words appearing in SMALL CAPITALS can be found in the appended glossary so as to advance the reader's basic comprehension of the primary themes. Becoming familiar with new concepts will help to connect the reader to a world that otherwise remains distant and off-putting.

Second, my citations will be kept to a minimum and appear at the end of the book rather than at the bottom of every page. Most of these are simply references to my sources, with only a few that serve as explanatory comments. This should leave the more casual reader unencumbered with details that may be of less interest, while those who wish to explore further resources will find them readily accessible.

The purpose of this book, then, is threefold. First, to explore central themes of the contemplative life for modern Christians through the lens of New Testament readings—most especially the gospels. Second, to reflect on what is unique to Christian MYSTICISM, particularly as this comes to expression in the interrelated doctrines of INCARNATION and DIVINIZATION. Third, to offer a variety of ways in which these aspects of the contemplative life might become actualized, or more so "embodied" in each of us through contemplative practice.

To that end, the first chapter provides an overview of the theology of DEIFICATION by exploring the relationship between the Scriptures and Christian mysticism. Deification is an ancient Christian doctrine that affirms the belief that through the incarnation, through which God took on human nature, so too humanity has been made "partakers of the divine nature" (2 Pet 1:4). I will explore the most prominent scriptural passages that support this doctrine and its implications for the Christian contemplative life.

Building upon the theology of deification, chapter 2 will reflect on the incarnation as the divine response to the human condition of alienation as portrayed in the biblical narrative of Adam and Eve (Gen 2–3). We will look at the real-world consequences of humanity's mythical "exile from paradise" and how the various aspects of the Eden myth inform a Christian understanding of the human EGO, the human struggle with insatiable longing, and the near-universal fear of mortality. In exploring the interplay between myth and history, I will explain how the incarnate Christ, whose presence permeates the cosmos, shifts the dynamic of the interior life for the Christian contemplative. The spiritual life can no longer be understood as humanity in search of God, but God in search of humanity.

Chapter 3 turns to the INFANCY NARRATIVES of Matthew and Luke, as well as the prologue of John, to reflect on the incarnation as the historical moment in which God interrupts humanity's perceived exile in an inconceivable offer of divine-human intimacy. An extended interpretation of Luke's parable of the Prodigal Son (Luke 15:11-32) will offer parallels with the Eden myth, now read through the lens of the incarnation. Understood now, not only as a past moment but an interior reality in the heart of the contemplative, the incarnation marks an end to our exile from Eden not because we have found our way back, but because God has united divinity with humanity in our deification.

Having established this union with God as a *fait accompli* through the incarnation, the fourth chapter is devoted to our struggle with our inner "demons" that prevent us from living fully into the reality of our deification. The chapter reasserts the necessity of the ascetical life for Christian contemplatives while redefining the role, purpose, and practice of asceticism for the modern church. Drawing from the rich history of ascetical practice in Christianity, I will redefine modern approaches to asceticism as a commitment to the "love of the beautiful." A love of beauty, however, not as the world defines it, but as the Gospel reveals it, especially as symbolized most starkly in the cross.

The final chapter weaves together the threads of the previous themes in an exploration of "contemplative discipleship" as the embodiment of prayer. For contemplatives living in society the relationship between prayerful solitude and active engagement in the world is explored through Meister Eckhart's interpretation of Mary and Martha in Luke 10:38-42. Here the theme of deification is extended to his unavoidable conclusion: discipleship is not about us serving Christ but Christ serving others in us. The interior movement of becoming an authentic disciple is a movement by which oppressive boundaries between oneself and others are transgressed and ultimately dropped, until one drops the greatest obstacle of all: the perception of separation from others. As deified members of Christ's body, or "other Christs" in the world, discipleship is patterned on the paschal mystery by which we all must take up our cross and die to self so that Christ might rise in us.

This work has been a long time in the making and I am happy to bring it to completion, or at least to that point where I might offer it to those who would be inclined to spend some time with it. Yet, I am well aware that what I have written here will remain static even as my intellectual interests and spiritual life continue to evolve. In some ways, I both hope and dread that ten or twenty years from now I will look back upon this work with some sense of embarrassment—much as an adult blushes when reading his or her childhood journal.

But whatever brings me to that future place of greater intellectual and spiritual maturity, it will not be without the responses of those who read this book. Indeed, I am poignantly aware that this work should end more properly with a question mark than a period. It is intended to be more inquisitive than authoritative, to invite questions rather than propose once-for-all answers. It is but one voice—and a small one at that—in a much broader conversation. But at its heart is a sincere, and—if I might admit—a loving attempt to share with you the beauty and joy I have come to know in my brief lifetime of contemplating Christ.

Chapter One

Words Made Flesh

Scripture and the Interior Life

We are talking about God; so why be surprised if you cannot grasp it?
I mean, if you can grasp it, it isn't God. Let us rather make a devout confession of ignorance, instead of a brash profession of knowledge.
Certainly it is great bliss to have a little touch or taste of God with the mind; but completely to grasp him, to comprehend him, is altogether impossible.

—St. Augustine of Hippo, Sermon 117.5

The ideas I lay out in this chapter are not easy to grasp but are beautiful to behold. I have struggled for many months with how to write this chapter and where to locate it in the overall scheme of the book. In many ways, it forms the lens through which to read all the chapters that follow. For that reason, I had to put it up front or risk all manner of explanatory tangents in subsequent chapters. There is very little in Christian theology or spirituality that can be unfolded in a linear fashion. One must be content to come into clarity in bits and pieces, much as the picture of a jigsaw puzzle comes slowly into view only as various fragments are assembled independently then joined together in ever larger segments. But the first thing most of us do when beginning to assemble a jigsaw puzzle is to look at the picture on the front of the box. Knowing what the completed puzzle will look like helps us tremendously in our task.

This chapter is my attempt to show you the big picture on the front of the box, that is, to familiarize you with the spiritual terrain we will explore throughout this book. Some of you may find this chapter to be technical or academic. But really, it is just *theological*, an example of what St. Anselm calls "faith seeking understanding." In my ministry as a priest and professor I have repeatedly encountered a real spiritual hunger and intellectual curiosity for something more than the standard parochial education our churches have afforded us. There are times when I have preached or lectured on a simple insight from the wisdom of our tradition and have received in response such unexpected reactions from my listeners. People will tell me they were astounded, deeply moved, even amazed by a particular concept or idea I shared with them. These experiences overwhelm me with a deep sadness. "Is that all it takes?" I think to myself. Are we, as a faith community, so intellectually and spiritually impoverished as to find ourselves spiritually satisfied with such a little morsel of insight? Our faith is a veritable feast of ideas, insights, and wisdom, but so many of us know nothing more than the scraps we have received in childhood.

This book is an attempt to speak to that intellectual curiosity and that spiritual hunger. With Augustine, I want to help my readers "to touch or taste God with the mind" all the while recognizing that "to comprehend is altogether impossible." If you are used to scraps, you may find the presentation of ideas in this chapter a bit overwhelming. If so, go slowly and give yourself time to digest it. You do not need to consume everything in one sitting. Once we have even a basic understanding of these ideas in place, the remaining chapters will more vividly come alive.

Allow me to offer just a few guidelines as you begin. First, you may not come away from this chapter with a perfect understanding. Most all of what I introduce here will resurface again later in the book as we go about assembling our jigsaw puzzle. Gradually the fuller picture will come into view. Second, when I introduce new ideas, I will usually repeat them to help you digest the concept. If a particular sentence seems difficult to grasp, rather than get hung up on it continue to the following sentence, where I will often try to convey the same idea in other words. Third, and most of all, enjoy learning about these new ideas. I have written this chapter because the theology is not only fascinating but beautiful. And not only beautiful but transformational. Many of you may encounter a dimension of Christian faith you have never seen before. If so, be patient with yourself as you try to embrace it—or, better, allow it to embrace you. I would venture to guess, if you returned to this chapter after reading the whole book, you would see just how far you have come in your own understanding.

In what follows, I will attempt to address common perceptions or difficulties contemplatives may encounter when first learning to meditate on the Scriptures. The Bible presents nothing of what we might call a technique or method of prayer. Yet, it is integral to the Christian contemplative as both a source of rumination and the foundation of the doctrine of the incarnation on which Christian mysticism is based. As we begin to flesh out the relationship between the Scriptures and the contemplative life, I will at the same time attempt to show how the Scriptures themselves demand we look beyond the sacred page to Christ revealed in our very flesh and bones.

Cracking the Geode

Have you ever heard someone refer to the Bible as a "page turner"? Me neither. Because the Bible is distanced from us historically, culturally, and linguistically it can often seem foreign and inaccessible, with little to satiate the modern spiritual interest in meditative techniques and esoteric wisdom. It is difficult to discern a unified spiritual vision or consistent ethic among its various books. The biblical endorsement of archaic social structures and worldviews often offends the very ethical and spiritual commitments these same Scriptures inspire among Christians today. For contemplatives in particular, the Bible may seem less of a spiritual oasis and more like a literary wilderness with little to offer the interior life of prayer. Yet within its pages God draws near to us, even as we find ourselves ever more distant from the ancient world in which its words were penned.

Perhaps the Bible is less like a precious gem whose natural luster lures us in and more like a geode—those rather unappealing if not unsightly rocks that must be cracked open in just the right manner to reveal an unexpected display of color and crystalline beauty. How, then, might the contemplative begin to crack open the Scriptures in order to peer deep into the transformative beauty contained within? In other words, how might we approach the gospels in a way that grounds the life and practice of contemplative Christians today?

Modern methods of biblical interpretation have made unprecedented strides in bridging this historical divide. It is as if we have been standing over an archeological site for centuries without picks or shovels or brushes. But new interpretive tools developed since the Enlightenment have unearthed aspects of Scripture to which we never before had access. We now know more than ever about the historical context in which the Scriptures were written, the theological intentions of the authors who wrote them, the interests of the audiences for whom they were written, and the manner in which the original texts of Scripture were copied and transmitted to later generations of Christians. Without engaging in the technicalities of these methods themselves, I will incorporate the insights we have gleaned from them whenever doing so will advance the spiritual interests of this book. Collectively called historical criticism, these modern methods of interpretation have been designed predominantly to reconstruct the past. While essential for sound interpretations, they remain inadequate for those who approach the Bible as a place of encounter with God in the present.

As Olivier Clément observes, the need to transmit the "archaic mentality" of Scripture to our own day justifies these scientific methods of interpretation. But, he concludes, "Science cannot give a meaning. . . . The meaning is revealed only to prayer."[1]

My focus is thus not on a critical examination of Scripture but on a prayerful rumination on the interior life informed by the gospels and the Christian mystical tradition. In other words, this book is not as much a contemplative commentary on the Bible as it is a biblical commentary on the contemplative life. The biblical narratives presented for reflection arose out of the contemplative interests I am seeking to address. For example, how does the incarnation serve as the divine response to humanity's search for God? Moreover, what is the role of asceticism, discipleship, and meditation for the Christian contemplative? It is this broader horizon, revealed only to prayer that will claim our attention throughout this book.

Slatted Fences

Some time ago I recall walking along a mountain road with a steep incline to one side, and to the other an extended slatted fence that stood some eight feet high. The wooden slats were rather wide but with only a few millimeters of space in between each of them. By any estimation the fence appeared a solid obstacle. In an effort to discover what lay on the other side, I shifted my focus from the slats to the thin spaces between them, and as I continued to walk past the fence I was suddenly able to see well beyond it, out onto a landscape that was immeasurably more expansive than the mountain road on which I was walking. I wondered how many had traveled this way before and never known the vastness of the landscape that lay beside them all along. The fence at once *concealed* and *revealed*, simply depending on my perception.

The Scriptures are much like that fence. What they conceal or reveal depends largely on shifts in our perception or where we place our focus. Ultimately, however, our sacred texts stand only at the perimeter of something that extends far beyond them. If we cannot peer beyond that perimeter we may "look and look but never perceive, listen and listen but never hear" (Matt 13:13-16). For the contemplative the words of Scripture, like the slats of the fence, serve both as delineators and as pointers. They delineate a uniquely Christian shape to the interior landscape of the heart. Yet, we must be attentive to the thin spaces, pregnant with meaning, that open up between them. Without those spaces—those imperceptible silences—the words would become confused and difficult to tell apart. And this is of great importance as we embark on what we might call a contemplative reading of the gospels. The fence—that is, the literary and historical context of a gospel—shapes the contour of the interior landscape but is not itself the destination.[2]

The image of the Magi whom we encounter in the opening pages of the New Testament may serve as a guiding metaphor. These archetypal pilgrims set out, much as we do now, on a sacred quest in search of an epiphany. And as with all pilgrims, we must walk simultaneously in two directions: the exterior and the interior. Two directions that are but one in Christ. For, in Christ there is no spiritual apart from the material, no movement toward God that is not at once a movement toward others. Contemplatives are not content to examine the gospels with the critical distance of an outsider but ruminate from deep within their hearts where that same star of the Magi might guide them to an inner epiphany of Christ. Thus, the gospels we read, the fence through which we peer, the pilgrimage on which we embark, ultimately lead not to a place but to a person.

Here we touch upon the uniqueness of Christianity among the world's monotheistic religions. At its center is neither a holy place, nor a sacred book, nor a revered symbol, but an embodied person, a human heart—that of Jesus of Nazareth whose Spirit indwells and pervades all and in whom all things are reconciled and unified (Col 1:20). As we will see, in Christ all perceptions of our separation from God and others are exposed as illusory. The name the gospels give to the historical realization of this unity is the "kingdom of God," best understood not so much as a location or future promise but as a present reality constituted by a new vision of human relationships rooted in the ministry, and more so the person, of Jesus himself. The kingdom is thus both an interior reality (Matt 5:3) and a historically tangible one (Matt 25:31-46). This union of the spiritual and the tangible reflects a uniquely Christian mysticism rooted in the incarnation.

The extent to which one can speak of Christian mysticism has been a subject of ongoing controversy. But this very question brings us to the heart of this chapter. What is Christian mysticism? How is it related to the incarnation? And what are the implications of this for the contemplative? In response, we must examine the intersection between scriptural interpretation, the doctrine of deification, and how these inform a contemplative reading of Scripture. Any one of these subjects could easily fill volumes of literature and still remain incomplete. Given my commitment to keep this book accessible to a wider audience, even as I strive to expand the reader's understanding of these themes, this chapter will necessarily remain incomplete. It is an attempt to lay the foundation for concepts that will be expanded and further clarified over the course of the book. I will begin by dispelling the most prominent misconceptions about Christian mysticism.

What Christian Mysticism Is Not

There is no universal definition of mysticism (see the appendix, "Mum's the Word: The Origins of Christian Mysticism," on p. 175, for a brief history of how mysticism became associated with Christianity). The term has become so loosely adapted to a spectrum of interpretations as to render it virtually meaningless. As a result, the subject of mysticism is generally surrounded by misconceptions that often evoke a variety of reactions ranging from rejection to suspicion to fascination. The spectrum of responses among Christians is no less polarized. It is looked on by some as an aberration of the faith and by others as the most authentic expression of Christian life and practice. I learned the hard way not to use the term "mysticism" loosely. On first mention, I have had college students and parishioners alike mistake mysticism for referring to Ouija boards and séances. But Christian mysticism has nothing to do with the occult, nor does it center on any kind of paranormal phenomena such as visions, dreams, locutions, levitations, or premonitions. As a whole, Christianity has never focused on esoteric practices or disciplines, nor is it primarily concerned with altered states of consciousness or otherworldly phenomena.[3] While there is no scarcity of numinous experiences reported by Christian saints and mystics, these experiences, when determined to be authentic, are peripheral at best and believed to be for the benefit of the broader community of faith rather than for the sole advantage of an individual.

Today, the fascination with so-called mystical experience is no doubt influenced by an increasingly therapeutic culture prevalent throughout much of Western secular society. Reflective of this, popular forms of meditation often center around personal health benefits, pain management, stress reduction, improved concentration, professional success, or better sleep habits. All of these are touchstones or entry points into the practice of meditation. For example, Mindfulness draws on the fundamental principles of meditation that lie at the foundation of most all traditional forms of practice. Deep breathing, good posture, the cultivation of silence, and interior attentiveness—these skills are all but universally recognized as the foundational components of meditation that different faith traditions have variously built on.

Traditionally, Christian contemplative practice has not emphasized meditation as a method of self-improvement but more so of self-forgetfulness. It has been less about what one experiences during prayer and more about how one is transformed through prayer. In other words, spiritual growth is not measured by the extent to which one experiences mystical phenomena or personal health benefits but by the extent to which one increasingly reflects the image of God (*imago Dei*) in the world (Gen 1:27).

In fact, the contemplative Christian tradition is nearly unanimous in its suspicion of mystical phenomena. The quiet simplicity of self-emptying prayer before God can easily erode into a lesser desire for an ecstatic experience of God. A meditation bereft of spiritual consolation is often the purest form of prayer because it is offered for its own sake. There is an ever-present risk of pursuing sensations that seem spiritually edifying but that have nothing to do with one's transformation into Christ. To guard against this temptation, the prevailing wisdom cautions the contemplative to consider mystical phenomena as like being touched by a flame. If the experience is genuinely of God, the scorching heat of the fire will immediately have its intended effect. There is no need to linger. If the fire is not of God, then it is but a bright light of distraction that serves no purpose but to reduce authentic prayer into a kind of spiritual thrill-seeking. In this case, there is even less reason to linger. And since it must be the community and not merely the individual who ratifies the authenticity of a mystic, we are left with the same prescription. Whether a mystical experience is of divine origin or mere mental distraction is often impossible to discern, and therefore those who commit themselves to a life of contemplative prayer should always and everywhere prefer simplicity and quiet, emptiness and tranquility over the fanfare of spiritual visions and consolations.

By way of analogy, imagine a woman is rushed to the hospital with appendicitis. She complains of intense pain in her side and after being examined by the doctor is admitted to surgery. Under the care of her surgeon she is anesthetized and the appendix is removed. Upon waking she is told the procedure was successful and she is well on her way to recovery. Imagine if she began to argue the surgery could not possibly have been successful because she did not experience the doctor's healing work during the time of the procedure. To this the doctor could only reply, "But do you feel better now? Is the pain gone? Is the diseased appendix removed? Has there been a transformation of your health for the better?" Clearly, the success of the surgery is based not on what the patient experienced *during* the operation but on the transformation of her condition afterward. So it is with contemplative prayer. One may not be conscious of the transformative work of the Spirit during prayer but the effects of that transformation are increasingly evident in the manner in which one outwardly embodies the love of Christ in the world.

Thus, Christians have largely dismissed the notion that the purpose of contemplation is to achieve altered states of consciousness. It is not. It is about living more deeply into a present state of consciousness. As Eugene Peterson observed, "The contemplative life is not a special kind of life; it is the Christian life, nothing more but also nothing less. But *lived*."[4] Yet, if it is that simple—that universal—why for so many does life seem empty? Why do so many feel an inner void rather than a sense of fullness or completeness? What does Peterson mean by "the Christian life" and how is this reflected in an authentic Christian mysticism?

Christian Mysticism: The Continuing Incarnation

Through the historical incarnation of Jesus of Nazareth, humanity, and by extension the universe, has been made one with God. This is essentially what it means to say Christianity is a mystical tradition. This is the interior truth to which the Gospel invariably leads us and the reason why it is called "Good News." The summit of the Christian life is the fullness of life in Christ, a fullness that cannot be attained by our own efforts, only accepted as a given. It cannot be achieved, only received as pure gift, pure grace. Thus, the contemplative life is not simply about adopting meditative methods and techniques but about entering into an interior silence that deepens our relationship with the triune God who dwells within. Contemplatives are integral to the life of the church and the world not because of any claims to so-called mystical experiences but because of the fullness with which they commit themselves to the Incarnate One. "I have come that they might have life and have it to the full" (John 10:10).

The mysticism of Christianity is a gritty mysticism—one that is earthy, elemental, and rooted in this-worldly experience. It is inseparable from Christ—the Word-Made-Flesh—and is thus inseparable from Earth and flesh. This grittiness is celebrated in the opening address of the First Letter of John:

> Something which has existed since the beginning,
> which we have heard, which we have seen with our own eyes,
> which we have watched and touched with our own hands,
> the Word of life—this is our theme.
> That life was made visible;
> we saw it and are giving our testimony,
> declaring to you the eternal life,
> which was present to the Father and has been revealed to us.
> We are declaring to you
> what we have seen and heard,
> so that you too may share our life.
> Our life is shared with the Father
> and with his Son Jesus Christ.
> We are writing this to you so that our joy may be complete
> (1 John 1:1-4; NJB).

The fullness of divine revelation begins with a historical encounter, with One who "existed since the beginning," yet whom we have "heard" and "seen," "watched" and "touched" in the flesh. The incarnation is after all *embodied* revelation, and the Body of Christ is the locus of God's revelation in whom "the whole fullness of deity dwells bodily" (Col 2:9). Thus, the telltale signs of a life lived in intimate union with God are not disembodied experiences of spiritual ecstasy but "life to the full" and "joy complete." Beyond a historical encounter with the embodied Christ, the New Testament points to a union with God that does not cease to be embodied but extends well beyond what we might call an "I-Thou" relationship. That is, beyond a relationship between two distinctive subjects—myself and God—toward a relationship that might be described as a kind of "shared subjectivity" or mutual "participation." In other words, we do not merely encounter Christ as a historical figure or an outsider, but we discover ourselves to be participants in his incarnation, which continues in and through us. Raimon Panikkar calls this the *incarnatio continua*, the "continuing incarnation."[5]

The eleventh-century monk, Symeon the New Theologian expresses something akin to the *incarnatio continua* through an eloquent poem that celebrates our own awakening to Christ embodied in us:

> We awaken in Christ's body
> as Christ awakens our bodies,
> and my poor hand is Christ, He enters
> my foot, and is infinitely me.
> I move my hand, and wonderfully
> my hand becomes Christ, becomes all of Him
> (for God is indivisibly
> whole, seamless in His Godhood).
> I move my foot, and at once
> He appears like a flash of lightning.
> Do my words seem blasphemous? — Then
> open your heart to Him
> and let yourself receive the one
> who is opening to you so deeply.
> For if we genuinely love Him,
> we wake up inside Christ's body
> where all our body, all over,
> every most hidden part of it,
> is realized in joy as Him,
> and He makes us, utterly, real,
> and everything that is hurt, everything
> that seemed to us dark, harsh, shameful,
> maimed, ugly, irreparably
> damaged, is in Him transformed
> and recognized as whole, as lovely,
> and radiant in His light
> he awakens as the Beloved
> in every last part of our body.[6]

Perhaps the most striking thing about Symeon's imagery is the degree to which Christ's body and ours are one and the same. It is not merely that Christ dwells in us but that Christ is "infinitely me." Symeon can hardly bring himself to distinguish between Christ's body and his own, as each "awakens" to the other. Further still, Christ who is "indivisibly whole" and "seamless" is therefore present full and entire in every part of oneself. Symeon beckons us to "wake up inside Christ's body" so that every part of us that is hurt, dark, shameful, ugly is not eradicated but transformed as we are made whole and beautiful in Christ. Such is the love of Christ. Such is Christ our Beloved.

As Symeon's poem celebrates with stunning candor, deification is the Christian way of naming our intimate participation in Christ's body, or rather Christ's participation in ours (cf. Heb 2:14). It is the inevitable outcome of the incarnation—a union that is mystical precisely because it is embodied.[7] The fourth-century bishop, Athanasius of Alexandria, penned what is the simplest and most celebrated formulation of deification: "God became human that humans might become God."[8] This is what Irenaeus of Lyon called "the wonderful exchange" (*admirabile commercium*) because it asserts that, in and through Christ, God and humanity *exchanged* their respective natures.[9] In other words, the incarnation does not end with the death of Jesus. Having taken upon himself human nature and exchanged with us his own divine nature, Christ continues to be embodied in us even now as risen Lord.

The intensity and immediacy of this bodily union with Christ goes beyond poetry and metaphor to something expressed in the Christian doctrine of DEIFICATION. Also known as THEOSIS or DIVINIZATION, these terms literally mean "to become God" or "to become Divine." Here again lies the grittiness of Christian mysticism and, as we will see, the cornerstone of our contemplative approach to the gospels in the chapters that follow. If the doctrine of deification really is the inevitable outcome of the incarnation, we should be able to approach the Scriptures in a way that illuminates the mystical heart of Christian faith: namely, that through the incarnation we have become "partakers of the divine nature" (2 Pet 1:4). Moreover, through incorporation into the mystical Body of Christ (1 Cor 6:15) we have ourselves become what Christian tradition calls "other Christs" (*alteri Christi*) in the world. The vocation of the Christian, then, is not to be "good" but to become God.[10] To realize oneself as "another Christ" is to awaken in Christ's body, to live fully as partakers of his divine nature so to become for others extensions of his ongoing presence in the world. That is, to be in our own unique way what he was in his earthly ministry: the presence and love of God in the world. This is not a vocation we attain apart from Christ but one that he attains through us, in the Spirit, by whose power we are made members of his own body.

This is the culmination—or TELOS—of Christian faith. The Greek word *telos* means "end," as in the ultimate aim or purpose for which something is intended. In other words, something reaches its *telos* when its purpose is fulfilled or has come to fruition. And the *telos* of Christian faith is the revelation that through Christ's incarnation our union with God has been made so complete that we actually share in God's divine nature. Authentic Christian mysticism is thus inseparable from the incarnation (God-made-human) and deification (humanity-made-God). That is to say, mystical union with God has been achieved through the incarnation by which God took on human nature and as a consequence humans are graced to participate in the divine nature. The fruition of the Christian contemplative life, then, is to embody Christ who has *already* become the very flesh of our flesh.

While flesh (Gk. *sarx*) itself might be subject to corruption and decay, in Christ the body (Gk. *soma*), physicality, materiality can never ultimately oppose God because the incarnation is, after all, *embodied* revelation: "The Word was made flesh and dwelt among us" (John 1:14; cf. 1 John 1). From the moment Mary conceived in the womb by the power of the Spirit, the Word-Made-Flesh never ceased to be incarnate—even now as Risen Lord. In other words, the incarnation refers not only to the birth of Jesus but more fully to the life, ministry, death, resurrection, and ascension—or what we refer to simply as the CHRIST-EVENT. That is why Christian spirituality can never be conceived apart from the material universe. Nor can the incarnation be limited to a singular moment that occurred in the past but, by the power of the Spirit, remains an ongoing and ever-expanding reality. As Anthony Kelly observes,

> Incarnational faith is not confined to the empty tomb, nor to the past history of episodic appearances of the Risen One. For his ascended Body is the limitless sphere of the church's present mission and eschatological hope, with Christ present to his disciples in every time, place, and nation.[11]

It is through the Christ-event that Christians understand the meaning of all that precedes him in salvation history and all that proceeds from him. Thus, Vladimir Lossky's assessment that the incarnation is the point of departure for all Christian theology does not undermine the significance of the Paschal Mystery but is in fact the only way to make sense of it.[12] There is an intimate link between Christ's incarnation, passion, ascension, and the descent of the Spirit at Pentecost, which can never be understood apart from one another. In an ancient cosmology where Heaven was "up," Hades was "down," and Earth was caught in between, we can understand the metaphorical language with which the early church grappled to say something meaningful about Christ's glorified body (Acts 1:9-11). But the era of Christ's appearances in the New Testament did not give way to a distant or absent Jesus now ascended into another *place*. Rather, here we glimpse the trinitarian dimension of salvation: the ascension of Christ to the Father, inextricably linked to the descent of the Spirit. If God is omnipresent, then what else is the ascension but the attribution of that same omnipresence to Christ? Precisely insofar as he is "seated at the right hand" of an omnipresent God (Mark 16:19), Christ too must be understood not as having gone *anywhere* but having gone *everywhere*.

Again, as Kelly rightly observes, "Jesus' risen and ascended life is a new phase of the incarnation, it promises a new mode of presence rather than the blank fact of absence. . . . That is to say the bodily resurrection and ascension of Christ inaugurates a new expansion of the incarnation and, consequently, a new way of relating to Christ (Col. 3)."[13] That new way of relating to Christ is ushered in by the descent of the Spirit at Pentecost, whose deifying presence forms the very sinews of Christ's body among the members of the church. The tradition of discrete appearances of the risen Christ dissipates not because Jesus has gone away to some distant heaven but because he has made of us his very body through grace. Insofar as the church is the Body of Christ, we might also understand it as the embodiment of the Holy Spirit in the world. The promise of Christ to be present whenever "two or three gather" in his name is not the promise of a separate presence but a presence constituted by the Spirit, in the very gathering itself (Matt 18:20). So, Kelly concludes:

> The Holy Spirit comes not as a substitute for a lost incarnation but as the transforming agent of its expansion. The Spirit, active in the conception of Jesus in the womb of the Virgin Mary, is working in every stage of the ongoing incarnation of the Word—in Christ's life, death, resurrection, and ascension. . . . When the Body of Christ is understood in its expansive totality, it includes the whole church and even the materiality of the whole universe.[14]

The deification of humanity—grounded in the historical inbreaking of the Word-Made-Flesh—has expanded to embrace the entire cosmos in a continuing incarnation. Christ is the pivotal moment in the evolution of the cosmos and in the history of salvation, through which everything that comes before and after is thrown into sharp relief. As we will see, if humanity is already divinized, so too by extension must be the universe, which is not merely a temple or sacrament of the Divine but the cosmic Body of Christ of which we are members and extensions. Put otherwise, the Risen Christ is the Cosmic Christ who has woven for himself the body of Creation, in whom "we live and move and have our being" (Acts 17:28). This is the meaning of Christian mysticism.

The fact that most Christians today would be confused and even scandalized by this almost unqualified union between Christ and humanity as expressed in St. Symeon's poem marks a radical failure of the church to communicate to the modern world its greatest spiritual treasure: *The incarnation has made mystics of us all.* In its wake, the modern invention of biblical literalism has rushed in to fill the void. As a result, Christianity has been reduced to a new kind of Pharisaism centered on moral scrupulosity and obsessed with personal salvation. Unable to see Christ immanent in one's own body, in material flesh, in creation itself, Christ remains a distant overlord rather than the Cosmic Christ whose life-giving energy pulsates through every living atom. Having forfeited the cosmic dimension of salvation history, we have no way of conveying what it means that in Christ heaven and earth interpenetrate the other. That all ground is holy ground. All water is holy water. All bread is Eucharist. All life—*not merely human life*—is sacred. The cosmos is itself a sacrament and the church a microcosm of the universe. Thus, Henri de Lubac sees in the church the sacrament of Christ's continuing incarnation: "If Christ is the sacrament of God, the church is for us the sacrament of Christ; she represents him, in the full and ancient meaning of the term, she really makes him present. She not only carries on his work but she is his very continuation."[15]

Oliver Davies has argued that the loss of this cosmological consciousness within Christianity was largely a result of the advance of the sciences over the past five hundred years, during which time the material world was ever more ceded to the realm of science, and spirituality was increasingly restricted to the internal and subjective:

> So deep were the changes brought by the new cosmology, over a period of centuries, that much of Christian theology has come to depart, often in profound ways, from the sensible emphases

> which characterized the classical tradition. . . . [And thus] . . . overwhelmingly the trajectory has been and continues to be one which leads *away* from the material as such.[16]

Our contemporary understanding of the cosmos and our place in it begs for new theological interpretations that cannot be ignored. The immensity of an evolving universe does not threaten or diminish Christian faith but provides a new and exciting context for exploring it. Theology—especially the study of Scripture—is never done in a vacuum but has always taken place in a particular philosophical, historical, political context from which we draw new imagery, advance new insights, and glean new perspectives. The new cosmology opened up by the modern sciences is no exception. The theological trajectory away from the material, lamented by Davies, is unsustainable. This is why a growing number of theologians today are seeking to bring theology into dialogue with the sciences. In a cosmos now deified in Christ, Christianity is essentially *mystical* precisely because it is incarnational. It is spiritual precisely because it is inseparable from the material. The interior life of the contemplative cannot be bifurcated from the physical universe. Theology and cosmology can no longer be segregated. Each informs the other.

Christian tradition has long observed that there are two books of scripture: the "big book," which is Creation, and the "little book" which is the Bible.[17] Having the same Author, these two books can never ultimately contradict one another.[18] Thus, if science is able to provide us new and clear evidence about the evolution of the universe and the interdependence of all things, these insights from the big book of scripture provide a compelling context for reinterpreting the little book with fresh eyes and new questions. Attention to cosmology throughout this book is not superfluous but necessary if we are to understand Christian mysticism as deification revealed in the materiality of the incarnation. We turn then to the role of Scripture and its relationship to the very doctrines through which Christian mysticism has been made explicit.

Contemplative Readings of Scripture: Incarnation, Deification, and Mysticism

The capacity for the Bible to serve as the basis for Christian mysticism emerges naturally, even inevitably, within the gospels themselves because they lay the foundation on which Jesus Christ is revealed as the embodiment of divine-human union. *Emmanuel*—God-with-us—becomes a cornerstone for the development of a Christian theology of union with the Divine (Matt 1:23).[19] The New Testament witness of Jesus Christ introduced rich theological tensions that later Christian tradition would seek to resolve. If God is one, how can Jesus and Spirit be divine? What does it mean to say that Christ is truly human and truly divine? How can titles and attributes that belong only to God now be used of Jesus and the Spirit: Creator, Redeemer, Lord? The early church addressed these tensions through the development of Christian doctrine. The uniquely Christian experience of God now as Father, now as Son, now as Spirit, culminated after nearly four centuries in the development of the doctrine of the Trinity. This came to authoritative expression in the Nicene Creed, which should be understood not as a description of God (which would be idolatry) but as a Christian way of modeling our experience of God who transcends description of any kind.[20] It is mystical truth expressed in precise theological language.

Thus, to speak of God as "Trinity" (three-and-one) is something akin to what Denys Turner would call self-subverting language: the use of language to establish a logical contradiction.[21] God cannot logically be *both* three and one in a numerical sense. The attributions are mutually exclusive, forcing us to recognize the profound failure of human language to grasp the divine. Thus, the doctrine of the Trinity is at once an attempt to model the uniquely Christian experience of God as essentially relational even as it forces us to recognize that no language is adequate of God. As the great sixth-century architect of Western Christian mysticism, Pseudo-Dionysius, observed, we should not think some ways of speaking about God are more right than others. Better to say that some ways of speaking about God are less wrong than others—and doctrine is no exception.

Nevertheless, doctrinal language holds a privileged place in theological discourse and shares a kind of circular relationship with Scripture that might be compared to a seed and the fruit it bears. Scripture is the seed and doctrine the fruit. Just as an orange seed once planted and nurtured will inevitably produce an orange, never a banana or a papaya, the witness of Scripture inevitably leads to the development of the doctrines that are now foundational to our theology. In other words, we discover the true potential of the seed through the fruit it bears. To smell the fragrance of an orange blossom, to taste the fruit of the tree, tells us far more about the seed than the seed itself. This is why, for example, the church's most universal summation of the doctrine of the Trinity in the Nicene Creed makes no mention of Jesus' ministry:

> For us and for our salvation
> he came down from heaven,
> and by the Holy Spirit was incarnate of the Virgin Mary,
> and became man [human].[22]
> For our sake he was crucified under Pontius Pilate,
> he suffered death and was buried . . .

The reason for this leap from the birth of Jesus to his death is because the creed is not a summary of the gospels but a frame or lens through which the life and teachings of Jesus in the gospels are to be interpreted. In other words, arising out of sustained reflection on the Scriptures, the creed articulates a precise theological model of the Trinity based in scriptural revelation but is not itself a definition. This is why, in his treatise *On the Trinity*, St. Augustine of Hippo must admit, "When it is asked 'Three what?' then the great poverty from which our language suffers becomes apparent."[23] Despite the "great poverty" of our language, for the Christian, *this* is the way of modeling God that makes most sense of scriptural revelation and its inherent theological tensions. And therein lies the circularity of spiritual interpretation. Reflection on the Scriptures leads to mystical truths that come to expression in the formulation of doctrine. These doctrines then become the lens through which we better understand the Scriptures themselves.

This too is how we should understand the doctrine of deification. Like all authentic doctrine, it has grown inevitably out of Scripture, and as a result has become a way to understand the Scriptures themselves more richly. For example, the confession Christ "came down from heaven . . . and became human" is as central to the doctrine of the Trinity as it is to deification. On the one hand, it clarifies the trinitarian nature of salvation, but it also confirms the union between God and humanity as a divine initiative, not a human achievement. This is central to Christian mysticism because it establishes divine-human union as universal in scope and a *fait accompli.*

Contemplatives intentionally live more deeply into the fullness of that union—not as a special class of spiritual elites, but in solidarity with all. Like spokes on a wheel that are furthest apart at the circumference but move closer together toward the center until they converge at the hub, so the movement toward God is at once a movement toward others. The interior and exterior pilgrimage is one and the same. This is because deification, or what Panikkar calls "Christophany," bears a twofold meaning: "The humanization of God corresponds to the divinization of Man. Christ is the revelation of God (in Man) as much as the revelation of Man (in God). The abyss between the divine and the human is reduced to zero in Christ."[24] We will take up this theme again in chapter 2, but first we turn to a brief selection of scriptural sources for the doctrine of deification.

We have looked at three images of Scripture that, when taken together, help to clarify the relationship between Scripture and the contemplative life. Scripture is like a geode that at times must be carefully pried open to reveal its inner beauty, hidden beneath a sometimes dull and antiquated exterior. It is like a slatted fence that points far beyond its surface to a vast interior landscape. And it is like a seed, sometimes bitter to the taste because of its cultural, linguistic, and primitive worldviews but, when cultivated in the heart, produces fruit that is both sweet and spiritually nourishing. A review of the foundational passages so central to Christian thought on deification should heighten our appreciation for Scripture as a resource for the contemplative. Each of these passages a geode, each a slatted fence, each a fertile seed if only we have eyes to see. While the following passages do not exhaust the scriptural witness to deification, they are central and by many estimations primary.

Partakers of the Divine Nature (Gen 1:26; Ps 82:6; John 10:34-35; 2 Pet 1:4)

Paul Collins makes the case that the constellation of passages including Genesis 1:26; John 10:34-35; and 2 Peter 1:4 "provide the strongest basis for a theology of deification."[25] To this we should add Psalm 82 to which John 10 makes reference. I will discuss these collectively, starting with the first three references cited below, and then take up 2 Peter afterward. The emphases in the following citations are my own.

Genesis 1:26

> Then God said, "*Let us make humankind in our image, according to our likeness.*"[26]

Psalm 82:6-7

> I say, "*You are gods,*
> children of the Most High, all of you.[27]
> nevertheless, you shall die like mortals,
> and fall like any prince."

John 10:34-36

> Jesus answered, "Is it not written in your law, 'I said, you are gods'? If those to whom the word of God came were called 'gods'—*and the scripture cannot be annulled*—can you say that the one whom the Father has sanctified and sent into the world is blaspheming because I said, 'I am God's Son'?"

Christian interpretations of Psalm 82:6-7 seem to begin as early as the second century with Justin Martyr. He interprets these verses as references to Adam and Eve, who before the fall were immortal (gods) but who having fallen like Satan (i.e., the "prince") now "shall die like mortals." Thus, Justin argues, as children of the Most High all humans are worthy of becoming gods, as were Adam and Eve, and each are to be judged according to their own actions.[28] Justin's interpretation of Psalm 82 centered around the growing interest among Christians to find messianic references in the Jewish Scriptures. Increasingly, the psalms and other Old Testament texts were interpreted as prophetic allusions to Christ or the church.

Stephen Thomas points out that the term "gods," as used in ancient Jewish literature, had multiple meanings. It referred to the false gods of the nations whom Israel was forbidden to worship: "you shall have no other gods before me" (Exod 20:3). As such, the absolute uniqueness of the God of Israel made clear that no human could ever become "God" in that unqualified sense. But Thomas also notes that the term "gods" referred to those heavenly beings believed to make up the divine council of heaven, as we see in the opening verse of Psalm 82, "God has taken his place in the divine council; in the midst of the gods he holds judgment." But more important, based on Genesis 1:26 ("Let us make humankind in our image, according to our likeness") Thomas observes, "There was, then, already in Judaism the idea that human beings can be 'heavenly beings' while at the same time living an earthly life."[29]

But as we have seen, the Christian reception of its first Scriptures from Israel was also accompanied by a unique and distinctive lens for interpreting those Scriptures: the person of Jesus of

Nazareth. Naturally, this led to interpretive debates and an ever-widening gap between Jews and Christians about the meaning and significance of those texts. The interpretation of Psalm 82 is no exception. In the decades following Justin Martyr, Irenaeus of Lyon would link the reference to "gods" in Psalm 82 with those who had been incorporated into Christ through baptism.[30] By the early third century, Clement of Alexandria made this association between "becoming gods" and Christian baptism explicit:

> Being baptized, we are illuminated; illuminated we become sons; being made sons, we are made perfect; being made perfect, we are made immortal. "I," says He, "have said that you are gods, and all sons of the Highest." This work is variously called grace, and illumination, and perfection, and washing.[31]

Clement's reference to "grace," "illumination," and "perfection" gradually become associated (and even synonymous) with the language of deification in later church fathers—many of whom emphasize its association with baptism ("washing").[32] Thus we see in the works of Justin, Irenaeus, and Clement a growing Christian tradition of interpreting Psalm 82:6-7 as a summary of the Creation and Fall of humanity and its restoration in Christ as attested to in John 10:34-36. This interpretive tradition might be summarized as follows:

God created humanity to be immortal children. But God's creative intentions were disrupted when, through disobedience, Adam and Eve attempted to become gods apart from God. As a result, divine-human intimacy was lost, and with it immortality itself. The human condition became defined as one of alienation, corruption, and death. However, reading Psalm 82 in light of John 10:35, the early fathers affirmed that "scripture cannot be annulled." That is, God's original plan for humanity could not ultimately be thwarted by human folly. Thus, imbuing the psalms with prophetic significance, Psalm 82:6 was understood to have been fulfilled in the incarnation. Jesus is the immortal and incorruptible Son of God in whom the fate of Adam is recapitulated and humanity restored to immortality. This new humanity was celebrated among those baptized into Jesus' death and resurrection. The language used by Paul to describe this new humanity was "adopted children of God" (Rom 8:12-23, 29; 2 Cor 6:16-18; Gal 3:26-29; 4:4-7; Eph 1:5) and by John, "reborn children of God" (John 1:12-13; 3:3).[33] This becomes one of the earliest scriptural seeds from which the doctrine of deification would grow.

The final text in this constellation of scriptural witnesses to deification is found in 2 Peter 1:4:

> Thus he has given us, through these things, his precious and very great promises, so that through them you may escape from the corruption that is in the world because of lust, and may become *partakers of the divine nature.*

As we have already seen, the phrase "partakers of the divine nature" should not be interpreted to imply a full-blown theology of deification. It is a seed from which that later doctrine would grow but is not itself the fruit. Stephen Finlan offers a concise history of early interpretations of 2 Peter 1:4 and concludes that the author of the epistle likely had in mind "ethical character" and "proper belief" as the preconditions that lead to the "inculcation of 'the divine nature.' "[34] In other words, right behavior and participation in the communal life of the church leads one to increasingly participate in divine character traits. However, reading 2 Peter in light of the broader testimony of Christian interpretation of Psalm 82 pushed the theology of deification beyond a mere participation in divine "character traits" to that "wonderful exchange" of divine and human natures on which the doctrine of incarnation would ultimately insist. So much so that the phrase "partaking of the divine nature" would become synonymous with deification itself.

By the time we reach the fourth century, Augustine has introduced the idea of the "whole Christ" by which he demonstrates something very near to Panikkar's *incarnatio continua*, that is, the expansive nature of the Mystical Body of Christ:

> Now, however, I wonder if we shouldn't have a look at ourselves, if we shouldn't think about his body, because he is also us. After all, if we weren't him, this wouldn't be true: *When you did it for one of the least of mine, you did it for me* (Mt. 25:40). If we weren't him, this wouldn't be true: *Saul, Saul, why are you persecuting me?* (Acts 9:4). So we too are him, because we are his organs, because we are his body, because he is our head, because the whole Christ is both head and body.[35]

Neither of Augustine's references to Matthew 25 and Acts 9 are intended in their context to articulate doctrine, yet both are early scriptural witnesses that would contribute to the weight of evidence in favor of the full development of the doctrine of deification. In both verses, the movement toward God and others is again one and the same direction. We should note as well that in both verses deification is already assumed regardless of whether the "little ones" (Matt 24) or the "disciples" (Acts 9) had themselves *realized* they were deified. Thus again, deification is not based in something we achieve, nor are we required to be conscious of it. It is rendered whole and entire by the incarnation. The contemplative life is but the manner in which we come to know that reality in our lives. But if the incarnation has made us partakers of the divine nature, so too must we see Christ in others (Acts 9), and not only see Christ but reverence and serve him in others (Matt 25). Once we awaken to the reality of our participation in the whole Christ, Jesus' testimony in John's gospel might finally be fulfilled: "On that day you will know that I am in my Father, and you in Me, and I in you" (John 14:20).

"Why Do You Persecute Me?" (Acts 9:4)

Following Psalm 82 and its associated verses, I want to briefly expand on Augustine's reading of Acts 9:4 in conjunction with two other New Testament witnesses so that we may better appreciate them as contributions to the Christian understanding of deification. In particular, how might these texts be more richly interpreted through the doctrine of deification in a way that informs the life of the contemplative today?

It is impossible to know with certainty the experiences that inspired Saul to develop his theology of Christ's body. But it is reasonable to surmise he was informed by his experience of the Risen Christ on the Road to Damascus as recounted no less than three times in Acts of the Apostles and alluded to throughout the Pauline epistles as well.[36] In each of the accounts in Acts, the risen Christ posed the question, "Saul, Saul, why are you persecuting *me*?" (cf. 9:4; 22:7; 26:14). As we have already noted, Augustine sees in this question a corporate reference to the "whole Christ," by which is meant Christ's disciples, the members of his body. Augustine elaborates on the meaning of this question for his understanding of deification:

> For Christ is not in the head or in the body, but Christ is wholly in the head and in the body. Therefore, what his members are, he is; but what he is, his members are not necessarily. For if he were not his members, he would not have said, "Saul, why do you persecute me?" For Saul was not persecuting him, but his members, that is, his faithful on earth. Yet he did not want to say, my saints, my servants, or the more honorable, my brothers, but "me," that is, my members for whom I am the head.[37]

As Augustine observes, the corporate nature of our deification is implicit in Paul's first encounter with the Risen Christ. Before we are saints or servants, sisters or brothers, we are incorporated members of his body. Contemplative discipleship, or any form of authentic Christian vocation, cannot be fully realized apart from this theological foundation. For many of us, our first encounter with Christ is as a historical figure whose word we hear through the gospel but whose living presence remains elusive. A Word that demands we go places we would rather not go, transgress boundaries that otherwise provide us a sense of safety and identity, and keep vigil in the midst of the world's darkness. We may well find ourselves drawn to this Word, even as we continue to resist it as foreign and threatening. Even Paul initially found the nascent church threatening to his own religious identity and sought to suppress its message. Recall that, according to Acts, Saul approved of the killing of the first Christian martyr, Stephen, and began "ravaging the church by entering house after house; dragging off both men and women, he committed them to prison" (Acts 8:1, 3). It was not until his transformative encounter with the Risen Christ that Saul would be led toward a new interior awareness of himself as a member of Christ's body. It was sometime after his inner transformation that Saul adopted his Roman name, Paul, to better assimilate himself throughout the gentile world (Acts 13:9).

Paul's initial opposition to Christ exemplifies the FALSE SELF and its agenda to keep Christ at a distance by reducing Christianity to a set of external rules and observances that we can fastidiously perform, all the while convincing ourselves of our righteousness before God without ever entering into an interior relationship with the risen and indwelling Christ. As we will see in chapter 4, Paul's assertion that he was "crucified with Christ" is a necessary precursor to its corollary, "It is no longer I who live but Christ in me" (Gal 2:19-20). Life in Christ is always preceded by a kind of death to self, to one's passions and attachments. Indeed, the cross stands at the center of Christian asceticism because it exposes the false self and its tyrannical demands, so that dying to our attachments Christ might rise in us. However, the Christian spiritual life is not reducible to ascetical practices any more than it is to the application of gospel teachings to our lives. If this were the case, Christianity would be tantamount to a reinvented Pharisaism (cf. Gal 5:18) and Paul would just as well have remained Saul. The application of Gospel teachings to our lives can only be a first—and at best a rudimentary—step toward the full flowering of contemplative discipleship realized as Christ alive in me.

"You Are Members of Christ's Body" (1 Cor 12:12-27)

Regardless of its origins, Paul's theology of the church as the Body of Christ holds out a near-perfect paradigm for understanding the Christian doctrine of deification. His theology is rooted in the historic Christ-event and at the same time preserves the *incarnatio continua* as an ongoing corporate reality without denying or confusing the manner in which an individual participates in the divine nature. In other words, Paul's theology holds in tension the idea that each of us are members of Christ's body and thus are really and truly deified. But none of us are individually the whole of Christ's body. That can be said only of the historical Jesus who continues to be incarnate as Risen Christ, through his body, the church (Col 1:18). We partake in Christ's divinity through the grace of the incarnation—the mingling of divine and human natures. It is through this lens that we can properly understand Paul's theology of Christ's body found variously throughout his epistles but spelled out perhaps nowhere more clearly than in 1 Corinthians 12:12-27:

> For just as the body is one and has many members, and all the members of the body, though many, are one body, so it is with Christ. For in the one Spirit we were all baptized into one body—Jews or Greeks, slaves or free—and we were all made to drink of one Spirit. Indeed, the body does not consist of one member but of many. If the foot would say, "Because I am not a hand, I do not belong to the body," that would not make it any less a part of the body. And if the ear would say, "Because I am not an eye, I do not belong to the body," that would not make it any less a part of the body. If the whole body were an eye, where would the hearing be? If the whole body were hearing, where would the sense of smell be? But as it is, God arranged the members in the body, each one of them, as he chose. If all were a single member, where would the body be? As it is, there are many members, yet one body. The eye cannot say to the hand, "I have no need of you," nor again the head to the feet, "I have no need of you." On the contrary, the members of the body that seem to be weaker are indispensable, and those members of the body that we think less honorable we clothe with greater honor, and our less respectable members are treated with greater respect; whereas our more respectable members do not need

> this. But God has so arranged the body, giving the greater honor to the inferior member, that there may be no dissension within the body, but the members may have the same care for one another. If one member suffers, all suffer together with it; if one member is honored, all rejoice together with it. Now you [*humeis*] are the body of Christ and individually members of it.[38]

While modern English does not convey a distinction, the Greek pronoun "you" in verse 27 is plural (*humeis*). Thus, we might paraphrase verse 27: "You people are together the body of Christ and each of you are individually members of it." Paul's language is precise. Apart from Jesus, no individual can independently or autonomously claim to be Christ. To be "another Christ" is to be a member of Christ's body, an extension of the one Christ in the world. Without sacrificing the absolute transcendence of God, the relationship between God and humanity in Christ can no longer be envisioned as an infinite distance or radical break but an organic participation. Deification does not eradicate our humanity but perfects it. Divinization does not diminish our individuality but fulfills it. Yet, there is a corporate reality to deification that Kelly touches on with regard to Paul's theology of the Body:

> For Paul . . . the Body of Christ is the sphere of the new creation. It implies something more than a sociological metaphor, for it looks to an incorporation of his "members," as body-subjects, into the transformed Body in its present vital relationship to the reality of the universe of space and time. Paul pushes Christian consciousness toward a distinctive realism in this regard. However this might be articulated, it goes further than any facile metaphorical application.[39]

As a "body-subject" I am a member of Christ's body, but Christ is not a member of my body. My unique identity can neither stand apart from that greater identity nor make any sense without it. Nor can we accurately look on anyone or anything apart from this fuller picture. The "distinctive realism" to which Paul "pushes

Christian consciousness" is to live into one's deeper identity as an ALTER CHRISTUS in the world. Beyond my own individuality, beyond my own distinctiveness as a nose, ear, or hand on the Body of Christ, my greater, fuller, and truer identity is that of the body to which I belong: Christ. If I am an ear, it can only be as an ear *on the Body of Christ.* If a hand, it can only be as a hand *on the Body of Christ.* The unity of Christ's Body does not eradicate my unique identity but fulfills and perfects it in the "fullness of communion" of all things. It is a "unity-in-difference" that cannot be reversed.

"I Am the Vine, You Are the Branches" (John 15:5)

Finally, then, drawing from the natural world, John 15:5 holds out a beautiful insight about deification that emphasizes the organic continuity between the incarnate Christ and humanity. Jesus says to his disciples,

> I am [*ego eimi*] the vine, you are the branches. Those who abide in me and I in them bear much fruit, because apart from me you can do nothing.[40]

The simplicity of this image should not be underestimated. Much as branches extend in organic continuity with the vine, so too does humanity share a continuous relationship with Christ. Likewise, deification does not eradicate the distinction between humanity and divinity as some have feared but takes the scriptural and doctrinal attestation of the incarnation to its unavoidable conclusion: we are extensions of Christ in the world. Where God ends and creation begins is marked not by an interruption but is a fluid continuum by which humanity has been grafted into the very life of God through the incarnation. Like Paul's theology of the Body, we cannot reverse the direction of this life-giving relationship. One cannot say, "I am the vine and Christ is the branch; cut off from me Christ can do nothing," for this would obscure the meaning of deification in light of Christian revelation. While the relationship between vine and branch is organic, it is also asymmetrical. The life of the branch is utterly dependent on the life of the vine, much as our divinization is dependent on Christ as its source.[41] To be cut off from the vine is death.

We should notice also that the language Christ uses in John 15:5 is present tense. He did not say, "I *will* be the vine and you *will* be the branches," but "I *am* [*ego eimi*] the vine and you *are* the branches." Thus, whatever we make of Christian salvation, it is not merely a future-oriented reality. The union between God and humanity is fully revealed in Christ and already accomplished in creation. Neither does the incarnation remain an abstract union of "natures"—human and divine—but is embodied in nature itself. Put otherwise, the metaphor of the vine and branches is not concerned with later theologies about the abstract union of natures in Christ, but speaks instead to the immediacy of deification as a realized union of persons—one's own person with that of Christ. Indeed, what good is an intellectual abstraction if I do not realize that I myself embody Christ in the world? Harkening back to the poem of Symeon the New Theologian we might then pray in our own bodies:

> Make my hands Your Hands, my feet Your Feet, my heart Your Heart. Let me see with Your Eyes, listen with Your Ears, speak with Your Lips, love with Your Heart, understand with Your Mind, and serve with Your Will. I commend to You my whole being; make me Your other self.

Reading from the Inside Out

Sometimes we do not understand the meaning of our story until we tell it. For in its telling, the spoken word becomes incarnate in us—embodied, as it were. A contemplative reading is embodied insofar as we realize the gospels are not only told *to us* but, more important, told *through us*. They are not merely iterations of past events but narratives that speak to one's own interior encounter with God—or, rather, God's encounter with us. The gospels can never be fully understood from the outside looking in, because they were written for participants, not spectators, and thus to apprehend their deepest meaning, we must allow them to draw us in and *inward*. If deification remains but an abstract theological concept we have not yet touched on the transformative power of the gospel.

There is a story from the Desert Mothers and Fathers that conveys the power of embodying even one verse from Scripture. When Abba Pambo was still a young apprentice he approached one of the Elders to learn a psalm. The elder began with Psalm 39: "I said I will take heed of your way, that I offend not with my tongue." After hearing this first verse, Pambo departed without waiting to hear the second half of the verse. He said to himself, "This one verse is sufficient if I can practically acquire it," by which he meant to realize the text in himself, to embody it. It was more than six months before he would visit the elder monk again. When he did, the elder admonished him for his long absence. But Pambo explained the reason he had been gone so long was that he had given himself over completely to the one verse the elder had given him but confessed he had still not been successful. After many years, one of Pambo's companions asked whether he had ever mastered the verse, to which he replied, "I have scarcely succeeded in accomplishing it even after nineteen years."[42]

Pambo's earnestness exemplifies what it means to read the Scriptures from the inside out. Virtually every passage from Scripture contains within it the entire Gospel. By acquiring one particular verse from a psalm, Pambo had to embody the whole Gospel. Because in order not to speak ill of someone, he had not to think ill of them. In order not to think ill of them, he had to not judge them. In order not to judge them, he had to be compassionate. In order to be compassionate, he first had to see his own need for compassion. In order to see his own need for compassion he had to admit of his own sinfulness. In order to admit of his sinfulness, he had to be humble. And in order to acquire true humility, he had to love God and his neighbor as himself. And upon this, says Christ, "hang all the law and the prophets" (Matt 22:37-39).

The relationship between the Scriptures and the modern contemplative is no less demanding. Those who strive to embody the

Scriptures must approach them not merely with the critical distance of a historian but with the receptivity of a disciple, not as a tourist but as a pilgrim. While critical readings of Scripture are invaluable as a source of theological *information*, an embodied reading seeks spiritual *transformation*. Rooted in the incarnation, the apex of an embodied reading is nothing less than the realization of oneself as an *alter Christus*. The point is not to arrive at a definitive interpretation of the text but to arrive at a more intimate relationship with the interior Christ. The gospels, after all, were written not that we might *know about* Jesus but that we may *know* him who continues to be incarnate in us. Echoing the pattern of the incarnation, contemplative silence for the Christian rises up in the midst of the Word, not apart from it.[43] "In the beginning was the Word . . . and the Word was made flesh" (John 1:1, 14). So too do the words of Scripture enter the silence of our own flesh.

Here again we are reminded of the slatted fence, comprised of the words of Scripture and the spaces between them. Silence amid the word. Beyond is an interior terrain replete with mountain peaks and misty valleys, rocky vistas and dense forests. Yet nothing is as it seems. Union with God is not achieved by human efforts to climb the mountain peaks but by Christ's descent into the misty valley of human history. Each of us must walk the interior landscape of the gospel in the solitude of our own hearts, only to realize that as members of Christ's body we never walk in isolation. We must each find our own way along the path of contemplation, if only to discover Christ is the Way. To touch on the gift of one's deification is to realize the gospels are not ends in themselves but point invariably to Christ within. "You search the scriptures because you think that in them you have eternal life; but it is they that testify to me" (John 5:39).[44]

Chapter Two

O! Happy Fault

Salvation History and the Interior Life

Midway upon the journey of our life
I found myself within a forest dark,
For the straightforward path had been lost.

—Dante Alighieri, *The Divine Comedy*

In my personal study, there hangs a reproduction of Giovanni di Paolo's famous fifteenth-century painting *The Creation of the World and the Expulsion from Paradise*, which, as its title suggests, seamlessly portrays the dual scenes of creation and the exile from Eden. Reflective of Renaissance cosmology, a two-dimensional earth dominates the lower left of the portrait, surrounded by concentric circles depicting the orbits of the sun and celestial constellations. In the upper left an anthropomorphic image of God, basking in golden light and held aloft by angels, points conspicuously toward the creation below. To the right of the portrait Adam and Eve take their first steps into exile, escorted by an angel in the foreground of a lush garden reminiscent of Dante's depiction of paradise in *The Divine Comedy*.

Artistically compelling, I have found di Paolo's masterpiece to be a rich source of contemplative rumination, vividly capturing that moment in which Christian tradition recalls humanity's "fall from grace." Di Paolo brings us to the threshold between life and death, full of tragedy and regret, alienation and loss, but without which we can hardly begin to appreciate the unbounded joy, eternal hope, and fullness of life held out by the Gospel. The first steps of Adam and Eve into their exile is at once the first step along the human pilgrimage back to God, or, rather, God's pilgrimage back to us. For the Christian, exile does not end in return but in the embrace of a God who rushes out to greet us while we are still on the way. Indeed, each of us is an Adam and Eve caught up in the divine embrace long before we realize it. Thus, the disastrous impulse of humanity's rejection of divine intimacy has come to be glorified throughout Christian history as the "necessary sin," the "happy fault" that provoked an unbounded—indeed incomprehensible—response of God's love and compassion:

> O truly necessary sin of Adam,
> destroyed completely by the Death of Christ!
> O happy fault
> that earned so great, so glorious a Redeemer!

So proclaims the Easter Vigil in a solemn chant known as the *Exsultet*, which commemorates the history of salvation through the all-encompassing lens of Christ's life, death, and resurrection. As we will explore below, the *Exsultet* does not evoke a historical Adam whose "necessary sin . . . earned so great, so glorious a redeemer." We are still in the realm of myth where the poetic impulse of a jubilant faith celebrates in one archetypal figure the universal significance of the incarnation for all: "where sin did abound, grace did abound the more" (Rom 5:20). Despite the prevailing view among many in the Western church, we are not bound to the conclusion the incarnation was an afterthought in the mind of God to reverse the unforeseen consequences of humanity's fall. Neither does the *Exsultet* require a strictly anthropocentric interpretation, as the cosmic orientation of the Vigil makes clear.

The universe is not merely a backdrop for the story of human salvation but is its object. Creation, incarnation, and deification are three inseparable moments in one continuous story of salvation. In other words, incarnation and deification are built in to the very plan of creation and bring it to its perfection. While the cross of the redeemer may well be the consequence of a fallen world, the singular catalyst for the incarnation is a love unrestrained and "hidden for ages in God who created all things" (Eph 3:9):

> The love of God knows no limits and cannot reach its furthest limit in the fullness of the divine abnegation for the sake of the world: the Incarnation. And if the very nature of the world, raised from non-being to its created state does not appear here as an obstacle, its *fallen* state is not one either. God comes even to a fallen world; the love of God is not repelled by the powerlessness of the creature, nor by his fallen image, nor even by the sin of the world: The lamb of God, who voluntarily bears the sins of the world is manifest in him. In this way, God gives all for the divinization of the world and its salvation, and nothing remains that he has not given. Such is the love of God, such is Love.[1]

Indeed, Paul assures us, "God proves his love for us in that while we still were sinners Christ died for us" (Rom 5:8). But if we are to contemplate deeply the uninhibited love of God in Christ we cannot ignore humanity's capacity for sin. If the human experience of divine alienation is typified in the mythical fall of Adam, the cross reveals the historical response of God who has fallen even lower still. So low, in fact, that forever after all human falling would be "a falling into him."[2] Here we encounter the heart of the gospel, the "condescension" of Christ, as it were, from its literal meaning "to descend with." The Philippians hymn speaks eloquently of the incarnation as an act of divine condescension in which Christ empties himself (KENOSIS) in radical identification with a fallen humanity, descending into the depths of suffering and despair "even unto death on a cross" (Phil 2:6-11).

At the center of the Christian contemplative life stands the scandal of the cross, the chief witness and paradigm of Christ's posture toward the very world into which he emptied himself: arms outstretched, vulnerable, and embracing the darkness that sought to destroy him. The scandal of this descent is the scandal of a God who has transgressed the abyss between divinity and humanity and is revealed in Christ not as emperor of the universe but as "crucified love."[3] Thus, if at times there is a sustained attention on the reality of darkness within the pages that follow, it is only to expose its impotence in light of the joy and power of the Gospel. "The light shines in the darkness, and the darkness could not overpower it" (John 1:5). The self-emptying of Christ crucified and risen lays bare the way of the Christian contemplative whose vocation it is to confront darkness both within themselves and in the world not through resistance, or worse retaliation, but by *absorption*. For Jesus, the consequence of this posture was his own death, which thereby rendered impotent the very darkness that railed against him. The practice of contemplative prayer is thus a kind of death-to-self through which each of us discovers that "it is no longer I who live, but Christ in me" (Gal 2:20).

There is a seventh-century hymn titled "Creator of the Stars," traditionally chanted at Vespers during the season of Advent. The hymn poetically captures this same Divine pathos that draws God near to us in the incarnation:

> Thou grieving that the ancient curse
> should doom to death a universe,
> did save and heal our ruined race
> By healing gifts of heavenly grace.[4]

Here, as in the Easter Vigil, the coming of Christ to heal the one human "race" is situated in the broader context of creation, much like di Paolo's own portrait of the expulsion. God grieves not only over the plight of humanity but for the fate of a "cursed universe," thus prompting the outpouring of divine love that brings the "healing gifts of heavenly grace" in Christ. The language of this hymn is inescapably archetypal, reminiscent of the great myths—both ancient and modern—where cosmic battles are waged between forces of good and evil. It is the universe that is under siege, an entire race destined for ruin. Yet, we must not fail to recognize here the fundamentally optimistic view that Christianity holds out toward the human condition. The divine response to the malady of sin is not condemnation but healing grace. Grace, which is nothing other than the very presence of the Spirit in the midst of our own brokenness and suffering.

Darkness and Beauty

While there can be no naïve denial of the human capacity for hatred, injustice, and violence, Christianity insists that these have neither the first nor the last word in a cosmos that God has deemed good and beautiful (cf. Gen 1:31). Perceiving this fundamental goodness, the Christian contemplative is one who falls in love with beauty and comes to embody that beauty through one's engagement in the world. Indeed, it is the vocation of the contemplative to shed the obstacles that prevent us from seeing truth and beauty in all.

It is all the more tragic, then, that Christianity has become associated in the popular mind with a body-hating worldview or with certain forms of doctrinal rigidity, institutional hypocrisy, scientific ignorance, and religious intolerance—assessments that too often bear merit. The rise of modern atheism in the West along with the precipitous decline in church attendance must be understood, at least in part, as a purifying corrective to the spiritual, moral, and imaginative failures of our religious institutions.[5] The consequence of these failures is the church's diminishing capacity to convey beauty. It is, after all, beauty that attracts the human spirit and beauty that compels the human conscience toward the good, not the dry, rigid formulas of doctrine, nor the clinical dissection of biblical texts, nor the ethical demands to love even before we ourselves have been made to understand not only that we are lovable (that is far too cliché) but that we are indeed *love itself.*

Without a commitment to a deep spiritual practice, the ability to recognize oneself and the world as begotten by love is too often masked by the scandalous proliferation of injustice, violence, and suffering. In our own day, global environmental degradation, the unrelenting incursion of the market economy into every corner of the world, poverty, war, injustice, terrorism, genocide, and hatred all threaten our capacity to experience the world as beautiful. But the Christian contemplative does not have the luxury to shrink from these stark realities or to be paralyzed by them. And this is why a commitment to the contemplative life can never be a flight from the world, can never be an escape from conflict or suffering, or, much worse, a cocooning in on oneself. It is, rather, a flight precisely from the illusion of disunity, the illusion of separation that dominates the overarching narratives of our world. Contemplation cultivates an intuitive awakening to the divine union symbolized by Eden that grounds the very core of our being. Thus, with Paul, the contemplative can gaze with unflinching honesty at their own capacity for hatred, injustice, and violence, confident in God "who saved us and called us with a holy calling, not according to our works but according to his own purpose and grace" (2 Tim 1:8).

To be sure, the rejection of certain religious tendencies that thrive on guilt and shame is an understandable, even necessary, rebuke of pseudo-theologies that are rooted not in the radical freedom of the gospel but in an infantile legal system of reward and punishment, carrot and stick, heaven and hell. Yet, an authentic spiritual response to an infantile religious system cannot resort to an equally immature denial of one's capacity to sin. Perhaps no one in the history of Christianity has been more cognizant of this than the fourth-century contemplatives of the Egyptian desert. Their entire lives were dedicated to an unrelenting struggle against their demons and the purification of their hearts through prayer and asceticism. It is perhaps precisely because of this that no collection of Christian literature is more full of joy, simplicity, and compassion as the *Sayings* of these same Desert Mothers and Fathers.[6]

By contrast, Jonathan Edwards's infamous sermon of 1741, titled "Sinners in the Hands of an Angry God," is often cited for its puritanical and negative view of humanity. Its reputation is well deserved as Edwards presents a theology of a wrathful God who "holds you over the pit of hell, much as one holds a spider, or some loathsome insect over the fire, [who] abhors you, and is dreadfully provoked."[7] While his theology is much broader than this one sermon can capture, his point is to induce fear of hell as motivation for fidelity to Christ. This is a far cry from the God who walked side by side with Adam and Eve in the cool of the evening breeze, and farther still from the God who revealed himself in Christ as crucified love. It is one thing to recognize myself as a sinner and quite another to be made to believe I am a "sinner in the hands of an angry God." How can one begin an honest assessment of one's interior life before such a fierce God? It is understandable how in modern times there has been such an overwhelming rejection of this kind of theology.

As a child, the Catholic hymnals that circulated in my parish came to reflect the strides that were taken to mitigate this perverted emphasis on God's anger and wrath and on the inevitable sense of guilt and shame that dominated the experience of many Catholics before the Second Vatican Council. This well-intended rejection of humanity's "wretchedness" in favor of our primal goodness resulted in the revision of certain traditional lyrics that were invariably trite and saccharine. The classic hymn "Amazing Grace," for example, now proclaimed "Amazing grace, how sweet the sound, that saved *someone* like me." After all, to be thought of as a "wretch" is psychologically inconvenient. But as an entire generation jumped onto the "I'm okay, you're okay" bandwagon, no one seems to have stopped to wonder: if the human condition is not really so wretched then is grace really all that amazing?

This was the same generation that spawned the self-help movement and invented the inner child as a metaphor for self-care. But all children—even inner children—must eventually grow up. And when we do, each of us must learn to admit, with candor and humility, that the expulsion from Eden is not a story about our primeval parents eons ago but reflects rather the state of our own interior lives. Like all myths, the story of Adam and Eve never happened historically, but it is always happening in the heart of every person.[8]

Eden is the myth of our coming of age. How easily we are seduced into forsaking intimacy with God in exchange for an illusory autonomy that, as we will see, is the source of all our misery. Such an honest personal inventory leaves no high moral ground on which I might stand to judge another, no high horse on which to parade my moral superiority. Rather, awakening to the reality of our self-imposed exile unexpectedly brings with it glad tidings of the extravagant grace of God who even now rushes out to embrace us. It is only before such a God that we are free to look at ourselves with unrelenting honesty.

The psychosis of denial and projection is the inevitable outcome among those who have embraced a pseudo-theology that tells us we are "sinners in the hands of an angry God." For if we are to believe that the God before whom we search our hearts is eagerly looking for a reason to condemn us, we will inevitably suppress and project our most negative traits onto others for fear of the condemnation that would follow if we admit them of ourselves. However, it is only through a sustained interior gaze that the contemplative comes to the joyful realization that grace is "amazing" precisely because humanity is capable of such wretchedness. We are otherwise left with mediocre grace or what Dietrich Bonhoeffer called "cheap grace," which is no grace at all.

The expulsion from Eden is thus not ultimately a tragedy but merely a prelude to the divine embrace of the incarnation. The contemplative intuition that God already embraces us is at once an intuition about how the story of exile ends. We are able to see the whole drama of salvation history, the unfolding of our own interior conversion in light of the Gospel. Exile ends in embrace, sin ends in grace, death ends in new life. Indeed, with Dante, the contemplative knows that the history of human egotism unfolds not as a human tragedy but as a "Divine Comedy." How, then, might a contemplative reading of the Genesis account of Eden help to frame our understanding of the movement of the Christian interior life?

The Myth of Eden

The scene of Genesis 2–3 is a dramatic one, situated in a paradisiacal garden where divinity and humanity coexist in intimate union and God is portrayed in anthropomorphic terms. That is, God is presented with human-like qualities: he walks (Gen 3:8), talks (Gen 2:16-17), and has limited knowledge (Gen 3:9). To the contemplative, however, the story of Eden does not as much present God as human-like but humans as god-like. Thus, Adam and Eve might best be understood in theomorphic terms: they see God (Gen 3:10), talk directly with God (Gen 3:12), co-create with God (Gen 2:19), and live in a realm that is God's own (Gen 2:15).[9] The Hebrew origin of the word *'adam* is not a name at all but a description, literally meaning "red," or one who is made from the red earth (*'adamah*).[10] In the Hebrew of Genesis, the gender of *'adam* is not accentuated until the creation of Eve, whose own name means something akin to "source of life."[11] Only with Eve's creation does *'adam* become the proper name "Adam," for, as we will see, we are never fully "someone" until we are "someone-in-relation."

The intimacy they share between themselves and with God is portrayed in terms of nakedness; humanity is depicted in naked union with the Divine. Until, that is, they attempt to assert their autonomy under the tree in the middle of the garden. Seduced into believing that the knowledge of good and evil is something that can be attained apart from God, both Adam and Eve eat of its fruit. Building on Thomas Aquinas's interpretation of this narrative we might identify the "tree of knowledge of good and evil" as symbolic of humanity's desire for self-assertion and radical autonomy, which is why it stands in the center of the garden where it is most certain to claim our attention.[12] Within each one of us this tree stands tall, with deep roots and enticing fruit. And whispering from its outstretched branches is a most cunning serpent, tempting us to become gods in our own right, "knowing good from evil" (Gen 3:5). Once the awareness of our union with God is severed it can be replaced only with a frenetic preoccupation to re-create an alternative identity. Yet, cut off from the ground of being, this projected identity can be nothing more than an illusory guise we name the false self.

The greatest idol for each of us, then, is the illusory perception of our autonomous self, and for as long as we gorge on its fruit we are cut off from our deepest identity, which can only be rediscovered in naked union with God. And this is the fate of both Adam and Eve who now, bloated on the fruit of this illusion, look upon their nakedness not as freedom or an invitation to intimacy but as a source of shame. Subsequently, God is unable to locate them in the garden and begins an almost desperate search to find them. "Where are you?" God cries out. "I heard the sound of you in the garden," comes the reply, "and I was afraid, because I was naked; and I hid myself." And there, crouching in primordial darkness, lay humanity, fallen and alienated.

What follows in the story is as much a question as an indictment, piercing through the darkness and unrelenting through the ages: "Who told you that you were naked?" (Gen 3:8-11). This, the narrator knows well, is the existential question to which each of us must respond: Who told you that you were naked? That you must hide from me, the Source of your existence? To what terrible lie have you succumbed that you should think yourself separate from me? The contemplative already intuits the answer: that humanity is caught up in a grand illusion of duality. Having succumbed to the temptation to assert our autonomy from God, we have as a consequence been blinded to the truth of our THEONOMY—that is, the awareness of God as Source, Essence, Destiny, and, thus, the governing principle of our existence.

Borrowed Clothing

Given the enormity of this moment in the narrative, it is easy to overlook the subtle gesture by God who "made garments of skins for the man and for his wife, and clothed them" (Gen 3:21). This is borrowed clothing; coverings that will conceal their nakedness even as they reveal something about each of them in this new world they are about to enter. Metaphorically speaking, we might say the clothing represents the EGO. And we do well to differentiate it from the false self. The ego is not an aspect of our deepest identity but a part of our psychological construct, worn throughout the course of our lifetime. It will be shed upon death as we ultimately return to our own nakedness before God. In many spiritual circles the ego is conflated with the false self, an easy mistake to make because the ego often operates under its influence. But there is an important distinction.

The false self is nothing more than a constructed identity we project to fill the void left in the wake of our self-alienation from God. It is nothing more than the generation of thoughts, feelings, and mental chatter—with no real substance behind it. In order to compensate for unmet needs, emotional wounds, and psychological scarring, we generate an internal narrative convincing ourselves of our own virtue and demonizing those who threaten the wounded or neglected aspects of ourselves. We project our sense of self into the world, thriving on competition, exerting our control, and manipulating relationships to avoid further pain and assert our own dominance. To such a person living out of the false self, death is terrifying because it marks the end of my world and therefor the end of *the* world.

The ego, by contrast, is something given, as Genesis 3:21 would suggest. Like garments of skin, it is a gift of borrowed clothing, part of our human psychology we can develop in a healthy way over the course of a lifetime. As long as we do not mistake the ego for the fullness of our identity, it can express something of our true identity in the world even as it conceals our primal nakedness. Like the daily clothing we wear, the ego can be put on or removed as needed. If our ego is taken up to express something of our true selves, it can be a tool for much good in the world. To claim, "I am a professor . . . a fireman . . . a nurse . . . a physicist" is to assume an identity in the world based on socially accepted credentials and experiences. These acquired identities we develop over the course of a lifetime do not constitute one's deepest self any more than a suit and tie, a nurse's uniform, or a pair of jeans. But they can serve as a means of allowing one's deepest identity to be expressed in the world.

Very often we fail to distinguish between our true selves and the garments we wear, leaving our egos vulnerable to the whims, desires, and emotional programming generated by the false self. But through gradual detachment from the false self, we learn to take up our egoic identity when necessary and set it down again when it is no longer needed. To extend the metaphor, the ego is like a tool, say, a hammer. It can be used to build up or tear down. When used to advance goodness and the well-being of others, these egoic identities can rightly be said to reflect something of one's true self. When one's ego is under the influence of the false self, we encounter the worst forms of idolatry, which historically have occasioned all manner of evil and oppression.

The question is, what role does ego play in the interior life? As we will see in chapter 4, the contemplative vocation consists initially of spiritual disciplines and practices designed to wrest the ego from the dominance of the false self. Ultimately our practices of prayer, asceticism, and virtue have but one aim: to render us naked before God in a perfect union of Love. While the ego can be donned in service of our most authentic vocation to love in the world, in the end, it remains borrowed clothing that must be discarded in order that we might "put on Christ," the new self.

In his classic work *The Doctrine of Spiritual Perfection*, Anselm Stolz harkens back to the importance of the "theology of dress" that has been all but lost in the modern era. "According to the older notion," he says, "dress is more than an outward sign. It bestows the dignity which it indicates."[13] He goes on to say, "St. Paul's exhortations to 'put on' Christ and to 'put off' the old man, suggesting at once the picture of a garment, presupposes this attitude toward dress. The same idea is expressed in the symbolism of monastic garb."[14] Stolz's general reference here to monastic garb might be nuanced further to clarify the point. In Western Christianity, the hooded cowl of the contemplative is not intended as an outward or public garment projecting yet another interior identity in the world. That is the role of the habit. The cowl is much more an intimate garment in which one's egoic self, lost beneath its voluminous folds, all but disappears. To don the cowl is to put on Christ, which is to return to our primal nakedness before God restored to us by the incarnation. How fitting that a garment intended to sacramentalize our nakedness before God is so capacious that one is all but required to sit in stillness or risk all manner of clumsy mishaps. It is a garment intended for prayer and prayer alone. Echoing a white baptismal gown, the cowl is a garment of light, of transfiguration, and therefore of deification. It is a reminder that one must be naked of the egoic self in order to be clothed in Christ. The theology of dress underlying both the baptismal garment and the cowl for the spiritual life of the Christian could hardly find better expression than in Colossians 3:5-15:

> Put to death, therefore, whatever in you is earthly: fornication, impurity, passion, evil desire, and greed (which is idolatry). On account of these the wrath of God is coming on those who are disobedient. These are the ways you also once followed, when you were living that life. But now you must get rid of all such things—anger, wrath, malice, slander, and abusive language from your mouth. Do not lie to one another, seeing that you have stripped off the old self with its practices and have clothed

> yourselves with the new self, which is being renewed in knowledge according to the image of its creator. In that renewal there is no longer Greek and Jew, circumcised and uncircumcised, barbarian, Scythian, slave and free; but Christ is all and in all!
>
> As God's chosen ones, holy and beloved, clothe yourselves with compassion, kindness, humility, meekness, and patience. Bear with one another and, if anyone has a complaint against another, forgive each other; just as the Lord has forgiven you, so you also must forgive. Above all, clothe yourselves with love, which binds everything together in perfect harmony. And let the peace of Christ rule in your hearts, to which indeed you were called in the one body. And be thankful.

One can readily see a "theology of dress" reflected in the movement from "stripping off the old self" (v. 9) and being clothed with the "new self, which is being renewed in knowledge according to the image of its creator" (v. 10). Interior freedom from the tyranny of the false (i.e., "old") self leads to a spiritual renewal stripped of an egoic identification in the world, opening one to the deeper awareness of oneself as the "image of God" (vv. 5-10). Indeed, the Christian spiritual life is a process of stripping off the ego and exposing the false self, driven by fear, desire, lust, and competition. The remedy, as Paul admonishes, is to "clothe yourselves with compassion, kindness, humility, meekness, and patience" (v. 12). But "above all, clothe yourselves with love, which binds everything together in perfect harmony" (v. 14). As we will see, asceticism amounts to nothing if in the end it does not open us ever more deeply to the possibility of loving and being loved.

With the renewal of the true self, the awakening of love for others, one can more clearly see the transient nature of social, cultural, and religious identity: "In that renewal there is no longer Greek and Jew, circumcised and uncircumcised, barbarian, Scythian, slave and free; but Christ is all and in all!" (v. 11). As always, for Paul, this cannot remain a theoretical love of a hypothetical neighbor but must be embodied most especially through "forgiveness" in the context of a living community (vv. 12-13). The fruit of these efforts is its own reward. What the ego once perceived as separation is now recognized as unity in the Body of Christ (v. 15). So it is with grace we gradually discover that freedom is not freedom from God but freedom from the domination and illusions of the false self. Unshackled from its demands, we uncover again our deepest identity as the image of God, the true self, that increasingly reflects the love of Christ in the world. Not until one's ego is replaced with love for another does Christian ethics attain its perfect fulfillment.

> Owe no one anything, except to love one another; for the one who loves another has fulfilled the law. . . . Love does no wrong to a neighbor; therefore, love is the fulfilling of the law. . . . Let us then lay aside the works of darkness and put on the armor of light; let us live honorably as in the day, not in reveling and drunkenness, not in debauchery and licentiousness, not in quarreling and jealousy. Instead, put on the Lord Jesus Christ, and make no provision for the flesh, to gratify its desires. (Rom 13:8-14)

Admonishments like these can be easily misunderstood or dismissed by much of the modern church where interior transformation is less emphasized than social action. Putting down the works of darkness and putting on the armor of Christ the light requires introspection and self-critique, discipline and conversion. It is much easier to remain focused on the external, garbed in the comfort of one's egoic identity (however noble it may be) in pursuit of active forms of discipleship engaged in the struggle against evil and injustice *out there*. While the fruit of contemplation is service to others, action without contemplation is far more vulnerable to projections of my own prejudices. Too often, well-intended discipleship is not informed by a deep interiority by which I learn that the most important aspect of the spiritual life is not applying the teachings of Christ to my life but removing the obstacle of my ego so that the indwelling Christ can work *through* me.

The biblical Adam and Eve made the mistake of trying to be gods apart from God. They were searching for an identity outside of God that they already possessed precisely in their relationship with God. And this is our own dilemma as well: we continue to seek for what is already ours. Certainly, to seek to be gods apart from God is idolatry. But to realize I am already divine is the heart of Christian revelation. The greatest idol for each of us, then, is our own fabricated self, entirely ephemeral, consisting of nothing, which is why it is called "false." This, of course, is the complete antithesis of our true self, that deepest core of our being that reflects the "image" (Gk. *eikon*) of God. Idols terminate in themselves; icons point beyond themselves to the divine. But the shadow of the false self is cast far and long, and one cannot ignore its tenacious demands to idolize oneself above all else. We are, as it were, full of ourselves, which is the very antithesis of the divine self-emptying of Christ in the world. Even after the contemplative is emptied of all other attachments, there still remains the "I" of the false self. This last temptation to idolatry is the first to have taken root in the Eden of human consciousness. It is also the most tenacious because overcoming it demands the complete loss of the self made in my own image, in order that I might be found in Christ.

It is no wonder the contemplative life is embraced by so few. It is risky business fraught with dangers and emptiness, great silences and voids, arid interior landscapes bereft of signposts and directions that would lead us to that spiritual oasis who is Christ alone. But the risks of not making the journey are far greater, leaving one with what can only amount to an insipid form of Christian faith, either stuck on religious externals, emotional hype, or the critical distance of the academy. Such "Christianities" are no doubt experienced as fulfilling and meaningful by some but inescapably remain safe, external, and in avoidance of the pearl of great price that lies otherwise hidden from plain view (Matt 13:45-46).

The expulsion from Eden, then, is not so much a punishment as it is the inevitable consequence of our own self-assertion that results in the frenetic preoccupation with our egocentric desires.

But how does a mythological narrative about human origins and our relationship with the divine speak meaningfully about the human condition for contemplatives today? In short, what is the value of the Genesis myth of Eden for the Christian interior life?

Myth and History

Our recently acquired insights about the origins and evolution of the universe offer a fresh context for understanding the intersection between the Scriptures and the Christian spiritual life. Our scientific worldview is not properly a corrective to the biblical narrative of the creation and expulsion from Eden because Genesis 1–3 does not, in fact, present a competing claim to the scientific origins of the universe. Rather, told in simple and primitive terms, Genesis 2–3 conveys a theological depth that provides a key insight into how we might interpret the human plight from a contemplative perspective today. Much like the parables that Jesus uses to convey spiritual rather than historical truth, we should not mistake Genesis 2–3 as evidence of the historical origins of humanity. Something much greater is at stake here. Something that will not allow this narrative to be relegated to the safety of a distant past but that demands we hear in its telling the story of our own relationship with the Divine and the tragedy our own exile. In fact, there was no past moment in history when humanity, however long ago, existed in perfect harmony with God.

On the contrary, our cosmologists are ever more convinced that it is not harmony but disharmony that set in motion the expansive origins of our universe. A spark of asymmetry introduced into an infinitesimal singularity gave rise to an inconceivably rapid expansion of the space-time continuum that we have come to call inadequately the Big Bang. Without asymmetry, which theologians might articulate as a "divine spark," the universe as we know it could never have existed. The ensuing evolution of stars and galaxies and planets, indeed life itself, could not have been without this asymmetry paradoxically built into the very structure of the universe—the chaos out of which the Divine breath hovering over the abyss brought order and life (Gen 1:1). Although the ancient scribes of Genesis knew nothing of this vast, incomprehensible process of evolution, these scientific insights into the origins and nature of the universe and our place in it, allow for a new and much richer context for exploring the sacred narratives themselves.

Despite the appearance of an indifferent universe governed only by chance, a gaze into its deepest mysteries inevitably reveals an extravagance that begs the question, "Why is there something instead of nothing?" The very fact of a cosmos whose evolutionary dynamic gave rise to self-consciousness—a consciousness that itself can ask such questions while peering back into the universe from which we evolved—betrays a fundamental beneficence beneath every vibrating atom. "Let there be light . . . let dry land appear . . . let the earth pour forth vegetation . . . let the waters spring forth swarms of living creatures" (Gen 1). Like pure white light through a prism, the singular Word spoken throughout eternity gave rise to a multiplicity of form, dimension, and color evolving as minerals, plants, and animals—each of them holy writ in the Book of Creation. Each of them giving praise to the God whom they magnify in their very being. Indeed, to be Divine is to eternally give birth to "the All" (Col 1:16). Creation is not a moment in the past but a perpetual birthing anew in this present moment. Each moment is indeed a new creation, full of infinite possibility. Myth, it turns out, serves as a hermeneutical key by which the contemplative unlocks the christological meaning of both history and the cosmos in light of ever-new insights into the universe itself. What, then, are the implications of an evolutionary universe for Christian spirituality?

The Hitchedness of All Things

The nature conservationist John Muir once wrote in his journals, "When we try to pick out anything by itself we find that it is bound fast, by a thousand invisible cords that cannot be broken, to everything in the universe."[15] "Bound fast," or, as he will say later, "hitched."[16] Everything in the universe is "hitched" to everything else. That is to say, the particularity of anything participates in the universality of everything. Muir's vision of the unity of all things reflects a specifically Christian character. Within a universe replete with an almost infinite array of forms, there is a fundamental unity that the New Testament Colossians hymn identifies as Christ:

> Who is the image [*eikon*] of the invisible God
> firstborn of all creation;
> for in him were created all things
> in the heavens and on the earth,
> the visible and the invisible,
> whether thrones or dominions,
> whether rulers, or powers;
> all things, through him and for him, have been created;
> And he is before all things,
> And all things in him hold together,
> And he is the head of the body, the church;
> Who is the beginning,
> firstborn from the dead,
> so that he might come to have first place in everything;
> for in him all the fullness was pleased to dwell,
> and through him, to reconcile all things to himself,
> by making peace through the blood of his cross,
> through him to reconcile whether the things on earth,
> or the things in heaven.[17]

For the Christian contemplative Muir's unifying hitch is not a *what* but a *who*. In Christ, "all things hold together." Creation and redemption are but a singular divine event by which all things are reconciled in Christ. The creative energy through whom the many forms of beauty and darkness in the universe are brought into being and forever hitched is thoroughly personal. Christ, "the image of the invisible God," presents us with a paradox: the human face of Jesus does not mask his divinity but unequivocally reveals it. Thus, the contradiction between God's transcendence and imminence is abolished in the incarnation. As Jürgen Moltmann observed,

> When the crucified Jesus is called the "image of the invisible God," the meaning is that *this is God*, and *God is like this*. God is not greater than he is in this humiliation. God is not more glorious than he is in this self-surrender. God is not more powerful than he is in this helplessness. God is not more divine than he is in this humanity. The nucleus of everything that Christian theology says about "God" is to be found in this Christ event. The Christ event on the cross is a God event.[18]

The God of whom Christ is "image" (*icon*) is precisely the God who is and remains invisible, unknowable. As we will discuss in our final chapter, even in the incarnation God remains revealed Mystery beyond words, descriptions, or categories. Thus, the Christian theology of a personal God does not denote a superhuman figure or even a Supreme Being who possesses human qualities to their absolute perfection. To speak of a personal God is an attempt to articulate—however inadequately—that God is first and finally *relational*. And if God, then so too the universe that has been created by God, infused with the Spirit of God, and even now held together in Christ.

For the Christian, the universe itself is trustworthy. It is neither an illusion nor ephemeral but is the first book of scripture and the primordial sacrament of God's love. It is and always has been revelatory of the unknowable God in whom it subsists and through which we are graced with a near infinite array of theophanies of the divine. Without sentimentality or banality, Christian revelation holds out a universe that is imbued with the beneficent, loving, and creative force we name "Christ."[19] Through the incarnation the destiny of the cosmos is intimately wed with our own.

Indeed, as far as the limits of human discourse will allow, the Colossians hymn tells us that the universe is *in* Christ. Christ is the One in, through, and for whom God created the universe and in whom "all things" continue to be held in existence. We are assured that in Christ, all "fullness" was pleased to dwell (1:19). Paradoxically, the epistle itself speaks also of the interpenetration of Christ in whom the "fullness of divinity dwells bodily" (2:9) and who "is all and in all" (3:11; cf. Eph 1:23). This reflects the general Pauline principle that we can speak equally of the universe being *in Christ* and of the divine Christ being fully present *within* the universe. Both are mutually interpenetrated by the other. Raimon Panikkar speaks eloquently of this immanence of the divine in Christ,

> In Jesus Christ the finite and the infinite meet, the human and the divine are joined. In him the material and the spiritual are one, and also the male and the female, high and low, heaven and earth, the historical and the transhistorical, time and eternity. From the historic-religious point of view the figure of Christ could be described as that of a person who reduces to zero the distance between heaven and earth, God and [humanity], transcendent and imminent, without sacrificing either pole.[20]

Through the incarnation our human nature is forever wed to the divine nature in Christ. Yet, the incarnation abolishes God's distance from us precisely in the preservation of his radical otherness. God is at once utterly transcendent and radically immanent, wholly other and yet interpenetrating the very heart of the cosmos. This paradox holds out the absolute transcendence of God and the intimate union rendered in the incarnation "without sacrificing either pole." As Paul Fiddes explains, "Transcendence and 'otherness' of God from the world is not about absence, but about a mode of presence in which God cannot be confused with the world."[21] It is a pan*en*theism (God-in-all) but not pantheism (God-is-all). For the Christian, this is an important distinction. Union with God does not depend on a universe collapsed into the very being of God. Rather, God's union with "all" in Christ is rendered through a sovereign divine initiative motivated by unconditional love. Put otherwise, union with the divine is not a given but a divine choice born of infinite love. While Christian faith cannot conflate God and Creation, the incarnation nevertheless renders them inseparable. In short, through the incarnation God "is all and in all" (Col 3:11) but is not reducible to the universe. It is precisely because God's otherness cannot be collapsed into a simple equation with "the all" that Christian contemplation is never simply meditation *on something* but is necessarily the deepening of relationship *with Someone*. As Hans Urs von Balthasar saw, "The otherness of God is not something tragic that needs to be abolished" but the very basis on which we can claim God is love. He sees in this paradox of otherness a reflection of the triune life of God:

> The Christian knows that the Other is in God's very essence: The Son who never becomes Father, and the Spirit who never becomes either Son or Father. . . . The Christian knows that this eternal Other is the precondition on which God can be called love and thus the eternal correspondence of love in God also justifies the correspondence between God and creation.[22]

Within the Triune God is an eternal unity-in-difference between Father, Son, and Spirit. God is pure relationship without multiplicity of being. In other words, within God's very self, there is at once space for the Other that, if removed, removes with it the possibility of love.[23] For love is not love until freely given to another. To name "Father, Son, and Spirit" or "Creator, Redeemer, and Sanctifier" within the eternal unity of God, we name what is in essence "Love loving Love." Indeed, a love so perfect, so diffusive, as to pour itself out into creation itself, incorporating (literally "embodying") creation within the godhead. The Christian model of divine-human union does not consist in the dissolution of all things (a drop of water falling into the ocean) but preserves the possibility of love in the fullness of communion of all things (a single body comprised of many members). This manner of union mirrors the very trinitarian nature of one God in three Persons.[24]

The eternal pouring-out or self-empting of God is not just a creative endeavor but a redemptive one. Intimately linked, the same

Christ hymn that celebrates Christ as creator also speaks of a divine-cosmic reconciliation in Christ that is radically inclusive: we are not saved *from* the world; rather, it is the world that is saved. Through "the blood of the cross" every last atom in the cosmos is caught up in salvation, as it were, and is even now being transformed into the kingdom of God. Salvation involves a radical continuity rather than a definitive break with the cosmos and its evolutionary history. It is this cosmic vision that Gregory of Nyssa had in mind in his late fourth-century *Catechetical Orations* 25, in which the incarnation renders at once a deified humanity and a THEOPHANIC universe, that is, a universe that itself is a theophany of God:

> Now that the Deity should come to be in our nature will not on any reasonable grounds seem a strange idea to those who do not take a very narrow view of existence. For who is so simple-minded as not to believe, when he considers the universe, that the Divine Being is in everything, *clothing Himself with it*, embracing it, and residing in it? For all things depend upon Him Who is, and it is not possible for anything to exist which does not have its being in Him Who is. If, then, all things are in Him, and He is in all things, why are they ashamed of the plan of our religion which teaches that God came to be in [humanity], seeing that we believe that not even now is He outside [humanity]?
>
> For if the manner in which God is present in us is not the same as it was in that case, yet it is none the less admitted that now, as then He is equally in us. Now He is commingled with us, in that He maintains nature in existence. Then He mingled Himself with our nature, in order that by this mingling with the Divine Being our nature might become divine, being delivered from death and set free from the tyranny of the adversary. For His return from death becomes to this race of mortals the beginning of the return to immortal life.[25]

For Gregory, Christ "clothes himself" not only with human nature but with the universe itself. He thus presents a Christology that extends the locus of the incarnation beyond human nature to include the entire cosmos as the embodiment of Christ. This is what many have since come to call the Cosmic Christ.

The overly anthropocentric view of Christianity that has dominated our theology since the Enlightenment has suppressed this more ancient cosmic Christology to which both the Scriptures and early fathers attest. But deeper attention to scriptural texts like the Colossians hymn or John 1:14 ("the Word was made flesh") frees us from an exaggerated Christian anthropocentricism. A theology of the Word-Made-Flesh opens the possibility to explore whether the humanity of Jesus is the most fundamental category of the incarnation. Humanity shares flesh with all known forms of material life. It is Christ's enfleshment that remains the most fundamental category of the incarnation.

So, we discover, the universe is more fundamentally a cosmic body defined by relationality than it is a meaningless abyss characterized by indifference. The contemplative gaze peering through the multiplicity of created forms perceives a sublime unity in Christ that underlies the manifestation of endless diversity, a primal unity or hitchedness of all things in Christ who "is all and is in all" (Col 3:11). To glimpse this unity-in-difference, even for a moment, is to see the face of Christ.

The Terrible Cry

As the universe evolves around us, so too does a universe evolve within us, tormented by what the Greek poet, Nikos Kazantzakis, calls the merciless "Cry" of Love demanding the impossible, struggling—sometimes violently—against our own inertia and sterility to birth God within ourselves. Eden and our expulsion from it is thus an interior reality that each of us in our own spiritual evolution is condemned to repeat, a condemnation that Christian tradition calls original sin. It is original not because it is historical but because it is novel. Novel (repeated "anew") in the life of every human person who is struggling to "become." Kazantzakis offers a striking insight into the benevolence of this "terrible Cry," which he depicts as the divine impulse behind the evolutionary unfolding of a universe that is still "becoming":

> Blowing through heaven and earth, and in our hearts and the heart of every living thing, is a gigantic breath—a great Cry—which we call God.
>
> Plant life wished to continue its motionless sleep next to stagnant waters, but the Cry leaped up within it and violently shook its roots: "Away, let go of the earth, walk!" Had the tree been able to think and judge, it would have cried, "I don't want to. What are you urging me to do! You are demanding the impossible!" But the Cry, without pity, kept shaking its roots and shouting, "Away, let go of the earth, walk!"
>
> It shouted in this way for thousands of eons; and lo! As a result of desire and struggle, life escaped the motionless tree and was liberated. Animals appeared—worms—making themselves at home in the water and mud. "We're just fine," they said. "We have peace and security; we're not budging!"
>
> But the terrible Cry hammered itself pitilessly into their loins. "Leave the mud, stand up, give birth to your betters!" "We don't want to! We Can't!" "You can't but I can. Stand up!" And lo! After thousands of eons, humanity emerged, trembling on their still un-solid legs.
>
> The human being is a centaur; his equine hoofs are planted in the ground, but his body from breast to head is worked on and tormented by the merciless Cry. He has been fighting, again for thousands of eons, to draw himself, like a sword, out of his animalistic scabbard. He is also fighting—this is his new struggle—to draw himself out of this human scabbard. Humanity calls in despair, "where can I go? I have reached the pinnacle, beyond is the abyss." And the Cry answers, "I am beyond. Stand up!" All things are centaurs. If this were not the case, the world would rot into inertness and sterility.[26]

Inertia and sterility, tending always toward death and decay—these are the paralyzing effects of original sin—that relentless impulse toward self-absorption, which the terrible Cry demands that we step beyond into the abyss of self-transcendence. This struggle is not limited to humanity alone but extends to the whole of creation. Plants whose roots must be violently shaken from the soil, worms that are otherwise content to squirm in the mud were it not for the pitiless demand hammering over eons, "stand up and walk!" Ours is an evolving universe coming to self-consciousness, a universe ever expanding into God yet groaning in despair under the weight of our own inertia. This is our exile. Even Paul, in his Epistle to the Romans, is sympathetic to the universality of creation's resistance under the futility of sin to give birth to God in the world:

> For the creation waits with eager longing for the revealing of the children of God; for the creation was subjected to futility, not of its own will but by the will of the one who subjected it, in hope that the creation itself will be set free from its bondage to decay and will obtain the freedom of the glory of the children of God. We know that the whole creation has been groaning in labor pains until now; and not only the creation, but we ourselves, who have the first fruits of the Spirit, groan inwardly while we wait for adoption, the redemption of our bodies. . . . And so, the Spirit helps us in our weakness; for we do not know how to pray as we ought, but that very Spirit intercedes with sighs too deep for words. (Rom 8:19-23, 26)

This inward groaning is not merely a theoretical condition but an apt description of the contemplative life. Hampered and limping under the weight of our exile, crippled by our addictions to our own selves, we resist the growth that can come only by stepping into the transcendent abyss of self-forgetfulness through silence, solitude, prayer, and self-giving. No better than the plants and worms of eons ago, we protest our own spiritual evolution with petty and vain excuses, "I can't. I won't. I have reached the pinnacle. There is nothing beyond!" With the whole of Creation, we groan and struggle and despair with relentless tenacity, fixed like centaurs firmly on the earth yet struggling under a merciless impulse to become more deeply human and, yes, *more fully divine*. Indeed, the evolution of the cosmos is itself the story of our own divine-becoming and, thus, the story not only of "God-over-us" but, as Matthew will attest, of "God-with-us" (Matt 2:23; 28:20). And again, not only of God-with-us but God-within-us (Matt 25:40; John 14:20; Eph 3:17). Karl Rahner referred to this process as "active self-transcendence," by which he meant that evolution unfolds under the "pressure" of divine love acting not on creation but from within creation.[27] As such, the universe and the creatures in it actively participate in their own self-transcendence. The ability for creatures to better themselves is intrinsic to their being yet is the manifestation of a power that belongs only to God. This is the terrible Cry that has been shouting for eons, provoking our own inward struggle to draw ourselves out of our "human scabbard." But when, like Adam and Eve, we attempt to make of ourselves "gods" apart from God we defy the very gift of self-transcendence by which we reflect the image of God. Instead, our divine likeness is diminished and we succumb ever more to the illusion that God is separate from us, hidden from us, distant from us.

Now under the self-proclaimed autonomy of the ego, our humanity masks rather than reveals the radiance of our divine nature. And in this the mortal blow to all the "children of Adam" becomes frighteningly apparent: "you are dust, and to dust you shall return" (Gen 3:19). It is not death as such that we should see introduced here. Death is a natural part of an evolutionary universe. Rather, it is a newfound *dread of our mortality* that becomes the consequence of an ego governed by the false self. The natural cycle of death looms now as the terrifying inevitability of one's annihilation. Life becomes a pointless and frenetic avoidance of the unavoidable, bereft of ultimate meaning, in a seemingly indifferent universe where God is thought to be nonexistent, entirely absent, or worse, merciless in the face of our mortal plight. Humanity's cry echoes in solidarity with the psalmist,

How long, O Lord, will you remain hidden? Forever?
Is your anger to go on smoldering like a fire?
Remember me; how long have I left?
For what pointless end did you create all the children of Adam?
    Who can live and never see death?
    Who can escape the power of Sheol? (Ps 89:46-48; NJB)

A History of Longing

These questions—as existential as they are universal—strike at the heart of our self-imposed exile. Yet, the gift of exile is longing: a hidden seed, planted secretly in the core of the forbidden fruit of ego, which we inevitably ingest in our frenzied consumption of all that is illusory. That wardrobe I accumulated leaves me unsatisfied. The dream home I always wanted has now become a financial albatross. The latest technological gadget I thought I needed is soon obsolete. That promising new book on spiritual enlightenment has proven just another fad. The spiritual practice I thought would save me has since grown dull and tedious.

The inevitable dissatisfaction that arises in the wake of our lists and wants and agendas is not arbitrary; it is the symptom of a divine ruse. To be human is to long. And nothing, save naked union with God, will ever fulfill that longing. Indeed, nothing can. All of us therefore begin the contemplative journey convinced we are in a state of exile, longing for the divine intimacy of Eden. As we will see, the incarnation is God's response to "all the children of Adam" who have cried out with the psalmist through the centuries, "How long, O Lord, will you remain hidden?" And this, the very gift of our longing, can only come about because we have already been found.

I recall a time several years back when my nephew was just a few years of age. Amid a large family gathering, he and I were engrossed in a game of hide-and-seek. When it was his turn to hide, he would consistently retreat to the most conspicuous of places—face down on the sofa, standing rigid behind a curtain, crouching beneath a slender floor lamp in the corner of the room. But regardless of his location, each of which he revisited with monotonous tedium, there he would be, eyes closed, head in hands, under the endearing assumption that if he could not see us, we most certainly could not see him. The room would then fill with the exaggerated inquiries of mystified adults in their apparent search to uncover his location. "Has anybody seen Ryan?" I would call out. "No, we haven't! Now where could he be?" others would reply with feigned ignorance. "Is he under here?" I would inquire lifting a teapot or place mat as if I might possibly find him there.

The joy of this game for the adults was to relish in the beauty of his innocence, and in doing so, the masquerade often became a secret test of his patience. Predictably, within a matter of minutes, he would let out an impatient sigh, as if by making noise we bewildered adults might finally catch a glimpse of him. Eyes now peering cautiously from behind ever widening fingers, then quickly covering up again with a stifled giggle. Finally, when he could bear his self-imposed isolation no longer, he would jump to his feet declaring, "Here I am!" as the room would spontaneously erupt with the shouts and laughter of "startled" adults slapping their foreheads and wondering out loud, "How could we not have known?" And almost as instantly as the cheers had settled would come his question and demand all at once: "Again?" So, turning my back for an instant, my nephew would nervously scurry off to the couch, the curtains, the floor lamp while I counted aloud, "1, 2, 3 . . ." And so, the game would go on.

The contemplative life is like that. We repeatedly attempt to hide from God, all the time secretly longing to be found. And when our self-imposed egoic isolation becomes too much for us to bear we momentarily jump out from behind all that hides us and declare, "Here I am!" But when the fanfare of my latest spiritual quest has died down (as inevitably it does) my childlike demand for attention insists on another round of hide-and-seek. Whether I run off to my career or frenetic activity or sex or alcohol or religion or power or money, all of them are glaringly conspicuous hiding spots from the Divine. So the many false starts to my contemplative practice begin anew, while with Adam and Eve I still crouch in darkness, frightened but secretly hoping to be found.

When we come to understand this relationship between exile and longing, we realize that Eden turns our understanding of revelation inside out. It is not God who "remains hidden" as the psalmist laments but we who are called to come out from the dark corners of the garden into the light of God from whom we repeatedly attempt to hide—but in vain. Revelation consists in our own self-revelation to God, who is ever present and always in search of us.

> Where shall I go to escape your spirit?
> Where shall I flee from your presence?
> If I scale the heavens you are there,
> if I lie flat in Sheol, there you are.
> If I speed away on the wings of the dawn,
> if I dwell beyond the ocean,
> even there your hand will be guiding me,
> your right hand holding me fast.
> I will say, "Let the darkness cover me,
> and the night wrap itself around me,"
> even darkness to you is not dark,
> and night is as clear as the day. (Ps 139:7-11)

The transcendent God who for this psalmist is inescapably present throughout the universe is the same God now intimately present in Christ, in whom the saga of our exile is to be finally and definitively ameliorated. Indeed, the gift of our divine longing can come about only because God already knows where we are hiding. What mystics have always known, even if some in the church have too long forgotten, is that if you are playing the game it is because you have already been found. This is the meaning of the incarnation. In Christ we are found.

Chapter Three

Exile Interrupted

Incarnation and the Interior Life

The whole world is risen in Christ. . . . If God is "all in all," then everything is in fact paradise, because it is filled with the glory and presence of God, and nothing is any more separated from God.

—Thomas Merton, *The Hidden Ground of Love*

The themes laid out in the previous chapter will resurface again throughout the remainder of this book because they define the very contours of the Christian contemplative life. If Genesis 2–3 provides a window into the universal spiritual condition in which humanity finds itself, the Christian doctrine of the incarnation offers a unique remedy, namely, the divine interruption of our exile and a return to the intimacy of Eden. Through the Word-Made-Flesh the union between God and creation is a *fait accompli* and Christ "is all and is in all" (Col 3:11). The contemplative vocation is the universal call to live into the intimacy of the incarnation. But what does that look like? If the incarnation is historically identified with Jesus of Nazareth, what does it mean for us to be "found in Christ" today? In other words, what good is the incarnation as a past event if it is not somehow also a present reality within each of us?

In response to these questions I will look first at a brief chronology of the infancy narratives of Matthew and Luke, as well as the Prologue of John, to understand what they tell us about the incarnation as a past event. Taken independently, each of these narratives interprets the meaning and events of Jesus' birth differently, providing important theological insights we would otherwise miss. Once we understand what is distinctive to each of them, we will weave them in to a cohesive narrative that is better able to speak to the Christian interior life. To that end, I will look to an unlikely parable in Luke 15:11-32, which I will read as a Christian retelling of the expulsion from Eden in light of the incarnation. Luke's parable reiterates the mythical story of exile in Genesis in view of the historical revelation of Jesus in the gospels. While these two narratives share obvious parallels, the distinctions between them are significant. The Genesis narrative ends in exile whereas the Lucan parable ends in union. The Genesis narrative marks the beginning of our spiritual plight and the Lucan parable points to the divine resolution. In short, Luke lays out for us a map of the Christian interior life, which rightly reframes humanity's search for God as God's search for humanity. Through a spiritual EXEGESIS of this passage we will revisit the statement that concluded our previous chapter: *In Christ we are found.* This will open the way for us to explore the relationship between the historical incarnation and the interior life of the contemplative.

The Birth of God in Scripture

The earliest proclamation of the church was not "Christ is born!" but "Christ is risen!" The church came to reflect on the birth of Jesus backward, as it were, in and through the experience of his death and resurrection. In other words, it was through sustained reflection on the meaning of Christ's passion and resurrection that the church gradually came to a deeper understanding of Jesus' identity as the Incarnate One. This is why the celebration of Easter predates that of Christmas by over three centuries.[1] The foundational experience of the empty tomb gave rise to the early oral and written traditions about Jesus' resurrection and teachings. These would have coalesced into the sources that lie behind the four CANONICAL gospels. The curiosity of second and third generation Christians inspired more detailed accounts of the resurrection. As the tradition evolved, so too did the desire to push back ever further into the early life of Jesus, inspiring more elaborate accounts of his birth and infancy. Thus, the infancy narratives of Matthew and Luke and the Prologue of John reflect some of the latest developments of the gospel traditions about Jesus.

If we review the gospels chronologically this evolution becomes more discernible.[2] Mark, the oldest canonical gospel, has no account of the resurrection and no infancy narrative. He opens with an adult Jesus at the time of his baptism by John (Mark 1:1-9) and closes with three women—from among his closest disciples—running in "fear and trembling" from the empty tomb (Mark 16:1-8). A number of divergent endings can be found among the various manuscripts of Mark's gospel. The remaining verses (Mark 16:9-20) that now appear in most translations are accepted as canonical even though they are not original to Mark.[3] The fact that these additional verses detail precisely the kind of elaboration on the resurrection narratives we would expect to see gives evidence of the development of the gospel tradition I am summarizing here. Moreover, Mark's gospel does not contain a birth narrative, which is further evidence that Mark is the earliest gospel in the New Testament.

The second oldest gospel, Matthew, introduces our earliest infancy narrative, in which Jesus, conceived by Mary through the Holy Spirit (Matt 1:18), is depicted as the culmination of God's revelation in the long history of Israel (Matt 1:1-17). Luke's gospel follows with a more elaborate account of the virginal conception as revealed by the angel Gabriel (Luke 1:26-38) in connection with the miraculous birth of Christ's forerunner, John the Baptist (Luke 1:8-25). As the anointed prophet of prophets, Luke depicts Jesus as a sign of contradiction destined for the rise and fall of many (Luke 2:34), as one who will bring down the powerful and raise up the lowly (Luke 1:52), who will be light for those who dwell in the shadow of death (Luke 1:78-79).

Despite a number of irreconcilable differences, the birth narratives in both Matthew and Luke attest that the divine identity of the Risen Christ was not something he acquired or adopted late in life but was always integral to his deepest identity. The latest gospel, John, however, steps even further backward into the eternal existence of the Word (Gk. *Logos*) made flesh historically in Jesus (John 1:1-14). So it is that the gospels only gradually come to articulate Jesus' divine origins in light of his miraculous birth and preexistence as *Logos*. In sum, Mark begins with an adult Jesus at his baptism, Matthew and Luke convey greater details of his virginal conception by the Holy Spirit, and finally John peers beyond the veil of time into the eternal existence of the Word who "was God" (John 1:1) made flesh in Christ (John 1:14).

Each of these gospels offers a unique portrait of Christ, to which the infancy narratives and John's Prologue contribute principal insights. If we are to grasp what each evangelist was attempting to reveal historically about Jesus, we should pay close attention to the details of their respective gospels. Where are they different from one another? Where are they similar? Sometimes, when the gospels present two different versions of a story, interpreters have attempted to reconcile them through a process called "harmonization." For example, the ubiquitous nativity scene placed under our Christmas trees does not actually appear anywhere in the Bible. The Magi appear in only Matthew's birth story, and the shepherds appear in only Luke's birth story. Placing them together at the crèche is an example of harmonization because we have blended two distinct versions of Jesus' birth narrative into a unified scene.

Prior to the advent of modern HISTORICAL CRITICISM, harmonization was valued as a way of rectifying tensions between two or more biblical narratives. With the contemporary emphasis on historical accuracy, harmonization has fallen out of favor because it confuses the theological intentions of the individual evangelists. For example, modern interpreters seek to understand the historical reasons why only Matthew's gospel introduces the Magi in his version of the birth narrative. The reason is primarily to indicate to his Jewish-Christian audience that Jesus is of a royal lineage to whom foreign emissaries of the pagan world come to pay him homage. By contrast, Luke's interest in depicting shepherds at the manger reflects his concern to show his affluent Gentile-Christian audience that Jesus' birth is first revealed to the poor and lowly, the nameless and powerless—a theme he continues throughout his entire gospel. When characters from both gospels are made to appear together before the infant Jesus, the distinctive meaning intended by each evangelist becomes obscured. Thus, for the historical-critical interpreter, harmonizing gospel stories does not necessarily bring clarity but has the potential to confuse the unique portraits of Christ intended by each gospel.

Earlier approaches to interpreting Scripture favored allegorical interpretations that sought to establish how Christ was revealed in both Testaments. In other words, allegorical interpretations asked, "What do the books of both Old and New Testaments reveal about Christ?" Or, better, "How does Christ speak through both Testaments?" There was a pervasive assumption among PATRISTIC interpreters that christological truths hidden in the Old Testament were more fully revealed in the New. Because it has God as its principal author, all of Scripture was assumed to be a continuous landscape in which everything was connected and intertwined. The question was "How?" Spiritual exegesis sought to answer it. To that end, they drew allegorical connections between seemingly unrelated texts throughout the Bible. For example, Israel's flight from Egypt was taken on its own terms as a literary account of the exodus to the promised land. But that same narrative also served as an allegory for the Christian spiritual life by which one struggled to leave behind enslavement to sin. Passing through the Sea of Reeds thus becomes an allegory for baptism through which Christians are led to the Promised Land of union with God.

Because of the far-flung speculation that some allegorical interpretations entailed, this method was never without its detractors. Nevertheless, many allegorical or spiritual readings of the Bible yielded rich theological insights that are again being rediscovered today. Even within this book one can see the use of allegory in relating the exile of Adam and Eve to the interior life of the Christian. With due respect for the advances made through modern methods of biblical interpretation, even the church's most central doctrines find their origins not in any one biblical book but through the integration of themes that have been interwoven from among them. Thus, while harmonizing or allegorizing stories from among the four gospels may well encroach on their literary or historical integrity, this kind of cross-pollination is the very stuff of our christological doctrines. The doctrine of the incarnation, for example, is largely indebted to the infancy narratives of Matthew and Luke and the Prologue of John.

If we attend to these narratives not merely through the use of historical criticism but through the mystical doctrine of deification, what insights might surface about the incarnation and its relationship to the indwelling Christ in the heart of the contemplative today? I will frame my response to this question with an overview of Luke 15:11-32.

The Birth of God in History

Whether intended or not, Luke 15:11-24 presents a uniquely Christian recapitulation of the myth of Eden and thus a reflection of the universal interior journey of "exile and return." In other words, the parable of the Prodigal Son is a microcosm of the pattern of salvation history. As we have seen, humanity's exile from Eden typifies a universal longing for the divine to which so much of Israel's sacred literature gives witness. But reflected in Luke 15 is a specifically Christian alteration of the pattern from "exile and return" to an "exile interrupted." The younger son is presented here not unlike Adam and Eve who mistakenly sought freedom apart from God rather than in relationship with God. While this parable may seem an unlikely place to begin a reflection on the incarnation, I believe we have in this story not only the Christian history of salvation in miniature but a reflection on the interior contemplative journey of the Christian. That is to say, this parable presents a recasting of Genesis 2–3 in light of the incarnation.

> Then Jesus said, "There was a man who had two sons. The younger of them said to his father, "Father, give me the share of the property that will belong to me." So he divided his property between them. A few days later the younger son gathered all he had and traveled to a distant country, and there he squandered his property in dissolute living. When he had spent everything, a severe famine took place throughout that country, and he began to be in need. So he went and hired himself out to one of the citizens of that country, who sent him to his fields to feed the pigs. He would gladly have filled himself with the pods that the pigs were eating; and no one gave him anything. But when he came to himself he said, "How many of my father's hired hands have bread enough and to spare, but here I am dying of hunger! I will get up and go to my father, and I will say to him, 'Father, I have sinned against heaven and before you; I am no longer worthy to be called your son; treat me like one of your hired hands.' " So he set off and went to his father. But while he was still far off, his father saw him and was filled with compassion; he ran and put his arms around his neck and kissed him. Then the son said to him, "Father, I have sinned against heaven and before you; I am no longer worthy to be called your son." But the father said to his slaves, "Quickly, bring out a robe—the best one—and put it on him; put a ring on his finger and sandals on his feet. And get the fatted calf and kill it, and let us eat and celebrate; for this son of mine was dead and is alive again; he was lost and is found!" And they began to celebrate. (Luke 15:11-24)

Since the sixteenth century, most English Bibles have referred to this passage as the Prodigal Son, though perhaps a more suitable title would be the Prodigal Father. The term "prodigal" means "extravagantly wasteful," "reckless," or "uncontrolled." More broadly, it implies "giving something away on a lavish scale." While the son is extravagant and wasteful in his use of money, the father, who is the central figure of the story (v. 11), conveys a love for his son that is more extravagant still. So lavish and uncontrolled as to be rightly called prodigal. The two other parables that comprise chapter 15 are the Lost Sheep (Luke 15:1-7) and the Lost Coin (Luke 15:8-10). Together these three have been called by some commentators "the heart of Luke's gospel" because they so distinctively reveal Luke's portrait of Christ as one who seeks out the lost, the exiled, and the outcast.[4]

In all three parables, it is God who actively searches for the lost. There is no divine passivity in response to the human plight of exile. The sheep does not find its way back to the flock but is actively sought out and returned by the shepherd (cf. Ezek 34:1-24). The woman's lost coin does not miraculously reappear but is found only by her strenuous efforts to "light the lamp, sweep the house, and search carefully" (Luke 15:8). So too is the young man's sojourn through a "distant country" (v. 13) ultimately interrupted by his father who goes out to embrace him while he is still on the way.

Patristic interpretations have made much of this distant country ravaged by a "severe famine" (v. 14). It represents a spiritual state of deprivation and darkness in which the young man, famished for God's word, is reduced in his spiritual hunger to seek nourishment where there is none to be had. The fact that he is so desperate as to desire the food of pig troughs—animals believed unclean in his own Jewish context—symbolizes the extent of his alienation from home (v. 16).[5] In his *Exposition of the Gospel of Luke*, St. Ambrose understands the son's plight as a kind of self-alienation rather than an exile from a literal place. He asks, "What is farther away than to depart from oneself, and not from a place? . . . Surely whoever separates himself from Christ is an exile from his country, a citizen of the world."[6] It is all the more moving that the son's return home is precipitated by his "coming to himself" in verse 17.[7] We see here a rare glimpse into the interiority of a New Testament character that bears deep significance for the Christian spiritual life. To "come to oneself," to truly *know* oneself in relation to the Divine, is the first step in recognizing the illusion of our autonomy. The journey to self and to God is one and the same movement.

Having recognized his error, the son intends to return home in hopes of persuading his father to receive him under the legal status of a slave (v. 19). His goal is survival, not daring to dream of reconciliation. But "while he was still far off" his father was "filled with compassion" and "ran and put his arms around his neck and kissed him." The fourth-century bishop and theologian Peter Chrysologus sees this parable shot through with allusions to the incarnation:

> The Father . . . runs out in his Son, when through him he descends from heaven and comes down on earth. "With me," the Son says, "is he who sent me, the Father" [John 8:16]. He "fell upon his neck . . ." when through Christ the whole divinity came down as ours and rested in human nature.[8]

This figure of the compassionate father who greets his son with a kiss is historicized in the incarnation. Christ is the kiss of God given to all humanity, indeed, to the entire universe. It is a physical embrace, not withheld as a future spiritual reward for a life well lived, but an embrace that interrupts the trajectory of human history. It is, as Chrysologus would have it, the moment in which the divine "came down as ours and rested in human nature." In this way, God's mythical search for humanity in Eden is brought to historical fulfillment in Christ.

It is striking that the father ignores his son's rehearsed speech (v. 22) and never utters a word of forgiveness. Instead, forgiveness is embodied: adorning his son with the "best robe," a "ring on his finger," and "sandals on his feet" (v. 22). Much as God clothed Adam and Eve at the beginning of their exile, here too the father clothes his son, not to send him out into the world, but to bring him home. As if to signal the end of humanity's exile in Christ, we see again a "theology of dress" by which the father transforms his son from vagabond to heir as he dons him with the finest of clothing. This is reflective of the son's true identity, indeed dignity, as child and heir of the father. This is what it means to "put on Christ," to be deified. And this is no private matter but a communal affair. The items lavished on the son bring about the restoration of his dignity and his reintegration into the community.

Union with God always entails a deeper experience of union with others. As if to contrast his isolation in a distant land of exile, the father calls for his servants to prepare a feast for his son who "was dead and is alive again" (v. 24). Exile, it turns out, is self-imposed (v. 13). Self-alienation carries its own penalty (v. 15). Reconciliation, then, is not about God overcoming a grudge but about the restoration of an individual to the community that makes them whole.

The divine-human reconciliation wrought through the incarnation simultaneously opens the way for the self-alienated individual to be re-membered as an extension of the Body of Christ. To remember is to be membered-again. Should we find ourselves isolated from the community of faith, we ask Christ to remember us as did the thief on the cross: "Jesus, remember me when you come into your kingdom" (Luke 23:42). That is to say, "make us members again" of your one Body. Our fractured selves are made whole again, unified and revivified in Christ. Our illusions of separation are overcome the more deeply we realize ourselves as members of Christ's Body: "Now you are the body of Christ and individually members of it" (1 Cor 12:27).

The observation by some commentators that Luke's parable is theologically problematic for failing to equate the father's forgiveness with the "sacrificial death of Jesus" misses the point.[9] As T. W. Manson observes, the point is that the love of God revealed in Christ *precedes* human repentance.[10] This is the meaning of Paul's statement that "God proves his love for us in that while we still were sinners Christ died for us" (Rom 5:8; cf. 1 John 4:10). However, early patristic theologians like Irenaeus and Peter Chrysologus would go further to see the "fatted calf" slaughtered in verse 23 as a symbol of Christ offered up in celebration of the union between father and son, between God and humanity.[11]

Be that as it may, unlike the Eden narrative, this first half of the parable ends not in the curse of estrangement and isolation but in the celebration of reunion and communion (v. 24). To be brought "home" is a return to Eden, a return to that place of celebratory and intimate union with the Divine. And to be one with God is to be one with the whole community of God's creation. Certainly, this is a prospect worthy of celebration. Or is it?

The second portion of the parable (Luke 15:25-32) introduces the elder son who is also distant from his father, even if in a more unexpected way.

> Now his elder son was in the field; and when he came and approached the house, he heard music and dancing. He called one of the slaves and asked what was going on. He replied, "Your brother has come, and your father has killed the fatted calf, because he has got him back safe and sound." Then he became angry and refused to go in. His father came out and began to plead with him. But he answered his father, "Listen! For all these years I have been working like a slave for you, and I have never disobeyed your command; yet you have never given me even a young goat so that I might celebrate with my friends. But when this son of yours came back, who has devoured your property with prostitutes, you killed the fatted calf for him!" Then the father said to him, "Son, you are always with me, and all that is mine is yours. But we had to celebrate and rejoice, because this brother of yours was dead and has come to life; he was lost and has been found."

This addition to the parable was directed at the Pharisees who were "grumbling" over the fact that Jesus was sitting at table with "sinners and tax collectors" (Luke 15:1-3). One hears their complaint in the elder son who, having "never disobeyed any command" (v. 29), resents his father for bestowing such compassion on someone he deemed so undeserving. The father's response to his elder son mirrors that of the younger: He "came out and began to plead with him" (v. 28). This parallel movement of the father now toward his elder son confirms that he is dealing not only with one estranged child but two: "Son, you are always with me, and all that is mine is yours" (v. 31).

There is an admonishment here for all who would mistake rote religious observance for genuine spiritual enlightenment, for all who have grown complacent with a ritualism unmoored from interior transformation. One can say a thousand prayers and never pray, offer a thousand sacrifices and never give of themselves, fulfill a thousand religious obligations and never know spiritual freedom. While the elder son may not have left home, or misspent his father's inheritance, he nevertheless squandered the opportunity for intimacy. His literal proximity to the father guaranteed nothing. Neither does one's membership in a particular church or faith community. Despite the fact that they shared the same household, this elder son was as inwardly estranged from his father as the younger. Like him, we often fail to understand that self-alienation is its own punishment and intimacy with the divine is its own reward. Again, St. Ambrose comments,

> We are not strangers and pilgrims, but we are "fellow citizens of the saints and of the household of God," for we who were far away have come near in the blood of Christ. Let us not look down on those who return from a distant land, because we were also in a distant land, as Isaiah teaches. "To them that dwelled in the region of the shadow of death, light has risen."[12]

This distant land is the place of our interior exile, the wilderness of our egocentrism and self-imposed isolation. This is the land of duality: me, you, us, them. With Adam and Eve and the wayward sons of Luke's parable, we dwell together in the "region of the shadow of death" because here in our egocentrism we live only for ourselves. There is nothing beyond the "I" of my existence. The shadow of death hovers over us because mortality can mean nothing other than total annihilation. As we saw, it is fear of this curse of death that gives rise to the false self, born of the illusion of our separation from God. And this is why the ego, when under the influence of the false self, will rage against anything that threatens its survival, its power, its self-preservation. Recall that the younger son's motivation to return home was *survival*. Yet his father offers him much more than mere survival. He offers rebirth and the fullness of life.

Likewise the infancy narratives of Matthew and Luke proclaim for us a new birth shrouded with poignancy and mystery, as one would expect in a story of the coming of the Messiah. Foretold by ancient seers, a virgin conceives and bears a son. His birth is hailed by angelic watchers in the night sky as bewildered shepherds hurry to see this new sign: an infant wrapped in bands of cloth and lying in a manger. A star hovers over the place where he lay as if the universe itself bent low to gaze upon the birth of Eternity in our midst. And following after come Magi, mysterious and elusive, traveling from foreign lands and bearing gifts in fulfillment of an ancient prophecy: "Nations shall come to your light, and kings to the brightness of your dawn" (Isa 60:3). So proclaims Zechariah in his *Benedictus*,

> In the tender compassion of our God
> the dawn from on high shall break upon us,
> to shine on those who dwell in darkness
>   and the shadow of death,
> and to guide our feet into the way peace.
> (Luke 1:78-79, *The Liturgy of the Hours*)

This is what Christ calls the kingdom of God. God's journey into every living soul. That great and redemptive interruption of our exile that breaks upon us not with the ferocity of a divine warrior but with the vulnerability of an infant messiah. Christ, whose light has arisen in history, extends now to the shadows of every human heart.

Thomas Merton, one of the most prolific contemplative authors of the twentieth century, speaks of the tenderness and majesty of this in-breaking in his poem "Carol."

> Flocks feed by darkness with a noise of whispers,
> In the dry grass of pastures,
> And lull the solemn night with their weak bells.
>
> The little towns upon the rocky hills
> Look down as meek as children:
> Because they have seen come this holy time.
>
> God's glory, now, is kindled
> gentler than low candlelight under the rafters of a barn:
> Eternal Peace is sleeping in the hay,
> And Wisdom's born in secret in a straw-roofed stable.
>
> And O! Make holy music in the stars, you happy angels.
> You shepherds, gather on the hill.
> Look up, you timid flocks, where the three kings
> Are coming through the wintry trees;
>
> While we unnumbered children of the wicked centuries
> come after with our penances and prayers,
> And lay them down in the sweet-smelling hay
> Beside the wise men's golden jars.[13]

Written entirely in the present tense, Merton will not allow us to imagine the incarnation as a past moment but assures us that "God's glory, *now*, is kindled" before our very eyes. Indeed, the glory of God enters the world much as it does our own hearts: "gentle as low candlelight" and "in secret." Like a lullaby, the placid cadence of his poem invites us to gather with the stillness of shepherds, vigilant amid the quiet tranquility of this "solemn night." The universe itself hovers like a shining star over a "straw roofed stable," as if hoping to glimpse but a small child, born among the nameless, yet who bears the name above all names. With great rejoicing and "holy music in the stars," we are drawn into the presence of this sacred mystery because we too "have seen come this holy time." With the magi, we come bearing our own gifts of "penances and prayers," journeying "through the wintry trees" of doubt and despair into the warmth of an inner epiphany of Christ.

Christianity, now an old and venerable tradition, is invited to return to the innocence of this holy night. A time before the church was torn by division or marred by those who would use its transformative power for destructive ends. A time before basilicas and cathedrals signaled the political might of Christendom, when Eternal Peace lay sleeping under the "rafters of a barn." If Christ is the new Adam (1 Cor 15:45), Bethlehem is the new Eden. And we "unnumbered children of the wicked centuries" now return to this little town "upon the rocky hills" battered and bruised by history, darkened by doubt, and scandalized by those who have carried out atrocities in the name of Innocence Incarnate. Here we stand before this epiphany of Christ, a divine love overflowing from eternity into history. In this child is the embodiment of a prodigal father who comes to us now amid "a noise of whispers." Inasmuch as the inner life of faith may be patterned on Luke 15, it is only because the infancy narratives of Matthew and Luke speak eloquently of God's historical in-breaking in Christ.

The love of the prodigal father is poured out in the incarnation, not only as a past moment, but as an ongoing reality that touches the deepest interiority of every living thing. Recall the *incarnatio continua*. More recently others refer to "DEEP INCARNATION."[14] Both of these terms point to a continuum between the historical incarnation in Jesus of Nazareth and the ongoing incarnation of Christ in humanity and the wider cosmos. That is, the historical enfleshment of God in Christ reveals a radical embodiment of the divine extending to every last atom of the cosmos. As we began to see in the previous chapter, modern insights into evolution and cosmology richly inform our christological doctrines. Yet, there is nothing new about a cosmological vision of the incarnation. On the contrary, the overly anthropocentric view of Christianity that has dominated

Christian theology since the Enlightenment has eclipsed this more ancient cosmic Christology to which both the Scriptures and early fathers attest. We turn now to these early witnesses.

The Cosmic Birth of God

"The book of *genesis* of Jesus Christ" (Matt 1:1).[15] It is with these words that Matthew opens his gospel and consequently the whole of the New Testament. The Greek word *genesis* means "origin" or "beginning," and Matthew's use of the term invites us to notice a resonance with "The book of *genesis* of the heavens and earth" we explored in the previous chapter (Gen 2:4). In a world shrouded in darkness from the consequences of Eden, a new beginning dawns in Bethlehem. Similarly, the Prologue of John's gospel reflects the same resonance, which serves as a retelling of the creation story through the Word-Made-Flesh. In one of the most succinct and sublime affirmations of Christ's divinity in the New Testament, John begins his gospel with an unambiguous echo of the creation narrative in Genesis 1:

> In the beginning was the Word, and the Word was with God, and the Word was God. He was in the beginning with God. All things came into being through him, and without him not one thing came into being. What has come into being in him was life, and the life was the light of all people. The light shines in the darkness, and the darkness did not overcome it. . . . And the Word became flesh and lived among us. (John 1:1-5, 14)

With this new beginning John makes an audacious claim. The Word that was eternally *with* God, that indeed *was* God, "became flesh and dwelt among us" in Jesus of Nazareth (John 1:14). It is difficult to overstate the magnitude and brashness of his claim here. John is asserting that the principal creative force of the universe is not a *what* but a *who*. This singular Word (*Logos*) spoken from the Father for all eternity, from whom all life came into being, is the very one who "dwelt among us" (John 1:14), who preached his message throughout the region of Galilee and walked the streets of Jerusalem.

John does not tell us in the beginning was silence but that "In the beginning was the Word." Yet what is the Word but "the ecstasy of silence," as Panikkar has said.[16] From the Greek *ekstasis*, the term means literally "to be or stand outside of oneself," or "to go elsewhere from oneself." The Word is the eternal silence of God overflowing outside of the Godhead. Yet to speak one must simultaneously exhale. A word cannot be spoken without the breath that carries it. And here we encounter again the mystery of the Trinity and the role of the Spirit in the life of Christ. Is it not, after all, the breath of the Spirit that carries the eternal Word across the threshold of time in the incarnation (Luke 1:35)? Is it not the breath of the Spirit that carries the incarnate Christ from death into life in the resurrection (Rom 8:11)? By the power of the Spirit, the Word is eternally spoken from the silent abyss of the Father and returns to the bosom of the Father (John 1:18)—not infinitely, but eternally, not time after time without end, but once for all time without end.

Paradoxically, God not only gives birth from all eternity, as Meister Eckhart understood, but is indeed born from all eternity. The Word through whom the universe was born is now born within the universe itself. D. H. Lawrence celebrates this divine ecstasy of the Word in his poem "God Is Born," in which he affirms that "God is not / until he is born" and "there is no end to the birth of God." No end and indeed no beginning to the birth of God:

> The history of the cosmos
> is the history of the struggle of becoming.
> When the dim flux of unformed life
> struggled, convulsed back and forth upon itself,
> and broke at last into light and dark
> came into existence as light,
> came into existence as cold shadow
> then every atom of the cosmos trembled with delight.

Behold, God is born!
He is bright light!
He is pitch dark and cold!

And in the great struggle of intangible chaos
when, at a certain point, a drop of water began to drip
downwards
and a breath of vapour began to wreathe up
Lo again the shudder of bliss through all the atoms!
Oh, God is born!
Behold, He is born wet!
Look, He hath movement upward! He spirals!

And so, in the great aeons of accomplishment and dēbâcle
from time to time the wild crying of every electron:
Lo! God is born!

When sapphires cooled out of molten chaos:
See, God is born! He is blue, he is deep blue, he is forever blue!
When gold lay shining threading the cooled-off rock:
God is born! God is born! bright yellow and ductile He is born.

When the little eggy amoeba emerged out of foam and nowhere
then all the electrons held their breath:
Ach! Ach! Now indeed God is born! He twinkles within.

When from a world of mosses and of ferns
at last the narcissus lifted a tuft of five-point stars
and dangled them in the atmosphere,
then every molecule of creation jumped and clapped its hands:
God is born! God is born perfumed and dangling and with a
little cup!

Throughout the aeons, as the lizard swirls his tail finer than water,
as the peacock turns to the sun, and could not be more splendid,
as the leopard smites the small calf with a spangled paw, perfect.
the universe trembles: God is born! God is here!

> And when at last man stood on two legs and wondered,
> then there was a hush of suspense at the core of every electron:
> Behold, now very God is born!
> God Himself is born!
>
> And so we see, God is not
> until he is born.
>
> And also we see
> there is no end to the birth of God.[17]

Lawrence's celebration of God's birth throughout the history of the cosmos does not diminish the uniqueness of Christ's incarnation but underscores its inevitability. The incarnation is not, as has been argued for centuries, a divine contingency plan in response to the historical Fall of humanity. Rather, it is the clarifying lens by which evolutionary history is to be properly interpreted. Denis Edwards explains,

> Jesus is part of the climax of that long [evolutionary] development whereby the world becomes aware of itself, and comes into the direct presence of God. He is someone who, like all of us in his finite and historically conditioned humanity, is a receiver of God's self-communication by grace. Jesus is unlike anyone else, however, in that in him we find a radical and complete openness to God's self-giving in grace. In this one product of evolutionary history, the cosmos accepts God in a definitive and absolute way.[18]

And thus, we see come to expression the universal birth of God in the particularity of Christ. In Christ, God is born *par excellence*. Or put otherwise, Jesus is the inevitable outcome of a God whose nature it is to give birth eternally.

St. Bonaventure explains the inevitability of the incarnation by building on the language of Pseudo-Dionysius, who attributes to God the quality of perfect "Goodness."[19] In his classic work *The Soul's Journey into God*, Bonaventure writes, "Good is said to be self-diffusive; therefore, the highest good must be most self-diffusive."[20]

In other words, "Goodness" by its very nature is self-giving, self-diffusive. Since God is the "highest Good," the perfect Good, it follows that God is perfectly self-giving, perfectly diffusive. The incarnation is not only God's self-emptying (*kenosis*) into the created order but also the taking up of creation into God's self. Through the incarnation God achieves a state of perfect self-diffusion in creation. That is, a state of mutual interpenetration with creation. Thus, Paul can say at once that we are "in Christ" and Christ is "in us" (cf. Rom 6:11; 8:39; 12:5; 1 Cor 1:30; 2 Cor 5:17, 19; Gal 3:28; Eph 2:10 with Col. 1:27, etc.).

Until we realize Christianity is a passionate love affair between God and humanity, we have not begun to fathom the meaning of the incarnation. For the incarnation—God's full embrace of the cosmos, and all it contains—is the inevitable outcome of a God who is love (1 John 1:1-14; 4:8, 16). This is because such a God could never tolerate the infinite gulf between divine transcendence and the finitude of creation. But an infinite gulf can only be bridged by the Infinite. It is not enough, then, that God should remain forever transcendent above creation, nor was it sufficient that the Source of all should enter into the very fabric of cosmic history as "God-with-us" (Matt 1:23). If it is true, as Augustine insisted, that "our hearts are restless until they rest in Thee," it is because we have been made in the image of a God who is forever restless until he rests in us. "Those who love me will keep my word, and my Father will love them, and we will come to them and make our home with them" (John 14:23; cf. Sir 24:11). The *incarnatio continua*.

Through the incarnation, humanity is caught up in this great divine dance, the endless mutual indwelling of Father, Son, and Spirit known as PERICHORESIS. Originating in the fourth century with the work of Gregory of Nazianzus, perichoresis means "mutual interpenetration." In Christian theology, it came to refer to the eternal relationship among the Persons of the Trinity—each eternally interpenetrating or mutually indwelling in the other. Gregory's original use of the term, however, described the manner in which the divine and human natures coexist in Christ. Both natures perfectly interpenetrate each other without confusion or diminishment of either. In short, Jesus is fully human and fully divine, not half of each. Thus in Christ, the eternal interpenetration of Father, Son, and Holy Spirit overflows and is emptied out into all of creation. The eternal movement of "God from God, Light from Light, / true God from true God" now unfolds in our very DNA. This union between God and Creation—Lover and Beloved—is so absolute that God indeed becomes "all in all" (1 Cor 15:28).[21]

The Birth of God Within

In his *Sermon One*, Meister Eckhart celebrates this cosmic dimension of the incarnation in relation to the deification of humanity:

> Here, in time, we are celebrating the eternal birth which God the Father bore and bears unceasingly in eternity, because this same birth is now born in time, in human nature. . . . We shall therefore speak of this birth, of how it may take place in us and be consummated in the virtuous soul, whenever God the Father speaks his Eternal Word in the perfect soul.[22]

The consummation of the Word in the soul is nowhere better typified than in the virtuous figure of Mary, the Virgin Mother, whom Gabriel declares "full of grace" and "blessed among women" (Luke 1:28). For Luke, the same Spirit who "in the beginning" hovered over the Abyss (Gen 1:1) now overshadows a young Virgin on the forgotten margins of an ancient empire:

> The Holy Spirit will come upon you, and the power of the Most High will overshadow you; therefore the child to be born will be holy; he will be called Son of God. (Luke 1:35)

This new overshadowing inaugurates a new creation marked not by the repetition of nights and days but by the dawning of an endless day. The Eternal is birthed in time even as the long road of cosmic history is now stretched to meet the horizon of eternity. To Mary "God the Father speaks his Eternal Word" in time, and the Word, eternally begotten from the womb of the Father (*de utero Patris*), is joined to human flesh in the womb of a Virgin. It is the manner of her conception that the contemplative seeks to emulate: an act of listening that opens the way for the ongoing birth of Christ in the world. Commenting on the Prologue of the Fourth Gospel, John of the Cross observed,

> The Father uttered one Word; that Word is His Son: and He utters Him forever in everlasting silence, and in silence the soul has to hear It.[23]

In silence, the Word is spoken from eternity, and in silence spoken into history. So too in silence the Spirit conceives the inconceivable and hope is born in the most unexpected of places. As with Mary, so also the contemplative.

Since the fourth century, the church fathers expressed the virginal conception metaphorically as an act of silent listening on the part of Mary. "Through her ear the Word entered and dwelt secretly in the womb."[24] Thus, Mary is the archetype of a contemplative in the world. "Here am I, the servant of the Lord; let it be with me according to your word" (Luke 1:38). This is Mary's *fiat*, her consent to the presence of God within her. Yet, as von Balthasar observed, Mary's *fiat*—her "yes"—is not a once-for-all consent at the moment of conception but an openness to the work of the Spirit within her for the duration of her life. She must say "yes" even when Christ seems to dismiss her (Mark 3:31-35); she must say "yes" when he all but refuses to obey her at Cana; she must say "yes" when he is taken into custody and tortured; she must say "yes" as he slips away on the cross.[25] She must say "yes" to his resurrection and "yes" to his ascension. Even after giving birth to the infant Jesus, she never ceases to give birth to Christ within.

This trusting receptivity becomes the womb from which we too birth Christ in the world; a fertile receptivity by which we too listen to the silent Word spoken in our hearts, urging our consent to birth Christ in the world and indeed to Christ's birthing in all things. As Paul reminded the church in Rome, "faith comes from hearing, and what is heard comes through the word of Christ" (Rom 10:17). Receptive listening is the basis for the contemplative vocation to birth Christ in the world. By the Middle Ages, we see the widespread sentiment that objective redemption is meaningless if not interiorized and relived subjectively within the heart of every Christian. In modern times, this insight on the subjectivity of the incarnation, falsely attributed to Meister Eckhart, nevertheless summarizes this tradition beautifully:

> We are all meant to be mothers of God. What good is it to me if this eternal birth of the divine Son takes place unceasingly, but does not take place within myself? And, what good it is to me if Mary is full of grace if I am not also full of grace? What good is it to me for the Creator to give birth to his Son if I do not also give birth to him in my time and culture? This, then, is the fullness of time: When the Son of Man is begotten in us.[26]

For the Christian, the incarnation is not just a powerful metaphor. It is a historical event. But as Eckhart insists, neither should we think of it as a singular moment in history, having come and gone with the life and ministry of Jesus of Nazareth. With Mary, we too must ceaselessly give birth to Christ in our own "time and culture." Eckhart says this is possible because at the deepest core of every person is what he calls the "Ground" of being. He describes this as a silent abyss beyond all form, thoughts, experiences, or perception. Like the Virgin's womb it is the eternal meeting place between the divine and human within every person. Each of us comes to embody the ongoing and ever expanding enfleshment of God across time and space, made manifest whenever Christ is "begotten in us."

The Birth of God and Herod

Yet, whether birthed in time or within our own hearts, the birth of Christ still carries Simeon's ominous warning to Mary that a sword will pierce her heart also (Luke 2:35), that her Christ child will be a "sign of contradiction" and the cause of many to rise and fall (Luke 2:34). So also, once we realize that Christ's birth cannot be relegated to the past and that "it means little if it does not happen in me," we are immediately confronted with the hostility and egoic fears that rail against this birthing within us. Even as the light of Christ has barely begun to glimmer, fear, death, and despair attempt to stake their claim. The inexplicable darkness that rails against the birthing of Christ in the world is already intertwined with the beauty and innocence, the hope and tenderness of Matthew's infancy narrative. Thus, any sentimental associations we may have about the nativity are quickly mitigated by the brutality of the events that unfold in Matthew 2:16-17. Here we are told of Herod, who, in a fitful rage for having been thwarted by the Magi, slaughters all the male children under two years of age in Bethlehem and its surrounding districts. Although we have heard this story proclaimed innumerable times from our pulpits, it is tempting to shield ourselves from its carnage by dismissing it as an event illustrative of an ancient, brutal, and uncivilized world. At the very least, a story of infanticide serves as an uneasy intrusion into the peaceful silent nights of our celebrated Christmas traditions. But the truth more difficult to bear is that stories such as this are not limited to a distant or even a recent past but continue to unfold in our modern world before our very eyes. And worse, in our very hearts.

The interior struggle of the contemplative is mirrored in Herod's attempt to suppress any apparent threat to his reign, his worldly identity, his need for control. Herod is the paradigm of the ego enslaved to the false self. This is not the last time that the gospel will call on the reader to confront the kind of havoc wrought by the human ego. Within the narrative itself these events are shown to occur within the context of a divine plan, as is indicated by

Matthew's recitation of a heart-rending prophecy that he asserts has now come to pass:

> A voice is heard in Ramah,
> Lamenting and weeping bitterly:
> It is Rachel weeping for her children,
> Refusing to be comforted
> Because they are no more. (Matt 2:18)

In this passage Israel's matriarch, Rachel, cries out from her grave for the slaughtered innocents as she did nearly six centuries earlier when the children of Israel had been marshaled in Ramah in order to be sent into Babylonian exile (Jer 31:15). It is debated whether Matthew 2:16-18 recounts historical events that unfolded in the time of Herod or were introduced in a series of historical parallels between Jesus and Moses. It is almost universally recognized that Matthew presents the life of Jesus in parallel with that of Moses. For example, the genealogies of both Moses and Jesus places them squarely in the line of Israel's patriarchs (Exod 1:1-5; Matt 1:2-16). Both men are born of Jewish parents, and both of their lives are under threat from the rulers of their day. Later in the Exodus, Moses passes through the waters of the Sea of Reeds, even as in Matthew Jesus passes through the waters of baptism. Afterward, Moses spends a period of forty years tempted in the desert with Israel (Josh 5:6) whereas Jesus, the new Israel, spends forty days tempted in the desert (Matt 4:1-11). Both of them deliver the Law from atop a mountain: Moses gives the Ten Commandments and Jesus the Sermon on the Mount (Exod 19–20; Matt 5–7).[27]

Matthew's purpose in drawing such parallels is to show historical and theological continuity between Israel and this new revelation in Jesus. It may well be that Herod's slaughter of the innocents represents another brush stroke in Matthew's portrait of Christ. Somewhere between history and theology is something we might call "theo-history," whereby historical details give way to Matthew's theological agenda in order for him to convey something distinctive or unique about his portrait of Christ as the "New Moses" or the "New Israel." From that perspective, Herod's actions are unmistakably reminiscent of those of Pharaoh in the book of Exodus (cf. Exod 1:8-22).[28] Whereas, Pharaoh feared a growing population of Hebrew slaves could lead to a successful coup of his dynasty, Herod feared the birth of an infant king destined to be the savior of his people. In both cases, the infants are saved through divine protection: Moses through the cooperation of his mother and sister (Exod 2:1-10), and Jesus through the miraculous dream in which Joseph took heed of a warning to flee (Matt 2:13-15).

Aside from questions of historicity, the hostility of these worldly kings betray something universal about the inner life of contemplation. It is the nature of the false self and its projected ego in the world to rail, like Herod, against the daily birth of Christ within us. No less in Pharaoh do we encounter the devastating consequences of the false self in action, unmasking the human ego as its weapon of choice. The actions of both kings serve as a reminder that the enemy we face in the false self is not merely a nuisance or spiritual inconvenience; it is not just that aspect of myself I experience as petty, negative, or self-interested, but rather it lies at the root of history's most unfathomable displays of cruelty and brutality. As we will explore in the following chapter, these are our demons, and they are *the* enemy of the spiritual life through which the moral atrocities of the world are conceived and executed. They personify that place of darkness in the human heart that Christ insists makes a person unclean (Matt 15:18).

Herod represents a devastating indictment of humanity's capacity for darkness. But attempting to veil this fact from our spiritual and ethical consciousness too easily leads to a dangerous complacency. A spiritual truth to which our culture and society have so successfully numbed us is that the contemplative life is not a luxury or a quaint pastime but a matter of grave spiritual, social, and now even planetary urgency. Contemplatives know this intuitively. The prayer of silence that confronts the tyranny of the false self and opens us to the transforming power of the Spirit is a moral imperative.

For the contemplative, Matthew's narration of the slaughter of innocents demands not that we recognize the false self in Herod but that we recognize Herod within ourselves. To speak of the inner egoic Herod and the indwelling Christ is not, of course, to suggest they are comparable. Christ is the source of my deepest identity, whereas Herod is an egoic projection of the false self that strives to exist autonomously from that source. Christ is the ground of my being; Herod is but an ephemeral illusion. And thus, despite our interior resistance, we must acquiesce to a new ruler whose kingdom has no borders and whose reign has no end. One who rules not with an iron fist from a mighty throne but with arms outstretched on a wooden cross, who dwells not in a distant paradise but in the hearts of those who are in this world but not of it.

In our spiritual struggle between the egoic Herod and the indwelling Christ, we must not put down our guard or forget our own capacity for injustice, hatred, violence, and evil toward those who stand in the way of our socially constructed and fabricated identity. For the false self has only one purpose: *survival.* A survival to which it will cling, like Herod, with desperate tenacity. And thus, left unbridled, any perceived threat to its own survival, its own control or power, will be met with calculated defiance—and with fury. And the root of this fury is always the same: *fear.* Ravenous fear. Herod, let us not forget, was *afraid* and so—we are told—was the "whole of Jerusalem" (Matt 2:3). Herod thrives on fear, but the love of Christ casts out all fear (1 John 4:18).

Yet we too are afraid, at least inasmuch as we identify with all that is false within us. For we know too well how this story ends. In his own death Herod's fears about his eventual impotence are ultimately realized and he will all but disappear from history, while the infant Christ, also destined to die, will nevertheless reign triumphant as the Lord of history. And not just history, but of every human heart (Phil 2:10-11). Yet again the macrocosm of history mirrors the microcosm of the interior life. We should not be surprised that our first encounter with Christ—and many encounters thereafter—feel more like confrontations, even threats, because the Herod within each of us understands the danger to our constructed identity posed by the reign of this new king. How many of us are willing to abdicate the thrones of our power and worldly identity, achievement, and control to the Prince of Peace? And to what lengths will we go to thwart the birth of the Christ Child within us even as we pretend with Herod that we wish to pay him homage (Matt 2:9)? The outward appearance of fidelity is easy to maintain even as the interior struggle between Herod and Christ rages on.

Von Balthasar understands the immediacy and tenacity of this struggle for the contemplative every time he or she enters into prayer: "Every solitary hour that is truly such contains a challenge. That is why there is so little real solitude. Although we pretend to long for it, we avoid it and start up a noise within ourselves."[29] This is what the inner struggle against Herod looks like. Not the savagery of the slaughter of innocents, but the subtle, gradual, almost imperceptible erosion of spiritual innocence. Our youthful enthusiasm grows cold in a season of doubt, dark nights, and inner desolation.

This is what later generations of Christians will come to identify as the onslaught of our inner demons. The Christian spiritual life consists largely in our ascetical struggle against them. But such confrontations mark the beginning of contemplative faith, not the end. The tenacious resistance to prayer and solitude roused by the many noises we start up in ourselves are all futile attempts to thwart the birth of Christ within us. But not until every attempt fails do we cry out in utter desperation, "I can't; you must!" And in the moment we recognize our impotence to save ourselves, our birth pangs have come to an end, and Christ indeed is born in us.

Chapter Four

We Are Legion

Asceticism and the Interior Life

O! how fallen you are from heaven,
Day Star, son of the Dawn!
O! how you are cut down to the ground,
you who laid the nations low!

—Isaiah 14:12 (my translation)

I am not sure whether demons actually exist, but I do know this: *they are real.* Whether they inhabit us as addictions, attachments, or entrenched patterns of self-destruction; whether they impose themselves on us as depression, anxiety, anger, lust, greed, or lukewarm complacency, none of us have been spared the struggle against demons—not even Christ (Luke 4:1-13). Despite medieval depictions of serpents and dragons, horrid beasts and gaping jaws, most often the demons who assail us do not appear ugly or frightening to behold. Quite the contrary. They are beautiful, seductive, and glimmer with an enticing allure—at least upon first sight (2 Cor 11:14). Lucifer, let us not forget, means "light bearer." And who among us is not drawn to light?

Enter temptation. Like moths fluttering ever closer to the flame, we do not fly headlong into the fire but toy with it, drawn in by its seductive glow until in one irresistible moment we are consumed by the very thing we ourselves desired to consume. There is a lesson here in the stillness of the flame and the sporadic flight of the moth. Not all our demons stalk us. They do not have to. They have honed the virtue of patience as well as any saint. They glow gently and with infinite equanimity until just the right moment—*our weakest*. And then with the subtle venom of suggestion they whisper softly, and with unerring precision, exactly what we need to hear. So, the Epistle of James: "One is tempted by one's own desire, being lured and enticed by it; then, when that desire has conceived, it gives birth to sin, and that sin, when it is fully grown, gives birth to death" (Jas 1:14-15). The serpent of Eden, after all, led an entire race into the illusion of sin and death with little more than a whisper (Gen 3:1). Our temptations come in the guise of many forms and faces, each designed with meticulous calculation to strike at the Achilles heel of even the most virtuous among us (Gen 3:15). These are our demons. And they are legion. Yet, no matter their countenance they share but one tail.

Christian asceticism is the interior struggle against these sometimes subtle but powerful influences in our lives. Popularly associated with the Lenten practices of prayer, fasting, and almsgiving, asceticism has a much richer and more central place in Christian spirituality than most modern conceptions would allow. The ultimate goal of asceticism is freedom, particularly the freedom to love without condition or attachments. The practice of asceticism has varied from age to age and person to person, but all ASCESIS has in common an effort to unmask our attachments and wrest ourselves free of their dominance. For this reason, asceticism is a way of life not limited to a few chosen eccentrics but available to all who have been baptized into the death and resurrection of Christ. "Discipline yourselves, keep alert. Like a roaring lion, your adversary the devil prowls around, looking for someone to devour" (1 Pet 5:8).

Savvy to the countless shimmering masks our demons wear so astutely, the church's rite of baptism calls for a renewal of our promises with a piercing question: "Do you reject the glamor of evil?" This is a blatant challenge to the allure of our demons. The question itself demands we see them for what they are: *a facade*. Indeed, the whole of the Christian ascetical life might be summarized as a sustained commitment to reject the glamor of evil in pursuit of that which is authentically good and beautiful, that is, to discern between the veneer of beauty that leads only to death, and the beauty of the Gospel that leads through death to new life. Through baptism all Christians are called to contemplate beauty through the lens of the Gospel—most especially the cross—which stands at the center of Christian ascesis. Although the wisdom of the world can see nothing beautiful in the cross, for Christians it stands as the power and wisdom of God. It is the intersection where divine goodness and beauty are intimately wed to divine truth, not in the form of a proposition, but in the form of an embodied—*and crucified*—person.

That Little Space

Among the early Christian contemplatives of the Egyptian Desert, the rather crude depiction of demons as physical beings (often in the form of wild beasts) obscures the psychological sophistication with which they understood the demonic. In other words, their propensity to caricature demons as wild animals or in physical form does not reflect ignorance about the more elusive realities they personify.[1] In his *Life of Antony*, Athanasius narrates stories of St. Antony emerging out of the tombs where he spent long nights in prayer battered and bruised from his nocturnal battles with demons. Such legendary accounts must be understood as graphic depictions of interior struggles.[2] But this externalization of interior realities was not just a mythical construct. It expresses something about the inextricable relationship between contemplative solitude, asceticism, and the Christian life of virtue.

There is a saying, "When one of the Desert fathers told another of his plans to 'shut himself into his cell and refuse the face of others that he might perfect himself,' the second monk replied,

'Unless you first amend your life going to and fro among others, you shall not avail to amend it dwelling alone.' "[3] There is a tangible correlation between the interior work of prayer and asceticism, on the one hand, and the social dimension of Christian ethics, on the other. The temptation for the contemplative life to become divorced from society under the guise of spiritual perfection is betrayed by a Christian ascesis ultimately measured by one's love of neighbor. Solitude is a means not of escaping others but of moving into deeper solidarity with them.

After decades of solitude in the desert, St. Anthony and his fellow monks were sought after for their wisdom on the assumption that their lives were infused with prayer and a commitment to ascesis. They were looked upon as mediators of sorts, between the spiritual world and humanity, capable of exposing the social ills of their day and exorcising the demonic in others. For the desert contemplatives "the demonic" referred to oppressive external forces as much as it did the darker aspects of their own psyches. They recognized that social maladies of conflict, oppression, and violence *among* humans were a direct consequence of all that is broken *within* humans.[4] The cosmic battle between good and evil is fought in the microcosm of every human heart.

Again, St. Antony taught, "He who wishes to live in solitude in the desert is delivered from three conflicts: hearing, speech, and sight; there is only one conflict for him and that is with fornication."[5] Even Christ, the archetype of redeemed humanity, is led by the Spirit into the desert to be tested in his heart (Mark 1:12). Here in the desert, solitude and solidarity are wed in Christ. Forever after, Christian solitude can never be isolation. Christ did not go alone into the desert, and neither do we. The heart, much like the desert, is a place of encounter—and Christ already precedes us. Much more than a physical organ or the seat of emotions, the heart refers to the deepest core of our being, where, led by the Spirit, we encounter God and also our demons. It is therefore the place of our most intimate prayer and our greatest spiritual combat. St. Macarius of Egypt puts it succinctly,

> The heart itself is only a small vessel, yet dragons are there, and lions; there are poisonous beasts and all the treasures of evil; there are rough and uneven roads; there are precipices; but there, too, are God and the angels; life is there, and the Kingdom; there, too, is light, and there the apostles, and heavenly cities, and treasures of grace. All things lie within that little space.[6]

Many years ago, while discerning a monastic vocation I decided to spend an extended retreat at a Trappist monastery in New England. Some days before my departure, a friend of mine took me to lunch to discuss my intentions. He asked, "What do you expect to find there?" Naively I responded, "Peace, quiet, and serenity, to better discern my vocation." "Oh no!" he said, "It won't be like that! There are demons there!" He was right.

Without an intimate circle of friends or the scaffolding of my social identity, without the usual distractions or diversions at my fingertips, the darker aspects of my life began to surface in the silence. Like medieval gargoyles suddenly come to life, painful memories, old wounds, feelings of insecurity and self-doubt all began to emerge from the arched corridors of the monastery.

As I came to discover, the demons who dwell in monasteries are no different from those that plague us in the world. They do not haunt their hallowed cloisters awaiting our arrival. We bring them with us. But with fewer hiding places than society might afford, we are left more vulnerable to their assault, even as they too, in their boldness of attack, are more clearly exposed. Though it may not seem so at first, this is the gift of the monastery—to expose our demons that we might more clearly recognize them and the ways they otherwise conceal themselves in the world.

Thus, what we usually refer to as a retreat is really more of an advance; an advance from the world into "that little space" of one's heart and back again. Whether we spend weeks, months, or years in a monastery, or daily close the door of our private room to pray in secret (Matt 6:6), regular periods of retreat from the usual hiding places of everyday life open the potential for a real advance in the interior life. Exposing the camouflage of our demons and the places we have learned to hide from them leads us inevitably into the arms of Christ crucified, spread over the world like great wings of the divine in whom we take refuge.

> Be merciful to me, O God, be merciful to me,
> for in you my soul takes refuge;
> in the shadow of your wings I will take refuge,
> until the storms of destruction pass by. (Ps 57:1)

Our demons can indeed unleash what feel like violent storms of destruction within us: rage, pride, passion, and jealousy—filling us with anxiety, robbing us of interior tranquility and peace of mind, dampening our spirits, and crippling our capacity to love without condition. At other times, they cloak themselves so cleverly we hardly realize the discord they sew within and around us. After entire lifetimes given over to asceticism, the desert contemplatives knew well that the oppressive powers of the demonic are often impossible to overcome. In the end, ascesis leads necessarily to surrender into the protective shadow of God's wings. This is why St. Symeon the New Theologian says, "If you feel oppressed, go into a dimly lit and quiet place. Lift both your hands up to heaven. Make the sign of the cross over yourself. Then lift up the eyes of your soul toward God. The oppression will leave you."[7]

Renegades and Parasites

If the ancients understood demonic forces with more sophistication than their depictions suggest, we might ask conversely whether in a more psychologically astute culture there is ongoing value in speaking of our demons at all. It seems to me there is. Whether figuratively or literally, until we are able to name our demons we are unable to excise them. The effect is the same. We know, for example, that for those committed to twelve-step programs, the naming of demons is a way of life from which all of us could profit. In such circles, it is customary to introduce oneself by first name accompanied with the public acknowledgment that "I am an alcoholic

. . . an addict . . ." and so on. Naming a demon is the first step to gaining control over it. This same psychology is reflected in the Christian rite of exorcism, which requires the priest to compel the possessing demon to reveal its name. Regardless of what we make of exorcisms theologically, there is a psychological insight worthy of our attention. The shadow side of ourselves must be named if we are ever to be liberated from its dominance. There is as much an ethical as there is a spiritual urgency to this liberation. To the extent that we remain oppressed by our demons, we also remain complicit in the harm they cause others. Thus, despite the many ways our demons oppress us, it may be helpful to characterize them as two types: the renegades and the parasites. In general, renegades are crude and self-destructive while parasites are more subtle but ultimately more dangerous. I will take each in turn.

The renegades consume us like spiritual cancers, unskilled and bent on our destruction. Usually emerging from the cracks of unhealed psychological wounds, emotional trauma, or addictive tendencies, the havoc they wreak is most often quite evident for the world to see: lives destroyed by substance abuse, sex addiction, rage, greed, and compulsive patterns of behavior that all but destroy one's capacity to live integrated, productive, and meaningful lives. Like renegade teenagers, they tap into our most base adolescent impulses, demanding instant gratification and stunting our capacity to mature into the more sublime joys of emotional and spiritual adulthood.

When triumphant, these demons reduce us to little more than a shadow of our former selves, isolated from family and society, full of shame, remorse, and self-deprecation. This pattern entrenches us more deeply in the very addictions that have now become our only source of pleasure, or at least temporary relief from our inner state of anguish. The only thing worse than the addiction itself is the prospect of freeing ourselves from it. Like Israel being led through the wilderness by Moses, the Promised Land seems too far off. Anything would be better than wandering through the desert wasteland of our hearts, not knowing where our emotional sustenance will come from next.

The moment we think we have mustered enough resolve to strike out in search of our freedom, we find ourselves with Israel longing for the days of our enslavement: "If only we had meat to eat! We remember the fish we used to eat in Egypt for nothing, the cucumbers, the melons, the leeks, the onions, and the garlic; but now our strength is dried up, and there is nothing at all but this manna to look at" (Num 11:5-6).

As it turns out, we love our addictions. Despite our enslavement to them, we prefer the meager scraps of fish and garlic they provide to real spiritual freedom. We prefer the routine safety and the comfort of our enslavement to facing the unknown wilderness of our heart. Addictions mask our deepest fears. Better to stick with the slavery we know than confront the fears required of real freedom. And therein lies the power of our renegade demons.

Yet the overt and blundering destruction left in the wake of these renegades pales in comparison to those more lethal still, who have honed the skill of coexistence with us. Like clever little parasites they make their home in us, comfortably existing alongside our virtues and cunning enough to leave us in stasis. Their aim is not that we should self-destruct but something far more insidious: that we should become ordinary, that we should be neutralized or worse, co-opted, in service of the powers of "this present darkness" (Eph 6:12). Better that we should remain complacent in the face of our hypocrisies and the world's injustices. Better that we should find ourselves just comfortable enough to lack the motivation to challenge the status quo of our interior lives, the state of the world, or the plight of others.

The last thing a parasitic demon wants is for us to engage in any real self-examination that might spark an inner conversion or moral uprising, especially one that leads to greater self-awareness or deeper solidarity with the oppressed or marginalized. They much prefer a host who is content enough to make for themselves an acceptable life without ever realizing what it means to live to the full (cf. John 10:10): to exist, but never to thrive, to be just content enough, busy enough, distracted enough, or sedentary enough to do nothing in the face of evil. While most of us will never be counted among the infamous tyrants or conspicuous villains of history, the only moral climate these demons need to flourish is one that renders us extraordinarily mediocre.

Spiritual parasites are the most difficult to recognize because they are so adept at discretion. These demons do not emerge from places of brokenness and trauma—quite the opposite! They rise up from our experience of comfort and the desire to maintain it. They walk with ease throughout the sprawling suburbs of our interior life where comfort and convenience are readily at hand. They are like perfect tenants who pay their rent on time, thrive in a swept and tidy house, and always manage to maintain a low profile. They are quiet and unassuming lest they draw our attention to their shrewd handiwork. They befriend us just enough that we feel no compulsion to call their presence into question, much less evict them from our lives. In fact, if we are honest, we might secretly admit to enjoying their company. They are helpful and flattering, willing to go the extra mile to please us, and display a near perfect etiquette, having mastered the language of spiritual decorum and social civility.

Their symbiotic appeal is a simple but time-honored strategy that has worked since the dawn of humanity. Like the serpent of Eden, they know how to present the perfect blend of truth and lies. They know how to put our consciences at ease with token actions that never really transform society but nevertheless exonerate us from feeling the need to try. They whisper, "Give this homeless person a dollar" or, better, "Buy her a meal so she cannot use the money for drugs." Any impulse to reach across economic boundaries, to befriend her, to forge a relationship is thwarted before we can form it into a fully articulate idea. Thus, what I have really done is purchased a ticket to a freer conscience. I feel much better about myself as I pass her every day on the same street corner. I have done my part. In the end, she remains homeless and I sleep soundly at night. *Perfect.*

How frequently do we click hyperlinks from the comfort of our desk chairs to add our voices to a "save the environment" campaign, or send a letter to our senators, or add our name to a growing list of citizens who are being rallied to rise up against some new social ill. This growing phenomenon of feel-good activism that benefits no one but ourselves has a name: "slacker activism" or "slacktivism." What better use of the internet than to make us feel good about our contribution to a noble cause without ever requiring personal investment or engendering real change.

For our demonic parasites, it is essential we are made to feel as though we have done our part without ever disrupting or threatening our acquired comfort level. They know just how much ineffective engagement we need in order to feel good about ourselves. Yet, they also know when to keep entirely silent lest we grow impatient or embarrassed by their impertinence and resolve to take up a case against them. In short, these parasites know how to coexist unnoticed alongside our virtues. With the low din of interior noise, mental chatter, and token contributions for a better world, they dull the cries from our deepest selves for a fulfillment that forever eludes us as long as we remain in their grip. We remain comfortable but never fulfilled because secretly we know we are living something of an accommodated lie.

Although it may be convenient to believe that the demonic parasites we harbor are harmless, innocuous, and ultimately manageable, they are in fact the very forces that make evil possible in the world. Moral paralysis and mental distraction are enough to allow the most egregious tyrants to carry out their work of oppression without resistance. They are enough to allow the most unjust social systems to remain in place because they do not adversely affect me personally—and indeed I may well be benefiting from them.

Yet, the moment we take up resolve to break from our complacency, the demon of pride is poised to step in. It is no small irony that pride has all but the same effect as the demon of complacency. One's efforts to save the world mask the same desire to be god apart from God. How many of us are tempted to be the whole solution rather than accept the powerlessness of being but a small part of something much greater than oneself? How easily pride is masked as altruism. But whether we grapple with the parasite of pride or complacency, at the root of their handiwork is the primal curse of

Eden: the illusion of our separation from God and one another, an illusion that is as much of a social crisis as it is spiritual.

The less we are attuned to the love that deifies us, the less we are aware of the love that humanizes us. And therein arises the illusion of separation between ourselves and others, reinforcing a system of competition over collaboration. One person's success depends on someone else's failure. Desperate to fill the void that opens in the wake of authentic human relationships, we accept our lot as social consumers who are all but destined to value things over people. In a global economic and political system, proficient at protecting the consumer from the devastating effects of their own consumption, we become willfully blind to what we do, and what we fail to do, to others. We participate in systems that thrive on the backs of the poor, exploit the environment, and increasingly militarize the world in order to "protect our way of life." Such claims must then be bolstered by the wholesale creation of national myths designed to convince us of our benevolence and exceptionalism.

Having accepted the global narrative of "us" versus "them," we have become adept at turning a blind eye and a deaf ear to any inconvenient truths that would otherwise expose the scaffolding of our self-constructed identities as individuals, societies, and entire nations who need to believe we are good, innocent, and innocuous. This is precisely the milieu of discord and fragmentation in which our demons thrive. It is the wisdom of the world against which the cross stands as a sign of contradiction.

A Part for the Whole

An honest assessment of these divisions within ourselves, our families, our communities and nations, points to the fundamental error of mistaking a part of something for the whole. As we have already seen, what Christian tradition has come to call original sin is in fact the original illusion of separation. It is the illusion on which the false self is based, the distortion that blinds each of us to our inheritance as an "image of God." In its place, we erect an idol of our own making. Once the idol of the separate self is securely on its pedestal, we are capable of perpetrating untold evils on the newly perceived "other." In the aftermath of the expulsion from Eden, Genesis narrates the swiftness and ferocity with which this illusion of separation unravels into competition, jealousy, and rage. Through sin, death enters the world. And not only death, but *murder*.

> Cain said to his brother Abel, "Let us go out to the field." And when they were in the field, Cain rose up against his brother Abel, and killed him. (Gen 4:8)

The fundamental distortion that lies behind the Bible's first recorded homicide is rooted in the reduction of "brother" to "other." Cain reduced his brother Abel to a competitor, a threat, forsaking his identity as kinsmen. This is symbolic of the way in which sin is born when we reduce the whole of someone or something into a mere part or portion of the whole. It manifests itself in sexual objectification: the whole person is reduced to their sexual "parts." It surfaces in ethnic and racial prejudice: an entire community is set apart as inferior, and personal uniqueness is reduced to a mere stereotype. It underlies the ongoing horror of human trafficking: the infinite worth of an individual stripped away for another person's profit margin.

This same dynamic underlies the alarming rate of our environmental degradation. The pervasive disconnect between modern societies and the natural world open the way for entire species of plants, animals, and ecosystems to be exploited in acquiescence to every human whim and desired luxury. The majestic beauty of elephants poached only for their tusks; the gentle magnificence of seal pups brutally clubbed to death for a tuft of their fur; the destruction of forests and their inhabitants to make room for new factories or farmlands, to meet the demands of wealthy nations; the perpetuation of suffering and mutilation of farm animals in the name of higher yields of meat production.

Thus, the illusion of separation and the reduction of the whole to its parts are corollaries of one another; both a result of our failure to perceive the unity of the kingdom of God within ourselves and the world around us. It is a kind of spiritual blindness that leads to moral failure, driven by our attachment to satiate every passion and material desire, rather than face the void within. The first casualty of this kind of moral failure is beauty, or rather our ability to be touched and transformed by beauty, a beauty that, once perceived, will forever compel us toward the good—toward truth itself. Indeed, beauty is as elusive as it is universal, but for the Christian contemplative, it is inseparable from the unifying vision of the kingdom of God, a vision that is able to perceive the whole in all the parts, the Body of Christ in each of its members.

One of the fruits of asceticism is interior detachment, called APATHEIA. The term literally means "without passion" and signifies a freedom from interior attachments to one's passions, agendas, and appetites. Without ascesis we are easily weighed down by anxieties about the future, regrets about the past, and existential angst about our mortality. We cling to egoic identities and agendas in order to convince ourselves we are important and that our lives have purpose and meaning. We define ourselves over against others to establish our identity in the world. We value others not for who they are but for what they can do for us.

Asceticism is the intentional effort to release any passions, projected identities, or agendas that deny us the naked intimacy of Eden, an intimacy in which we know we are beloved of God. Without cultivating *apatheia*, the freedom to fully love others will forever elude us because the intimate knowledge that we ourselves are beloved of God will not yet have taken root in our hearts. This is the love that sent the galaxies spiraling in their course, the love that raised Jesus from the dead, the love that is as personal as it is universal. Prayer, asceticism, and the practice of virtue open us to the beauty of our union with all things in Christ.

Gospel Beauty

Trying to speak or write about beauty is like attempting to explain a joke. Once an explanation becomes necessary it is already too late—the humor lost, the moment passed. Throughout Western history one of the most enduring and contested philosophical debates about beauty has been whether it is fundamentally *subjective* ("in the eye of the beholder") or *objective* (an aspect or quality of the object itself apart from one's individual perception or interpretation of it). Of course, exclusive claims to either the subjective or objective approach ultimately collapse in on themselves. If beauty were purely subjective, we would have no way of communicating anything substantial of our own experience of beauty to another. And yet, even while allowing for differences between cultural constructions, personal temperament, and individual aesthetics, there nevertheless remains a striking consistency across time and culture as to what we humans find beautiful. Who would contest the loveliness of a brilliant sunrise or remain indifferent while standing beneath the canopy of a redwood forest? On the other hand, beauty cannot be understood on a purely objective level. A telescope peering deep into the night sky cannot, of itself, appreciate the magnificence of the cosmos or be humbled by its vastness. Only the human subject gazing through the instrument can experience awe at what the telescope registers.

Historically, these two poles between subjective and objective approaches to beauty have vacillated, sometimes with greater emphasis on one or the other. The classical world into which Christianity was born could hardly understand itself apart from beauty.[8] For the Greek philosophers, beauty was primarily understood as an objective quality expressed in outward forms of symmetry and proportion, harmony, and the coherence of many parts into a synthesized whole. The more perfect these qualities, the more inherently beautiful an object was perceived to be. This understanding of beauty gave rise to some of Europe's most magnificent cathedrals, to sculptures like Michelangelo's famous *David*, and to the mathematical symmetry that underlies our most beloved classical compositions.

The eighteenth century saw a turn toward a more subjective exploration of beauty in philosophers like David Hume and Immanuel Kant, even as the Industrial Revolution continued to further objectify and commodify beauty, which was in a sense to lose any real connection to it. Indeed, already in 1802, the English Romantic poet William Wordsworth criticized the world born of the Industrial Revolution as one that had become absorbed in materialism and had tragically distanced itself from nature:

> The world is too much with us; late and soon,
> Getting and spending, we lay waste our powers:
> Little we see in Nature that is ours;
> we have given our hearts away, a sordid boon! . . .[9]

Only in the past half century or so has Christianity seen a resurgence in a theology of aesthetics, as we see, for example, in Hans Urs von Balthasar. He lamented that, by the twentieth century, Western society had largely relegated beauty to a mere facade, a commodity that is to be marketed, controlled, objectified, or exploited.[10] Thus, in contemporary society, it has become almost necessary to relearn how to perceive beauty in our lives. The modern resurgence of the Christian contemplative life has much to do with an aesthetic impulse—a quest for the beautiful—in a world ever more bereft of it. If we are to be spiritually alive, fully actualized human persons, it is imperative that we bear witness to beauty and, indeed, embody and mediate it. This the contemplative shares in common with poets, artists, musicians, architects, mathematicians, and physicists, all of them compelled by the love of the beautiful. Songwriter and activist Phil Ochs was right to insist, "In such an ugly time, the true protest is beauty."[11]

Christian ascetical practices do not seek to introduce beauty into the world as if to impose it from the outside. They simply bear witness to the beauty that remains after we cast aside all that is false and fabricated, that which remains when our attachments are set aside and we are liberated to love freely, without condition. If we do not see beauty, we are not looking. If we do not hear beauty, we are not listening.[12] The Christian contemplative is, after all, one who is compelled by the love of the beautiful or, better, who realizes his or her own beauty as beloved in the eye of the Beholder. That is why to see deep beauty—beauty, and not just sentimentality—requires that we also leave ourselves open and vulnerable to the world's suffering, to stand powerless and brokenhearted in a world in which Christ continues to be crucified in the poor and oppressed, the outcast, the aged, the innocent, and in the alarming exploitation of our planet. It requires us to reject the veneer of hostility and anger of even our worst enemy in order to see more clearly the face of Christ in them. This is the vocation of the contemplative because it is the Way of Christ. Not only of Christ the teacher and preacher, but of Christ crucified.

Where we discover genuine beauty, we have happened upon truth, and we recognize truth precisely because we discover it to be beautiful. Recall John Keats:

> beauty is truth, truth beauty, —that is all
> Ye know on earth, and all ye need to know.[13]

Yet, Gospel beauty is quite countercultural to the commodified beauty that von Balthasar lamented in contemporary culture. To this society the Gospel holds out for us a counterintuitive experience of beauty that is as transformative as it is scandalous. It is a beauty that can be relegated neither to the objective nor to the subjective; rather, it arises precisely in the relationship that emerges between the Beholder and the beheld. To behold beauty is to be fully awake. To realize you are beheld as beautiful is to be spiritually alive. Thus, beauty is neither sentimentality nor a luxury but rather a spiritual necessity.

To see beauty in the cross, then, is essential to the fulfillment of the human vocation to become other Christs. This is because the Christian ascetic must remain vulnerable to the world's horror, standing as it were at the foot of the cross—or, better, embodying Christ crucified—so that we may remain authentic witnesses to the unsurpassable beauty of resurrection faith.[14] We cannot live the light of Easter while flinching from the darkness of Good Friday.

The cross abides not despite the world's horrors but precisely in the midst of them when we see the world in Christ, or perhaps when we attain the interior freedom to see others as Christ in the world.

Love of the Beautiful: The Profile of a Modern Ascetic

A viable asceticism today must be reclaimed as a life committed to the love of the beautiful, not the adoption of morbid exercises that segregate the body as a special target for punishment or abuse. The enemy is not the body but the demons of disconnect and disintegration that would have us objectify the body as a threat or obstacle to the spiritual life. Ascesis does not condemn the flesh but participates in its redemption. It is an active cooperation with the indwelling Spirit of Christ to restore unity within the whole person—mind, body, and spirit—that we might reclaim our original beauty as images of the Divine in the world, that is, a beauty reflected in the corporate nature of the incarnation—the Word-Made-Flesh *in us*.

Yet, an authentic Christian asceticism can never cultivate an encounter with beauty divorced from suffering. Compassion, which literally means to "suffer with" (Lat. *cum passione*), is an act of loving participation in the suffering of others. Thus, Christian ascesis is transformational not only for the individual but also for society. It does not ultimately turn us inward, away from the world, but gives us an increasing capacity to open ourselves to the world's suffering—all the while embodying a ray of hope, a persistent joy, and a heart of compassion. In the truest sense the Christian ascetic is in the world but not of it (John 17:15-17). Therein lies the paradox of the contemplative vocation: to mediate the interior world of the heart and that of society. To be in the world but not of it is to be immersed in its beauty and its suffering without discrimination.

There is a prevalent misconception that ascesis is a matter of self-denial for its own sake—a kind of spiritual athleticism or religious feat that must be accomplished as a way of proving one's worthiness to God. But this offends the free gift of grace as well as the true spirit of asceticism, which is designed not to make us worthy but to lead us to the realization of our total dependence on God in every moment. Ascesis unshackles us from our attachments to the renegade demons that grow out of our psychological wounds, but no less from the parasitic demons that thrive on our creaturely comfort. Whether stuck in our wounds or clinging to our comfort zones, both result in a kind of self-absorption that prevents us from embodying the very pattern of God's self-emptying love for others. Asceticism is a commitment to live in a way that is whole and holistic, disarmed by an honest interrogation of one's own heart.

The examination of conscience is an honest appraisal of one's interior life before God, whose unconditional love makes it possible to admit of one's demons without fear or denial. Ascesis is not a morbid obsession with one's guilt or sense of unworthiness but a celebration of the experience of being loved unconditionally by God. When we fail to confront our inner demons, we risk projecting them onto others. The battle is either fought within or it is thrust onto others whom we literally "demonize." This is why Jesus challenged the angry mob gathered around an adulteress, "Let the one without sin cast the first stone" (John 8:7). His admonishment was in fact a call to arms, a revolutionary summons to make war on the only battlefield that really matters: *one's own heart*. But let us not mistake asceticism for spiritual athleticism. Athletic discipline is undertaken to succeed and triumph. Asceticism is undertaken precisely so that, in failing, God might triumph in us. With Paul, we succeed when we accept we cannot save ourselves:

> For we know that the law is spiritual; but I am of the flesh, sold into slavery under sin. I do not understand my own actions. For I do not do what I want, but I do the very thing I hate. Now if I do what I do not want, I agree that the law is good. But in fact it is no longer I that do it, but sin that dwells within me. For I know that nothing good dwells within me, that is, in my flesh. I can will what is right, but I cannot do it. For I do not do the good I want, but the evil I do not want is what I do. Now if

> I do what I do not want, it is no longer I that do it, but sin that dwells within me. So I find it to be a law that when I want to do what is good, evil lies close at hand. For I delight in the law of God in my inmost self, but I see in my members another law at war with the law of my mind, making me captive to the law of sin that dwells in my members. Wretched man that I am! Who will rescue me from this body of death? Thanks be to God through Jesus Christ our Lord! (Rom 7:14-25)

Any attempt to prove oneself "worthy" is the very thing that becomes an affront to God because such efforts imply a lack of faith in the one thing necessary: *faith in Christ*—the one who has raised us beyond the categories of worthiness and unworthiness to that of *Beloved*. This is not to suggest morality and virtue have no role in the contemplative life. They do. But historically there has been a stubborn tendency in Christianity to communicate a secret form of Pharisaism that places the ethical cart before the horse. The trap we keep falling into is the temptation to make salvation conditional on an adherence to a new set of laws or regulations. It is as if Christians prefer the safety of their slavery to the law, unable to accept the radical freedom of the Gospel we claim to profess. "But" says Paul, "now we are discharged from the law, dead to that which held us captive, so that we are slaves not under the old written code but in the new life of the Spirit" (Rom 7:6).

The salvation wrought through deification—membership in Christ's body—is a gift freely given. Morality does not lead to salvation; it flows from it. We are not called to a life of virtue so that we might be saved but because to act otherwise is beneath our dignity as members of Christ's body. Paul's language in Romans 7:4 is not an imperative ("you *must* die to the law") but a statement of fact: "*you have died* to the law through the body of Christ, so that you might belong to one another." Deification is the basis on which questions of virtue flow from the lived experience of oneself as a member of Christ's body. Is this not implicit in Paul's question to the Corinthians?

> Do you not know that your bodies are members of Christ? Should I therefore take the members of Christ and make them members of a prostitute? Never! (1 Cor 6:15)

The incarnation is thus the foundation and basis of all Christian morality because at its base is not first a commandment to love but rather a commandment to love rooted in the revelation that *we first are loved* (John 3:16). This is the truth Christianity must communicate above all else: *that each of us are loved because we are incarnations of love itself.* Only insofar as we effectively embody this truth can we begin to speak meaningfully of either a Christian ascesis or a Christian ethic. Thus, the opposite of worthiness is not unworthiness but gratitude (*eucharistia*). This is the root of the Christian spiritual life.

Self-examination leads not to self-deprecation but to gratitude for God who "proves his love for us in that while we still were sinners Christ died for us" (Rom 5:8). In the vacuum left by our failure to examine ourselves, the egotistical lie of our autonomy stands ready to rush in, projecting our moral failures onto others in order to avoid the hypocrisies we cannot bear in ourselves. "First take the log out of your own eye, and then you will see clearly to take the speck out of your neighbor's eye" (Matt 7:5). The ascetic thus knows better than anyone "the cross is the judgment of judgment."[15] Stripped of their capacity to judge, only compassion remains. Exposing the ills of society does not then come from a place of judgment, but from solidarity with those who suffer, particularly at the hands of their own demons.

As we move into a deeper solidarity with others, contemplation does not shield us from a broken heart but commits us to a lifetime of broken hearts. As we live more deeply into our deified nature, we live with increasing compassion for others. The lines between ourselves and others are blurred the more we realize we are but a part of the whole. Each of us is but a single member of Christ's body. As this spiritual awareness takes root in one's spiritual consciousness, it gradually counteracts the demonic distortion by which the part of something is mistaken for the whole. To die to oneself is not only to live for an abstract resurrected Christ but to live for Christ *in you*. The more one recognizes that all are members of Christ's body, the less one is able to see another's suffering apart from their own. To harm another is to harm oneself. To judge another is to condemn oneself. As Evagrius of Pontus observed, a contemplative is "someone who considers himself as one with all, because he unceasingly thinks he sees himself in everyone."[16] Thus, for the sanctified person, the underlying motivation for the Golden Rule is no longer ethical; it is spiritual. But so too is it logical. Once we recognize others as inseparable from ourselves in Christ, where is the wisdom in causing them harm?

> The sanctified person is someone no longer separated. And he is only sanctified to the extent that he understands in practice that he is no longer separated from anyone or anything. He bears humanity in himself, all human beings in their passion and their resurrection. He is identified, in Christ, with the "whole Adam." His own "self" no longer interests him. He includes in his prayer and his love all humanity, without judging or condemning anyone, except himself, the last of all. He is infinitely vulnerable to the horror of the world, to the tragedies of history being constantly renewed. But he is crushed with Christ and rises again with him, with everyone. He knows that Resurrection has the last word. Deeper than horror is the Joy.[17]

We cannot know authentic joy or inner tranquility by rising above the suffering of others but by entering into the source of our own suffering in solidarity with others. This is the way of Christ—the paschal mystery. To bear humanity in oneself is to identify with all humanity in our shared suffering and in the promise of resurrection. To "judge" and "condemn" oneself, according to Clément, is to examine with fierce honesty our own vulnerability to the influence of our demons. It is to recognize we are so caught up in their tenacious demands that there is no room to judge another. The perception that one is separate and therefore somehow morally superior to another is the greatest obstacle to one's ability to identify "in Christ" with the whole of humanity. And that is precisely the obstacle our demons strive to keep firmly in place.

The Eastern Christian compendium on the contemplative life known as the *Philokalia* translates "love of the beautiful." The thread that weaves together the collected works of the *Philokalia* is the Jesus Prayer, which is inextricably linked to the practice of "watchfulness" over one's thoughts, passions, and emotions. As we will explore more fully in chapter 5, the invocation of the name Jesus brings one into the intimate presence of the indwelling Christ. The Name is a lens through which one first notices one's thoughts and impulses before compulsively acting on them. The invocation is at once prayer and ascesis in which the trickling streamlets of disparate thoughts that run through our consciousness are concentrated into a powerful river that flows only of love. With this kind of interior integration of consciousness, we are gradually freed from our impulses and, as a result, more nimble in our ability to respond to the needs of others.

In this way, ascesis cultivates the freedom to love—and to love perfectly. "Be perfect therefore, as your heavenly Father is perfect" (Matt 5:48). But again, let us not mistake being perfect with being worthy. To be perfect is to be the most authentic self I can be, not so that I might love, but so that Christ might love through me. The more I die to my own attachments, agendas, and judgments, the more free I am to be myself. "I have been crucified with Christ; and it is no longer I who live, but it is Christ who lives in me. And the life I now live in the flesh I live by faith in the Son of God, who loved me and gave himself for me" (Gal 2:19-20). Or, to paraphrase Paul, it is not we who love but Christ who loves in us. This is the fruit of divinization.

Prayer and ascesis become two arms of the same interior movement that extend outward to embrace others in the struggle against injustice, oppression, and cruelty in the world. Thus, the ascetical movement of the Christian contemplative is not one of ascent to the heights of spiritual ecstasy but of descent into the material world after the pattern of Christ's own self-emptying (*kenosis*) in the incarnation (cf. Phil 2:5-8). More pointedly, Christian mysticism is not an ascent that rises above the world's suffering but a *kenosis* that descends into it. It is inescapably a participation in the cross of Christ in order to share in his resurrection. As Andrew Louth observes,

> In contrast to earlier forms of mystical theology based on the Platonist premise of the soul's natural kinship with God, Athanasius posits a great ontological gulf between God and all else—souls included. This gulf can only be crossed by God: man can only know God if God comes to him, comes *down* into the realm of corruption and death that man inhabits. And this he does in the Incarnation. Athanasius' understanding of the Incarnation and his understanding of the monastic life thus link up with each other. In the light of the Incarnation, those who desire to identify themselves with this God who comes down must follow the same movement. No longer will they be drawn upwards to holiness in ever greater likeness to the invisible God; now they will find themselves being drawn down into the material world with the Word made flesh. So, in the *Life of Antony*, we read nothing of the soul's assent to God in contemplation, but rather of its descent into the world given over to sin, a descent to the place of the demons there to do battle with them.[18]

The Desert Mothers and Fathers were among the earliest Christians who would have understood their radical commitment to interior ascesis in light of Christ's descent into the desert to do battle with demons (Mark 1:12-13; Matt 4; Luke 4:1-13). Indeed, desert monasticism was spurred in part by a desire to participate in Christ's own death and resurrection in an age when Roman persecutions against Christians had largely dissipated. The desert ascetics sought a kind of inner spiritual martyrdom of dying to themselves in order that Christ might live fully within them. St. Jerome referred to this desert way of life as "white martyrdom" in contrast to the bloody "red martyrdom" suffered by Christians of earlier centuries.

Historically, Christian asceticism arises more from this kind of imitation of Christ. With the exception of gospel narratives where fasting and almsgiving are presumed (i.e., Matt 6:1-4, 16-18), the origins of Christian asceticism find little support in the teachings of Jesus. He does not prescribe dietary restrictions or specific times for fasting. Neither does he insist on other forms of asceticism that would later evolve within the Christian tradition as a means to fend off demons. In fact, Jesus and his disciples were often criticized by his contemporaries for not observing fasts or sabbath rests when Jewish law would otherwise prescribe doing so (Mark 2:18–3:6; 11:19). Christian asceticism is not rooted in Christ's teachings but embodied in his person.

Despite a clear victory over the demons throughout the course of Jesus' ministry, they continued to assail him with ever greater vehemence (cf. Mark 5; Luke 22:3, 53). This battle is nowhere more decisive than in his passion and death on the cross. Aware of this escalation, Luke concludes his narration of Christ in the desert with an eerie foreshadowing of things to come, "Having exhausted every way of putting him to the test, the devil left him, until the opportune time" (Luke 4:13). The opportune time was of course his weakest. Not when he began his public mission but when, by all worldly standards, he was faced with the definitive failure of his mission in a public execution. His cry of dereliction—"My God, my God, why have you forsaken me?"—is not merely a poetic reference to Psalm 22:1 but a devastating insight into the interiority of a suffering messiah. Hanging over the precipice Jesus cries out into the Abyss. In response, there is only a great and terrible silence—and death (Mark 15:34).

The cross is an enigma. To gaze upon it is to see terror and beauty reconciled. Not a beauty born of appearances or facades but a beauty turned inside out in kenotic love. Is not our commemoration of Christ's passion called Good Friday because we see something radically beautiful, not in his pain and suffering, but in the magnitude of the love that bore it? To celebrate the death of Christ is to celebrate the death of death.

> Death has been swallowed up in victory.
> Where, O death, is your victory?
> Where, O death, is your sting? (1 Cor 15:54-55)

This affirmation of faith is as countercultural as it is scandalous. The crucified Christ is victorious through defeat; foolishness to the world, no doubt, but for Paul, the cross reveals the wisdom and power of God:

> Since in the wisdom of God the world did not recognize God through wisdom, God was pleased through the foolishness of our proclamation to save those who believe. For Judeans demand signs and Greeks desire wisdom, but we preach Christ crucified, a scandal to Judeans and folly to Gentiles, but to those who have been called, both Judeans and Greeks, Christ the power of God and the wisdom of God. For God's folly is wiser than human wisdom, and God's weakness is stronger than human strength. (1 Cor 1:21-25)[19]

The cross is a uniquely Christian symbol of beauty, not immediately apparent to anyone who has not encountered the Spirit of Christ alive in themselves. While beauty itself remains as universal as its description is elusive, the beauty of the cross is manifested in God's unconditional love, liberating forgiveness, and intimate relationship—all of which lay at the heart of the Christian spiritual life. To experience beauty in the cross one cannot merely look on Christ's disfigurement as would a bystander but must recapitulate the Paschal Mystery in their very being. The cross then becomes the posture of the contemplative in the world: arms outstretched, naked and vulnerable, dying to oneself in order that love might reign not through triumph over the world but in self-sacrificial defeat, not in human strength but in divine weakness. Thus, with Christ crucified, the ascetic does not retaliate against evil but absorbs it in love and thereby renders evil and death impotent.[20]

The beauty of the gospel is the beauty of the cross that makes us whole. Like its intersecting beams, all things are united at its center where the Incarnate One hangs crucified between heaven and earth. Here we see not a punitive God of justice exacting a human sacrifice but a kenotic God of love pouring out the divine life so to reconcile all things to himself (Col 1:19-20). And who among us cannot hear in the words of the prophet Isaiah the horror and the gratitude that has come to unique expression in the cross of Christ:

> Surely he has borne our infirmities
> and carried our diseases;
> yet we accounted him stricken,
> struck down by God, and afflicted.
> But he was wounded for our transgressions,
> crushed for our iniquities;
> upon him was the punishment that made us whole,
> and by his bruises we are healed.
> All we like sheep have gone astray;
> we have all turned to our own way,
> and the LORD has laid on him
> the iniquity of us all. (Isa 53:4-6)[21]

This is the descent of the Word-Made-Flesh, the descent into holiness and wholeness that all Christian ascetics must traverse. These are the wounds that heal. This is terror and beauty reconciled. Christian ascesis arises naturally within the larger pattern of a contemplative life devoted to the imitation of Christ. Central to that pattern is the Paschal Mystery, the dying and rising of Christ. With Paul, we are called to bear the wounds of Christ crucified in our own bodies not because Christianity is body-hating but because the body is the very parchment on which is revealed the holy writ of incarnation:

> May I never boast of anything except the cross of our Lord Jesus Christ, by which the world has been crucified to me, and I to the world. For neither circumcision nor uncircumcision is anything; but a new creation is everything! As for those who will

> follow this rule—peace be upon them, and mercy, and upon the Israel of God. From now on, let no one make trouble for me; for I carry the marks of Jesus branded on my body. (Gal 6:14-17)

Thus, the command to "take up your cross and follow me" becomes a summation of the Christian ascetical life (Matt 10:38; Luke 14:27). It is not enough that we should be Christ in the world; we must be Christ crucified. Indeed, the way of Christian asceticism is the Way of the cross. Without asceticism, the contemplative life remains incomplete. And without contemplative prayer, discipleship remains vulnerable to the influence of our demons by which we can easily confuse the will of God in us with a desire for a world of our own making. The oppressive influence of our demons has social implications and liberation from them frees us not only for our own sake but for the purpose of becoming more authentic disciples in service of others.

Asceticism and Discipleship

Christian ascesis is inseparable from social engagement, discipleship, and virtue. Asceticism is prayer turned inside out. It is a loving attention to one's oppressive patterns and compulsions in order to love others with radical freedom. It is attentiveness to the impact of one's actions in order to be part of the solution to social ills rather than a contributor to the problem. It is a willingness to keep vigil with those who suffer, that we might embody the beauty of God's love in a broken and violent world.

In what is the most vibrant account of Jesus' exorcisms in the gospels, Mark 5:1-20 narrates the ghastly story of the Gerasene man oppressed by demons. He lived among the tombs unable to be restrained, howling night and day, all while continually taking up stones to inflict wounds on himself. As Jesus approached, the man saw him from a distance and "ran and bowed down before him." Here is a metaphor for all of humanity, who, despite our demons, tend toward the divine as surely as a compass points to true north.

The Gerasene of Mark's gospel personifies the aescetic who even while under the influence of his demons runs toward Christ and bows before him. Yet even the weakest magnet in close proximity to a compass can easily misdirect its needle. To run toward Christ is at once to run away from false magnets so that one's spiritual needle points faithfully in the direction of true north, to Christ himself.

Thus, once the Gerasene man reached Jesus, he shouted at the top of his voice:

> "What have you to do with me, Jesus, Son of the Most High God? I adjure you by God, do not torment me." For he had said to him, "Come out of the man, you unclean spirit!" Then Jesus asked him, "What is your name?" He replied, "My name is Legion; for we are many." (Mark 5:7-9)

"Legion," let us not forget, was the name given to the largest cohort of soldiers in the Roman army, numbering some five thousand men. Here, Mark is literally "demonizing" the oppressive power of Rome that was particularly virulent in the mid-60s when he was writing. Like a Roman legion, the demons we harbor are oppressive. They thrive in a climate of fear and internal disintegration, which in turn isolates us from a full participation in our communities. We become like the living dead, preferring to keep company with our demons for the gratification they provide or because of the shame they induce, even at the expense of life-giving relationships. As Mark narrates, our demons are a source of torment from which we need healing, not condemnation; reintegration, not segregation. In a culture in which swine were the epitome of uncleanliness, we can better appreciate the significance of Jesus outwitting the demons by driving them into a herd of pigs, who, in a frenzy, throw themselves off a cliff.

It is one thing to name and even exorcise one's demons. But there is a communal dimension to this kind of liberation. Christian ascesis opens the way to freedom from the tyranny of the ties that bind us. But it is not a freedom for its own sake. It is a freedom that must itself open the way to a fuller life in service of the Gospel. To cultivate a spiritual life that is neat and tidy because it isolates itself from the messiness of the world deprives the interior life of its fulfillment. That is, the exorcism of "unclean spirits" must open the way to a new kind of possession by the Holy Spirit, whose divinizing presence in us leads to authentic discipleship. Spiritual liberation that is not manifested in social justice or transformed into service risks opening us to a worse spiritual condition than before, one that is easily overtaken by the spirit of pride, arrogance, a sense of superiority, hypocrisy, and condescension. These are the other spirits that threaten to fill the void of one who strives for interior purity and perfection apart from service of others. The *Sayings of the Desert Fathers* express this in a tale of two brothers:

> A brother asked an elder: "There are two brothers; one of them [fasts] six days in a row . . . giving himself a great deal of hard labour but the other one takes care of people in distress; whose task will God more readily accept?" The elder said to him: "Even if the one who [fasts] for six days were to hang himself up by the nostril he cannot be equal to the one who cares for people in distress."[22]

Jesus warns of such demons when preaching to the crowds about the dangers of hypocrisy and complacency in Matthew's gospel,

> When the unclean spirit has gone out of a person, it wanders through waterless regions looking for a resting place, but it finds none. Then it says, "I will return to my house from which I came." When it comes, it finds it empty, swept, and put in order. Then it goes and brings along seven other spirits more evil than itself, and they enter and live there; and the last state of that person is worse than the first. So will it be also with this evil generation (Matt 12:43-45).

R. T. France observes in his commentary on Matthew that "this cautionary tale does not relate directly to any of the exorcisms recorded in the gospel, but is a comment on a danger associated with exorcism in general. A person liberated from demonic possession remains vulnerable to further possession if they remain 'vacant.'"[23] Based on Jesus' teaching throughout the gospel, France concludes that this vacancy must be filled by discipleship. Therein lies the power of ascesis. We must be like the Gerasene man. Freed of his demons, he is sent home, back to his community, where Mark 5:20 tells us, "he went away and began to proclaim in the Decapolis how much Jesus had done for him; and everyone was amazed." The fruit borne of asceticism is the reintegration of the whole person within themselves and within the community of which they are members. This is the basis of contemplative discipleship in the modern world.[24]

The questions then remain: How does the modern contemplative engage in an ascesis that opens the way for real interior and social transformation? How does one identify their demons even as they open themselves to the reconciling grace of the cross in the midst of daily life? How do our interior practices "crucify us to the world" in a way that reconciles individuals and transforms society?

The Royal Way

Today, asceticism is often associated with eccentric hermits or religious fanatics, evoking morbid practices of self-deprivation that are deemed as unhealthy as they are unappealing. We hear of medieval monks sleeping in their coffins to remind themselves of their mortality, daily self-flagellation to mortify the flesh, extended periods of sleep deprivation to induce visions, the wearing of penitential garments to inflict bodily pain as penance for one's moral weaknesses. Many of these practices were no doubt well-intended, but it is hard to escape the sense they harbor a certain body-hating sentiment that in hindsight has no place in an incarnational faith. The body is not our enemy but a gift, a temple of the Spirit, the very expansion of Christ's own incarnation in the world.

Despite occasional historical excesses, the Desert Mothers and Fathers adopted relatively modest ascetical practices. We even read of cautionary tales warning that ascesis or the ardent memorization of long scriptural passages cannot themselves become replacements for an authentic embodiment of the Gospel.[25] Abba Poemen, one of the most cited monks in the *Sayings of the Desert Fathers* was particularly known for his moderate approach to asceticism, which he called the "Royal Way." This was a reference to Numbers 20:17, in which Moses sought to lead Israel through the Transjordan by a wide, easily accessible route of the same name. For Poemen, this Royal Way provided a metaphor for a way of asceticism that was accessible to a wide range of people, not merely a few spiritual elites.[26]

> Abba Joseph asked Abba Poemen, "How should one fast?" Abba Poemen said to him, "For my part, I think it's better that one should eat every day, but only a little, so as not to be satisfied." Abba Joseph said to him, "When you were younger, did you not fast two days at a time, abba?" The old man said: "Yes, even for three days and four and the whole week. The fathers tried all this out as they were able and they found it preferable to eat every day, but just a small amount. They have left us this royal way, which is light."[27]

If, at times, ascetical practices have tended toward excess, we should not forget this broader history of moderation when examining approaches to asceticism today. It seems, however, that in modern consumerist societies we are in little danger of falling into such excesses. To the contrary, what passes as asceticism today has been largely reduced in the popular mind to giving up cigarettes, coffee, or sweets for Lent, often with ulterior motives such as losing weight, starting a new health kick, or getting back in shape. While these goals are noble in themselves, the spiritual value of the Royal Way has been all but lost. Most notably, ascesis has become largely unmoored from contemplative prayer even though historically the two were inseparable. Indeed, they are extensions of one another.

While prayer is not itself an ascetical practice, asceticism is the leaven of our contemplation. It gives rise to our prayer by stripping away ego, making our hearts supple and our wills more responsive to the movement of the Spirit. The ability to release the relentless thoughts and impulses of the false self in each moment is an ascesis in its own right. Without asceticism our prayer remains dense, heavy, weighed down by worldly cares and concerns. The leaven of asceticism raises us to that place of interior tranquility, rest, and self-forgetfulness. The *Philokalia* calls this HESYCHASTIC prayer.[28] As we learn to release our cares and anxieties in surrender to God we gradually become the very embodiment of the Lord's prayer, "Thy Will be done."

Thus, meditation is to the mind what asceticism is to the body. Meditation is the practice of dying to oneself that Christ may live in us. Asceticism is the practice of dying to one's neighbor that we may reverence Christ living in them. Here we see the union between prayer and asceticism rooted in the death to self for the sake of another. "There is no greater love than this, than to lay down one's life for another" (John 15:13).[29] The love of God and neighbor are not two loves but one, fundamentally rooted in a single interior movement by which the foothold of the false self is gradually displaced by love itself. Both require detachment from the ties that bind us and the impulses that control us: compulsory thoughts, addictions, and behaviors—in a word, our demons. Both involve an interior exodus from the slavery of sin to freedom in the Spirit of Christ. Both require sustained effort and yet both succeed only in failure.[30]

Try as we might, we fail to love as much as we are loved. Neither can we pray as we ought. And too often our demons have the upper hand. But the beauty of these failures is that in and through them we come to realize our utter poverty before the richness of God's love. We come to realize our total dependence on the mercy of God. We come to realize we cannot save ourselves but can only accept our deification in Christ despite ourselves. Our failures become the seeds of God's success. Paul understands this as a radical abandonment to God's grace:

> A thorn was given me in the flesh, a messenger of Satan to torment me, to keep me from being too elated. Three times I appealed to the Lord about this, that it would leave me, but he said to me, "My grace is sufficient for you, for power is made perfect in weakness." So, I will boast all the more gladly of my weaknesses, so that the power of Christ may dwell in me. Therefore I am content with weaknesses, insults, hardships, persecutions, and calamities for the sake of Christ; for whenever I am weak, then I am strong. (2 Cor 12:7b-10)

We should not miss in Paul's experience a description of what we would call the death of ego: to be "content with weaknesses, insults, hardships, persecutions, and calamities for the sake of Christ." He is describing spiritual freedom by which the ego is no longer vulnerable to manipulation by the false self. Asceticism exposes our weaknesses and attachments, opening us to the ever-present need for God's sustaining presence in our lives. When the scaffolding of our distractions and the false pretenses of our self-sufficiency fall away, we at once discover our inability to save ourselves and the freedom of realizing we do not have to: "My grace is sufficient for you, for power is made perfect in weakness." To fail in the ascetical life is not to fail in the spiritual life but to discover the sustaining presence of Christ dwelling in us.

Asceticism is not an effort to make oneself worthy before God but rather to learn what it means to completely abandon oneself into the hands of God in every situation. For the desert contemplatives, anxiety and worry were interior signs of a lack of trust in God. It is perhaps also a subtle form of idolatry, whereby the ego is given central place in the inner sanctuary of the heart, which belongs to God alone. By contrast, *apatheia* is the expression of faith in a state of total surrender of one's cares to God. Among the gospels the virtue of *apatheia* is perhaps nowhere better expressed than in Luke 12:22-31 where Christ's admonishment to "consider the lilies" is not meant to dismiss the deleterious effects of real economic poverty but to make a clear association between worry and a lack of faith. Instead, he teaches, strive for the kingdom and all necessary things shall be given as well. The resulting interior equanimity allows one to love others without conditions or attachments. Douglas Burton-Christie explains,

> The *telos* of the monks' life in the desert was freedom: freedom from anxiety about the future; freedom from the tyranny of haunting memories of the past; freedom from an attachment to the ego which precluded intimacy with others and with God. They hoped also that this freedom would express itself in a positive sense: freedom to love others; freedom to enjoy the presence of God; freedom to live in the innocence of a new paradise. . . . Taken together, these images comprise a montage expressing the ultimate goal of renunciation and detachment for the desert fathers: Freedom from worry, anxiety, and care, born of a sense of total dependence upon and confidence in God.[31]

No one ensnared by anxiety is really free to love because by rousing one's passions and attachments our demons enslave us to their demands. Addictive behaviors carried out under a cloak of shame gradually take precedence over meaningful relationships. The accumulation of personal grudges coupled with a persistent spiritual malaise leaves one cynical toward others and disappointed in oneself. Paradoxically, as Macarius understood, when we discover the reality of God's mercy toward us it becomes the source of our own mercy toward others. That source is an immediate and liberating encounter with God's peace and love, a living in the present moment without anxiety. The *telos* of Christian prayer and ascesis, as Burton-Christie suggests, is the freedom to love God and others fully present, fully alive in the here and now. While most contemplatives will find it easy to love God (or at least their conception of God), loving other people often presents personal as well as spiritual challenges. But therein lies the key to the Royal Way.

Precisely because the Royal Way of asceticism extends beyond the predictable rhythm of the monastic life, it must be adaptable to the variety of commitments and daily responsibilities that face Christians living in the world. In other words, we might approach asceticism as more of a posture that informs everything we do rather than a prescribed program of distinctive practices. Without attempting to be exhaustive, I will look broadly at three such postures that exemplify how one might take up this Royal Way of asceticism for themselves. First, the ascesis of personal love; second, the ascesis of impersonal love; and finally, the ascesis of entrusting the world to God.

Other People: An Ascesis of Personal Love

"Hell is other people." So maintains the French playwright and philosopher Jean-Paul Sartre through one of his characters, Joseph Garcin, in *No Exit*. While this sentiment as it is popularly understood may often ring true experientially, a more optimistic Christian view would contend "asceticism is other people." That is to say, the darker aspects of ourselves we are forced to confront through our relationships with others do not present hopeless roadblocks to our spiritual development but a vocational call to love ourselves and others more authentically. For Christian contemplatives, this call to love is both the foundation and summit of Christian ascesis because it is likewise the foundation and summit of the whole Christian life. The British Carmelite Ruth Burrows wrote:

> In true love for our neighbor lies all the asceticism we need. Here is the way we die to self. What are the disciplines, artificial practices of penance and humility compared with this relentless pursuit of love? Perfect love of the neighbor means complete death to the self and the triumph of the life of Jesus in us.[32]

The most challenging forms of ascesis are not the ones we choose but the ones that are thrust on us through life's circumstances, especially when involving our relationships with other people. Modern suburban life presents any number of interactions or situations that may be interpreted either as roadblocks or as invitations to love, depending on our ascetical posture. Commonplace experiences we have come to accept as necessary evils of modern-day life are in fact schools of love: long lines, crowded subways, heavy traffic, fractured families, hostile neighbors, dysfunctional work places, and so on. If we perpetually experience these things as personal assaults or affronts to our inner peace, then we will never find the interior stillness we seek. As Burrows suggests, "artificial practices of penance" must give way to more nimble forms of ascesis that have as their basis the "relentless pursuit of love." These need not be heroic acts of grandiosity but may well be the moment-by-moment accumulation of a secret generosity toward others. As Jesus poetically admonished, even the left hand need not know what the right hand is doing (Mark 6:3).

And herein lies an invitation to ascesis in the modern world: to see difficult encounters with others as invitations to embody the love of God that we might see the face of Christ in all. It is a commitment to let go of our inner ranting, judgment, and resentment over a world that is not as we would have it. It is to learn the meaning of love and forgiveness cultivated for even the most difficult personalities. It is a summons to patiently counter egocentrism with compassion, even where truth must be told and respectful boundaries must be drawn. It is one thing to discover oneself in the context of loving relationships, but asceticism involves the more difficult practice of discovering oneself in hostile relationships.

> You have heard that it was said, "You shall love your neighbor and hate your enemy." But I say to you, love your enemies and pray for those who persecute you, so that you may be children of your Father in heaven; for he makes his sun rise on the evil and on the good, and sends rain on the righteous and on the unrighteous. For if you love those who love you, what reward do you have? Do not even the tax collectors do the same? And if you greet only your brothers and sisters, what more are you doing than others? Do not even the Gentiles do the same? (Matt 5:43-47)

The way we think about, talk about, and "greet" our enemies does in fact reveal something about ourselves and the demons we harbor. There is grace even in the midst of our most hostile relationships, a grace that reveals our shadow side, our appetite for revenge, gossip, and power. If we are attentive to this, we can find the sacred dimension of divine revelation about ourselves and thereby find the key to transforming these relationships into sacred encounters with self and God.

One's spiritual authenticity lies in the direct correspondence between one's words and actions, and thus the interior work of prayer and ascesis must become embodied in real-world action. Solidarity with others calls for a kind of fasting from our own emotional reactivity to difficult personalities. We let go of judgment long enough to cultivate a love born of compassion for their suffering.

The commitment to love one's enemy is a commitment to see Christ in them. It is a personal commitment to love them beyond the distortions of their ego, the projections of their false self, and the ravages of their demons. It is a faith commitment that this person is first and finally beloved of God. It is an ethical commitment that requires one to admit the distortions of their own ego, the projections of their false self, and the ravages of sin in their life. It is a spiritual commitment to see the log in one's own eye before attempting to remove the speck from the eye of another (Matt 7:5).

Traffic Light Asceticism: An Ascesis of Impersonal Love

I have often invited my students to consider the practice of "traffic light asceticism." For many of us a green light means "go" and yellow means "go faster." Red, of course, means "stop because the law requires me to do so." If we look just beneath the veneer of this hurried attitude we quickly see a kind of self-centeredness that persistently puts one's personal needs and agendas before the safety and well-being of others. The fact that I am late for work or for my next appointment is no one's fault but my own. The fact that I grow impatient in traffic or become aggressive with other drivers is a sure sign of egotism in play. But for Christians who are summoned to love neighbor as oneself, it is legitimate to ask how that love is manifested for the stranger. And here we see the link between ascesis, social justice, and ethics. For the Christian, social justice is the extension of personal love to the stranger. Where I cannot love someone personally, I can contribute to the creation of a society in which the health, safety, and well-being of all people, indeed all sentient forms of life, are promoted and respected. To stop at a red light not because the law requires me, but because love compels me, is to extend personal love to the stranger. For the modern ascetic, a red traffic light becomes an invitation not merely to stop, but to rest, breathe, and pray for those whose paths in life cross my own at a busy intersection. If only we cultivate eyes to see and ears to hear, all mundane encounters become sacraments revealing the presence of Christ in those around us.

The perpetual inclination to put myself, my agenda, and my interests before all else is the biggest obstacle to this manner of seeing and hearing—resulting in a culture that thrives on the spiritual blindness and deafness of its members. As a result, there is a pervasive sense of disconnect between myself and others, myself and creation. I choose to ignore the suffering of the laborers who make my clothing, the migrant workers who harvest my food, the torturing of farm animals perpetuated by the modern meat industry, the abundance of plastics that are filling our oceans, the burning of carbon fuels that are destroying our ecosystem. But traffic light asceticism is an exercise in fasting from this kind of willful ignorance. It is the cultivation of an intentional life in which one increasingly abides in the awareness of the impact of one's choices and actions on others.

The parasitic demons that have settled within our shadows either lull us into complacency or cripple us with paralysis at the magnitude of suffering and destruction left in the wake of human civilization. Too big to acknowledge or assimilate, we succumb either to denial or a persistent state of anxiety that masks our larger questions of disconnect and narrows our concerns to a myopic preoccupation with ourselves. Self-absorption becomes the antidote for facing the reality of the world and one's ethical responsibility to it. If I can only keep myself busy I will feel important enough to justify my hurried, anxiety-ridden life. I insulate myself from any suggestion that my real fulfillment lies in the abandonment of my self-preoccupation for the sake of others. Because to do so is to risk accepting how little I have loved compared to the infinite love of God I have come to know in Christ (John 3:16). It is to risk acknowledging how little I have done in the face of suffering and, worse, how much my own way of life contributes to the suffering of others.

The demon of anxiety lurks just beneath the surface of so much of what we do on a regular basis that we hardly notice how much of our behavior is ruled by it. How easily we can lose sight of the fact that these annoyances can only exist in a world of privilege where there are in fact markets, systems of public transportation, and a lawful society. How easily we can forget that coping with long lines at a grocery store is infinitely better than the struggles of so many who must cope with a scarcity of healthy food and clean water, or who lack the necessary transportation to attend school or a village market where they might eke out a living. How accustomed many of us have grown to living in well-ordered societies rather than war-torn regions overrun by gangs, terrorist organizations, or despotic governments. As von Balthasar observed,

> Solitude: the great disappointment of many who wish to be virginal for God's sake. They seek silence, a consecrated space, but in silence they find themselves and forget that true solitude, Christ's solitude, is that of the person deprived of rights, the person abandoned defenselessly to all the importunities of men: here there is no protection, no "enclosure," but only floating, adrift on the high seas. Here many a pious person has become a philistine.[33]

Traffic light asceticism is but a symbol for the cultivation of an intentional life in and through the mechanisms of daily life. It is an ascetical posture that sees in the mundane invitations to contribute to a just society by extending personal love to the stranger. It is a way to transform daily frustrations, annoyances, and pet peeves into opportunities to love: to see in every red light an invitation to enter the hermitage of one's heart, to see in every long line a sacred procession into the present moment where God comes out to greet us, to realize in every minute choice the global consequences of our personal decisions. Each of us carries a "consecrated space" in our heart where we can enter solitude even in the midst our most crowded cities; a solitude not of isolation but of solidarity with all. Every moment is an invitation to enter the interior "enclosure" that opens the way to an identification with Christ in all.

But there are times when our actions—no matter how virtuous, well-intended, or authentic—are not enough, when no matter how much we love others, or work toward a peace born of justice, the world is confronted with bewildering acts of hatred or violence that defy description. There are times when all we can do is let God be God, and with Christ abide in the midst of a suffering we can do nothing to alleviate. This too is an ascetical practice, and perhaps the most difficult to take up because we must be content to admit our powerlessness, live with unanswerable questions, and relinquish our desire to conform the world to our vision of it. Herein lies the power of our powerlessness—the practice of keeping vigil.

Keeping Vigil: Solidarity in the Midst of Suffering

Macarius of Egypt once observed of the ascetical life:

> Those who have been deemed worthy to become children of God and to be reborn by the Holy Spirit from above, who have within themselves Christ, illuminating and bringing them rest, are guided in many and various ways by the Spirit. They are invisibly acted upon in the heart, in spiritual tranquility, by grace. . . . Sometimes they find themselves immersed in weeping and lamenting over the human race and in pouring out prayers on behalf of the whole human race of Adam. They shed tears and are overwhelmed by grief because they are consumed

> by the love of the Spirit toward [human]kind. At another time, they are so enflamed by the Spirit with such joy and love that, if it were possible, they would gather every human being into their very hearts, without distinguishing the bad and good. . . . Sometimes they are lifted up in "joy unspeakable" (1 Pt. 1:8).[34]

Macarius describes here a spiritual solidarity with all of humanity that can only arise from the heart of one who knows what it is to keep vigil. That is, to be entirely present to reality with a heart full of compassion and a mind free of judgment. Such a one is "reborn by the Holy Spirit," "guided in many and various ways by the Spirit," and "consumed by the love of the Spirit." Thus, to keep vigil is an ascesis born of the Spirit by which one is so identified with the whole of humanity as to all but lose the ability to distinguish between themselves and others.

This kind of solidarity can only be born of grace, whereby one is infused with an unshakable inner tranquility "illuminating" and "bringing them rest" even amidst the conflicting emotions that inevitably arise. There is no need to suppress one's emotions or alter them. One simply remains tranquil in the midst of them, opening one's heart to an unbridled empathy that is not content to witness the joy and suffering of others as would a bystander, but participates in their experience as members of the same Body of Christ.

Indeed, the ecstasy and the anguish of keeping vigil is the ecstasy and anguish of being "consumed by love," "overwhelmed by grief" and "inflamed with joy." It is an ascesis of entering into solidarity with all—especially with all who suffer. Like the faithful women of Calvary who kept their courageous vigil of tears at the foot of the cross, we are summoned to abide, unblinking, before Christ still crucified in our midst.

To keep vigil is to hold out a tenacious refusal to medicate, distract, or isolate oneself from the world's suffering. It is to accept the influence of our own demons and our capacity to contribute to the world's darkness—if not by action then too often by omission. If we limit our contemplation to the good and uplifting, to the sublime and transcendent, our faith will become dishonest and inauthentic. We cannot be people of the resurrection while still denying the cross. We cannot be Easter people if we have not witnessed Good Friday.

In his Letter to the Galatians Paul proclaimed, "May I never boast of anything except the cross of our Lord Jesus Christ, by which the world has been crucified to me, and I to the world" (Gal 6:14). To boast in our weakness in the midst of suffering is not to sink into nihilism but to embody a uniquely Christian optimism that insists on the light of the resurrection even while standing in the shadow of the cross. It is this same optimism that echoes in the heart of the contemplative who forgives the world's darkness if only to prove that faith not fate, love not hate, life not death have the final say. "Father forgive them, they know not what they do!" (Luke 23:34). Indeed, we are to become in Christ the very light that darkness cannot overcome and the embodiment of hope that makes a mockery of despair.

To be crucified to the world through the ascesis of vigil-keeping is to participate in the frailty of Christ by which we come to know the inner anguish of the cross "My God, my God, why have you forsaken me?" (Matt 27:46). It is to allow this question to become our own and to hang mid-air, as it were, vulnerable and naked, with no foothold or grounding, and to remain faithful—literally "full of faith"—knowing now, as Christ did then, no response will ever come. None, that is, except in Christ himself, through whose resurrection we are given not a decisive answer but a new and definitive question: "Who do you say that I am?" (Mark 8:29). Christ, we discover, is not the answer but the question. In response, each of us must take up again the mantle of our contemplative vocation to crucify ourselves to the world or, as Paul would encourage, "Boast in your weakness so that the power of Christ may dwell in you" (2 Cor 12:9).

To keep vigil then, is above all, to stay awake; to keep watch with Christ in the Gethsemane of history where so many innocents have been arrested, held prisoner, and executed for the cause of righteousness (Matt 26:38). No less in our own day, we are confronted with an almost unbearable weight of grief and bewilderment in the face of barbaric violence, acts of terrorism, mass shootings, endless warfare, refugee crises, and environmental destruction. With each new headline a dread sense of familiarity is ushered in. We have been here before, we have heard the talking heads and the politicizing, the accusations and judgment, and the questions for which there will never be answers. The temptation to seek distraction in blame and argument, anger and judgment, mundane diversion or avoidance is the temptation to fall asleep. What we really desire in all of these is to hide behind our anonymity, to keep the world at arms-length and the suffering of others impersonal. Yet, each of us bears a moral and spiritual obligation neither to edit the world's ugliness nor to remain complicit in its presence.

Solidarity with those who suffer is impossible without the deeply personal act of vigil-keeping whereby we consciously remain present to the experience of another. Who is to benefit if we are crucified to the world in an abstract or impersonal way? It is *your* heart that must be allowed to break with the hearts of mothers and fathers, spouses and siblings, in whose loved ones Christ has been crucified yet again through some new persecution or act of violence. That is why vigil-keeping is perhaps the most rigorous ascetical practice the contemplative life will demand of you. With Macarius it is *you* who must "gather every human being into your very heart, without distinguishing the bad and good." It is *you* who must refrain from the duality of judgment and accusation, so to enfold both victim and perpetrator in the tender mercy of God. And with relentless compassion, it is *you* who must hold this contemplative gaze with weeping and tears and dread. And as you do, reveal to all whom you encounter that the world is beautiful still, because you make it so—because *your* love makes it so.

Chapter Five

Becoming Prayer

Discipleship and the Interior Life

> *I believe that the cross will not be satisfied until that point when it has destroyed in you everything that is not the will of God.*
>
> —Paul Claudel, *The Satin Slipper*

"You can read all the cookbooks in the world," an old monk once told me, "but until you feel the heat of the oven, you will never bake a loaf of bread!" No book about the contemplative life can ever replace the heat of the oven. As the Desert Mothers and Fathers famously taught, "Go into your cell and your cell will teach you everything." The cell is the place where one learns to pray or, rather, where one becomes an apprentice of the Spirit who prays through us:

> The Spirit helps us in our weakness; for we do not know how to pray as we ought, but that very Spirit intercedes with sighs too deep for words. And God, who searches the heart, knows what is the mind of the Spirit, because the Spirit intercedes for the saints according to the will of God. (Rom 8:26-27)

The contemplative life is a school of love by which the Spirit intercedes in us with sighs too deep for words. It is a life radically oriented toward God who is radically oriented toward us. To cultivate silence and solitude, prayer and asceticism is to cultivate the love of God in one's heart. This is the mind of the Spirit and the will of God: that we come to know ourselves as other Christs in the world. This is what it means to live into our deification. And in this school of love the cell is of central importance. In the foreword to her translation of the *Sayings of the Desert Fathers*, Benedicta Ward observes:

> The aim of the monk's lives was not asceticism, but God, and the way to God was charity. . . . The monks went without sleep because they were watching for the Lord; they did not speak because they were listening to God; they fasted because they were fed by the word of God. It was the end that mattered, the ascetic practices were only a means. The cell was of central importance in their asceticism. . . . The point was that unless a man could find God in this one place, his cell, he would not find him by going somewhere else. But they had no illusions about what it meant to stay in the cell: it meant to stay there in mind as well as in body. To stay there in body, but to think about the outside world, was already to have left it.[1]

To stay in the cell with both mind and body is to feel the heat of the oven. But what does that mean for contemplatives living in the world? As Ward observes, the cell is more than just a physical location; it is a spiritual state. To find a cell—a place of prayerful solitude into which one can advance at regular intervals—is a great gift for those who wish to embrace the contemplative life: a room (or the corner of a room!) with a door that can be closed, a park bench, a patch of grass under a favorite tree, a solitary pew in the back of a cavernous church where one can get lost in an otherwise bustling city. Wherever your cell might be—find it and go there. Go there often. And once you are there, remain there even when you feel the heat of the oven—the dryness, the boredom, the distraction, the display of memories good and painful, the waves of feelings, questions, and emotions. And yes, the demons.

The location of the cell does not matter. It is only a doorway to the spiritual cell you carry in the little space of your own heart. And if your circumstances do not permit you a stable place to return, there is nothing to prevent you from entering the interior cell of your heart even in the midst of daily life. St. Francis de Sales instructed,

> Always remember . . . to retire at various times into the solitude of your own heart even while outwardly engaged in discussions or transactions with others. This mental solitude cannot be violated by the many people who surround you since they are not standing around your heart but only around your body. Your heart remains alone in the presence of God.[2]

St. Francis of Assisi, among the most beloved contemplatives of the church, did not himself live in a monastery but famously declared, "The world is my cloister, my body is my cell, and my soul is the hermit within!"[3] The expansive sense of the world as one's cell—the arena of divine encounter—assumes that true solitude need not be sought out but is something we carry with us, in our own bodies, even as we engage the world around us. For Christians living in mainstream society, the relationship between solitary prayer and socially engaged action is central to our understanding of contemplative discipleship.[4] This is because contemplative discipleship is not merely the result, or outcome, or flowering of a life of prayer but is its very embodiment. It is not simply that meditation gives rise to action or occurs alongside it but that prayer and action mutually interpenetrate one another. We might speak at once of prayerful action and action shot through with prayer. The disciples whom Jesus taught to enter daily solitude and pray in secret (Matt 6:6) were the same disciples sent out into the world two by two (Mark 6:7).

Through the cultivation of interior silence, Christ transforms us into salt of the Earth and light of the world (Matt 5:13, 14). In his darkest hour he implores the apostles, "Stay awake, praying at all times for the strength to survive all that is going to happen, and to stand before the Son of man" (Luke 21:36). In Paul's first letter to the Thessalonians he writes, "Always be joyful; pray without ceasing; and for all things give thanks; this is the will of God for you in Christ Jesus" (5:16-18). And again, in Colossians 4:2, "Be persevering in your prayers and be thankful as you stay awake to pray." The life of a Christian is a life of incessant prayer, joyfulness, and wakefulness; a wakefulness that cultivates interior serenity and gratitude even in the midst of one's going out into the world.

Thus, the vocation to "pray without ceasing" is not an appeal to say prayers without ceasing but rather to *embody* prayer in all we do. It is less about saying grace and more about eating *gracefully*, eating *thankfully*. It is less about what one experiences in the solitude of meditation than it is about how solitary prayer expands into one's entire life, one's whole existence: much like the ripple effect of dropping a stone into a pond. Our actions radiate outward from the ground of our being. This is the action that arises not from the thoughts and judgments of our mind but from the silence of compassion that we embody. We do not go forth from our solitude to serve the world but serve the world by including those around us in its circumference. This intersection between prayerful solitude and a compassionate engagement in the world is something we might call "contemplative discipleship" and is the theme of this chapter.

Contemplative Discipleship

The church cannot be reduced to a social program. It is first and foremost a spiritual entity: the *incarnatio continua*, or "continuing incarnation." Thus, for the church to be an effective agent of transformation in the world, its members must first be transformed in Christ. Contemplative discipleship is the fruit of contemplative discipline: an interior awakening to Christ in all. The Christ who dwells within, and of whom I am an extension, is the same Christ I serve in all. The two cannot be separated. Contemplative discipleship is the fruit of prayer, action born of interior stillness, speech born of silence. To forget this is to conflate Christian discipleship with social activism.

To be sure, the relationship between contemplation and active ministry has been open to a broad spectrum of interpretations throughout the history of the church. Traditionally, members of monastic orders discouraged active engagement in the world because it was seen as a distraction to a life devoted to incessant prayer and interior transformation. MENDICANT orders, like Franciscans and Carmelites, have sought ways to synthesize contemplation and active ministry around their communal life. The establishment of oblates and Third Order movements were designed to assist the laity in adopting the rule or charism of their monastic counterparts as best they could while living in the world. These various approaches to the contemplative life—monastic, mendicant, and oblate—have been perceived somewhat hierarchically, often privileging the monastic vocation over others. This tendency is reflected in much of Christian spiritual literature because it has been written largely within monastic circles.

However, as hierarchical distinctions between religious orders and the laity have given way to a renewed emphasis on the universal call to holiness (1 Thess 3:13; 5:23), it is incumbent to ask anew what it means for modern Christians to commit to a life of prayer that is not merely an adapted or diluted form of monasticism. Raising such questions should not engender a sense of competition among the many authentic contemplative vocations in the church; nor should one insinuate there are sharp distinctions between them when in fact they are distinguished only by different accents or emphases.

In an earlier age, before one was expected to be a hermit to be a contemplative, the Christian summons to prayer was more clearly universal in its scope. The writings of the early church fathers abound with instructions on the life of prayer ordered to the daily rhythm of creation—sunrise, midday, sunset, midnight.

Prayer is not merely a discursive activity of the mind. We pray, too, with the body: standing, kneeling, lying prostrate, facing east, enfolding oneself in the sign of the cross. As in death, we lie down at night with Christ who was laid in the tomb. Before dawn we rise in prayer, signing ourselves again in praise of the living Christ whose resurrection light fills the darkness. At the break of day, we awaken to pray facing east where the sun rises as surely as the Son rose from the tomb. In the bright light of midday, we pause to remember the darkest hour of Christ's crucifixion. Days and seasons, springtime and winter, sowing and harvest, the rhythms and cycles of the cosmos betray an intimate link between creation and redemption. All of nature is a theophany of divine presence, a doxology of praise, a cosmic liturgy to which the Christian is called to the fullness of participation.

All time is sanctified and all creation permeated with the paschal mystery of Christ's dying and rising, inviting Christians to pattern their entire lives in wakeful vigilance with Christ. So, the concluding antiphon of Night Prayer:

> Protect us Lord as we stay awake;
> watch over us as we sleep,
> that awake we may keep watch with Christ,
> and asleep rest in his peace. (*The Liturgy of the Hours*)

Many have suggested contemplative prayer is not a prayer of speaking but a prayer of listening. Yet, this does not go far enough. Contemplative prayer is a prayer of *being*. This is why the practice of meditation is almost universally associated with deep breathing. Our breath most immediately binds us to life. Contemplative prayer opens us to the fullness of life, the fullness of being. It is not something I do in addition to my daily activities as much as it is a way of doing everything else that I do. Meister Eckhart insists that for all who truly possess God, the work they do in the world is more genuinely God's work than their own:

> Now if a man truly has God with him, God is with him everywhere, in the street or among people just as much as in church

> or in the desert or in a cell. If he possesses God truly and solely, such a man cannot be disturbed by anybody. Why? He has only God, thinks only of God, and all things are for him nothing but God. Such a man bears God in all his works and everywhere, and all that man's works are wrought purely by God—for he who causes the work is more genuinely and truly the owner of the work than he who performs it.[5]

To see Christ in all is to see Christ not only in all people but so too in all times, in all places, and in all things. As Merton observed, every moment contains a fertile seed that has the potential to give life.[6] A regular commitment to solitary prayer and asceticism tills the soil of our hearts to better prepare us to receive the life-giving seeds of the Spirit. But tilled soil is no guarantee of a good crop, and a singular seed generously sown may unexpectedly flourish in a field left fallow. In the same manner, prayer and ascesis cannot be reduced to a method or technique that will guarantee a desired outcome or enlightened state. As Origen of Alexandria summarized eloquently,

> [One] prays unceasingly who combines prayer with necessary duties and duties with prayer. Only in this way can we find it practicable to fulfill the commitment to pray always. It consists in regarding the whole of Christian existence as a single great prayer. What we are accustomed to call prayer is only a part of it.[7]

On the Jesus Prayer

The part of prayer we frequently mistake for the whole of it is often called "meditation" or "active contemplation." As we will see below, Meister Eckhart says that the only way of prayer is the "wayless way." Moreover, if it is true that all of Christian existence is "a single great prayer," then to present a so-called method of prayer runs the risk of falsely conveying the idea that prayer is an independent category of the spiritual life rather than a manner of being that pervades all we do. Yet, if we are to understand what it means to stay in the cell in "mind as well as body," as Benedicta Ward observed, we must know what to do with the mind while the body is resting in the solitude of the cell. Recall Ward's assessment: "To stay [in the cell] in body, but to think about the outside world, [is] already to have left it." In other words, if silence and solitude are necessary ingredients for baking the bread of prayer, what do you do with those essential ingredients once you have them? Or rather, what does God do with them in you? It is one thing for St. Francis to urge us to retire into the solitude of our hearts, "even while outwardly engaged in discussions or transactions with others," but what does that look like interiorly? Moreover, for contemplatives living in society, how does the prayer of interior silence come to expression communally?

There are numerous books on prayer—both ancient and modern—that explore these questions thoroughly.[8] Without attempting to summarize or evaluate them here, I will simply introduce the way of prayer that I have embraced for over thirty years. If you find yourself drawn to it, adopt it; if not, find a way that most moves you to love.

The *Invocation of the Name* or, more simply, the *Jesus Prayer*, is a prayer that can be traced back to the New Testament (Luke 18:10-14) with more explicit references dating to the early seventh century. The form of the prayer is brief: "Lord Jesus Christ, Son of God, have mercy on me, a sinner." Yet as long as the name "Jesus" is invoked, the prayer may be reduced to any portion of this phrase, as, for example, "Lord Jesus Christ, have mercy," or simply "Jesus." When praying the Jesus Prayer, one simply calls upon the name "Jesus" repeatedly in the heart. It may be whispered on the lips or invoked interiorly in silence. The prayer is not prayed as if to call Christ from a distant place. It is prayed to the indwelling Christ of whose body we are extensions. It is prayed to Jesus, intimately present, and thus should be prayed quietly, whispered softly as if to our beloved, not forced or strained.

As thoughts, emotions, and memories arise you will find yourself distracted or you may realize at some point you have dropped the repetition of the name. Do not become anxious or frustrated. Simply return to the invocation of the name. Distraction is not a sign of failure. It is simply the mind doing what it has evolved to do: to think, evaluate, imagine, observe. Give thanks for a healthy mind and gently allow the name of Jesus to rise up again in your heart. Some find it helpful to associate the recitation of the name with their breathing. This can help ground your prayer in the silence of your body rather than in the chattiness of your mind. That is to say, allowing the prayer to ride upon your breath helps to ground you in the present moment by keeping you conscious of your body—uniting both body and mind in the cell of your heart.

Inasmuch as Jesus is the Word of God, the Holy Spirit is the breath of God. As we pray the name of Jesus we too breathe the Spirit, echoing the very love of God in whom Word and Spirit are spoken from all Eternity. Thus, the association of your prayer with your breath is a participation in the life of the triune God within you, and should thus instill a sense of peace and interior recollection. As you pray, you need not strain your breathing in any way. Breathe naturally, and if it feels right, repeat the name slowly and gently with each breath.

Consider finding regular times in a given day or week to set aside all other activity and simply pray the Jesus Prayer: ideally, twenty minutes a day twice a day. Work up to this slowly and make accommodations as your life circumstances demand lest you become weary. When you grow tired, stop. You can return to it at any time, even—*and especially*—in the midst of activity and engagement in the world, whether walking or driving, running errands or conversing with a friend. When you sense judgment arising in you toward anyone, allow the name of Jesus to rise up instead, gradually purifying your heart and mind of negativity, prejudice, and criticism. At times the prayer, "Lord Jesus, have mercy on me" may become "Lord Jesus have mercy on *us*" and " . . . have mercy on *them*" invoking the name of Jesus upon all beings and upon all situations. As you lie down to sleep, return to the prayer so that your heart might continue to ruminate on the name even as you sleep ("I slept, but my heart was awake" [Cant. 5:2]). When you arise, let the name of Jesus be the first word to cross your lips.

When invoking the name, you need not attempt to conjure an image of Jesus but simply rest in his presence without any need for imaginative projections, thoughts, or concepts. With time and attention, you will find that the prayer begins to pray itself within you. With every breath you will find the name breathing you. Over time the prayer begins to cultivate a pervasive intuition of the divine presence because to invoke Jesus, the Christ, is to invoke the Trinity. As St. Basil the Great observed, "The invocation of Christ is the confession of the whole, since it is clear that God is the one anointing, the Son is the one anointed, and the Spirit is the anointing, as we have learned from Peter in Acts: 'Jesus of Nazareth, whom God anointed with the Holy Spirt (10:38).' "[9] Thus, to invoke the name of Jesus is to call upon the triunity of God's holy presence.

The Jesuit theologian Walter Burghardt famously described contemplation as "a long, loving look at the real."[10] I might add, for the Christian contemplative that long, loving look is accompanied by a dark intuition that the *Real* is gazing back. Not gazing back from the outside in, but from the depths of one's own interiority. The Real—*Ultimate Truth*—is not an abstract concept but an embodied person (John 18:37-38). To invoke the name of Jesus in all times and places is to enter the cell of one's heart and remain there even in the midst of daily life. The interior cell becomes that sanctuary whereby we come to gaze lovingly on our Beloved and know that our Beloved is gazing back.

The fourth-century Prosper of Aquitaine, a protégé of St. Augustine, introduced the now-famous theological axiom, *lex orandi, lex credendi*, which loosely translates, "the way of prayer is the way of belief." In other words, the way we pray reflects what we believe about God. This is particularly evident in the church's liturgy but is no less true of the individual. The Jesus Prayer is a response to the vocation to "pray always" (1 Thess 5:17) because it reflects a commitment to a life of interior solitude even in the midst of community. It is not a prayer we "say" or a meditation we "do." It is rather, a prayer of *becoming*. That is, of becoming another Christ in the world. *Lex orandi, lex credendi.*

Christian contemplative prayer can never ultimately be divorced from the liturgy or the sacramental life of the church because the interior cell and the communal sanctuary are deeply intertwined. Even the Desert Mothers and Fathers emerged weekly from their solitude to join the *synaxis* or "ingathering" for the celebration of the liturgy. Then as now, the sacraments celebrate and realize the hidden mystery of our deification and bring us into deeper connection with those who celebrate what it means to be Christ's body. Like a continual heartbeat of the church, the liturgy is the place where the blood cells, dispersed throughout the body, are joined together in the chamber of the heart where they are rejuvenated and given new life-breath before being sent out again to vivify the whole Body of Christ. It is here that the hidden mystery of our deepest identity as "other Christs" is celebrated and fully realized. This, most especially in the sacrament of baptism—which unites us corporally with Christ, and the Eucharist—which is first and foremost the sacrament of deification.[11] So, Augustine insists, the church is before all else the Body of Christ:

> If, therefore, you want to understand the body of Christ, listen to the apostle telling the faithful, "but you are the body of Christ and its members" (1 Cor 12:27). So if you who are the body of Christ and its members, it is your own mystery that has been placed on the Lord's table; what you are receiving is your own mystery. You say *Amen* to what you are, and when you say that, you affirm what you are. You hear, "the body of Christ," and you reply, "Amen!" Be a member of the body of Christ in order to make that *Amen* true.[12]

It is in the great "Amen!" of the liturgy that the Jesus Prayer, and indeed the entire contemplative life, is summed up and celebrated. It is where we publically profess our identity as other Christs, even as Christ's presence in the Eucharist makes it so. In the great eucharistic acclamation, the meaning of contemplative discipleship is brought into sharp relief. We do not serve Christ by serving one another, rather, we serve Christ *in* one another. It is one act of service, not two. Put otherwise, the command to love God and neighbor is not a summons to possess two loves but one: as other Christs in the world, we love God in loving our neighbor (1 John 4:20-21). It is within community that our discipleship is both nourished and tested. If we fail to reverence Christ in one another we cannot authentically reverence his sacramental Presence on the altar: "Whatsoever you do to the least of my sisters and brothers you do unto me" (Matt 25:40). Likewise, solitude with Christ in the interior cell of one's heart is fulfilled in solidarity with the same Christ present to us in the poor, the oppressed, the suffering, the alienated. It is Christ "who is all in all" (Col 3:11) whom we encounter in solitude, sacrament, and society. Thus, whether we reverence Christ in silence, in community, or in service we affirm our own mystery as members of Christ's body. Let us then, with Augustine, make our "*Amen*!" true.

The Contemplative Vocation: To Become Another Christ

As the contemplative mind begins to shift from thinking about God to being in God, so too is there an evolution from praying to Christ as an object of devotion to living in the Spirit as members of Christ's body. Christ is no longer an object of analytical thinking, imaginative projection, or external devotion outside and beyond ourselves, but the very subject of our subjectivity, the heart of our heart, and the soul of our soul. If Jesus remains no more than an external, historical figure whom we attempt in some way to emulate, or whose teachings we seek to apply to our lives, our objectification of him inevitably becomes a barrier to our internal transformation. Instead, there must be an internal shift from analytical thinking to a simple contemplative resting in God beyond the use of words, discursive thought, or imagination. As I have observed throughout this book, Christ's mediatorial role between humanity and divinity is rooted in his person—*his Body*—of which we are members. Herein lies the distinction between *saying* prayers and *becoming* prayer.

An externalized Christianity limited to the application of Christ's words and teachings to one's life has not really embraced the scandal of the incarnation—the Word-made-*flesh*. Christ remains but a historical figure or spiritual teacher whose ideas we may admire and seek to emulate but whose living, indwelling presence we never really come to know. This reduction of Jesus to a historical figure apart from his indwelling presence was the basis of Aldous Huxley's argument that Christianity could never produce an authentic mysticism. He wrote,

> Contemplation of persons and their qualities entails a great deal of analytical thinking and an incessant use of the imagination. But analytical thinking and imagination are precisely the things which prevent the soul from attaining enlightenment. On this point all the great mystical writers, Christian and Oriental [*sic*], are unanimous and emphatic. Consequently, the would-be mystic who chooses as the object of his love and contemplation, not the Godhead, but a person and personal qualities, thereby directs insurmountable barriers between himself and the higher states of union.[13]

Analytical thinking and the "insurmountable barrier" it creates for a Christian mysticism of union with the divine is overcome once we intuitively grasp Christ's teaching on the vine and branches (John 15:5) or Paul's theology of Christ's Body (Rom 12:4-5). But as members of Christ's Body and extensions of his presence in the world, the question is, where does the vine end and the branch begin? Where are the boundaries of Christ's body? And where are the boundaries between you and me? As we will see, contemplative discipleship sees continuity where the analytical mind sees division. Contemplative discipleship embodies unity where the analytical mind perceives separation. In his response to Huxley, William Johnston describes this contemplative shift as one in which Christian mystics "will speak of the life of Christ growing within them to such an extent that they can say it is not I that sees: Christ sees through my eyes; He listens through my ears; He speaks through my lips; He blesses with my hands; He loves through my heart. Christian mysticism is not a looking at Christ and an imitation of Him, but a transformation into Christ."[14]

This "transformation into Christ" is the theological basis for understanding a contemplative vocation in the world. The term "vocation" is derived from the Latin *vocare*, which means "to call." To follow one's vocation is to respond to the universal call to holiness, which is the call to love. How we best love in the world will depend on our particular set of skills, passions, shortcomings, and so on. By way of analogy, we are like prisms, each refracting the pure light of Christ in the world through our uniqueness and particularities. Some refract red, some green, some blue or violet. The source of the light is One, but the manner in which it is refracted is virtually infinite.

The discernment of one's vocation compels us to consider the manner in which we uniquely refract the light of Christ in the world. And this requires genuine humility; that is, the ability to see the truth and admit it. This is not the kind of false humility of self-deprecation that so many have mistaken for virtue. Rather, to be truly humble requires one to admit of their gifts and strengths, their particular charism, as well as an honest assessment of one's limitations. It requires one to discern the unique manner in which they refract the light of Christ in the world or which member of the body they manifest. If you have a particular talent and find therein your passion, you have an ethical responsibility to admit it and place that gift in service of the broader community. "No one after lighting a lamp hides it under a jar, or puts it under a bed, but puts it on a lampstand, so that those who enter may see the light" (Luke 8:16).

Thus, if in my uniqueness I refract the light of Christ as the color red, I must strive to be the brightest red I can be. If I refract green, I am to be the most vibrant green I can be, and if blue, then the deepest blue possible. Like Paul's theology of many members comprising one body, the paradox lies in this: I best reflect the light of Christ not by adopting some image of Christ "out there" but by becoming more authentically who I already am. If I am violet, I cannot pretend to be orange or, if orange, I cannot pretend to be yellow.

Christianity has too often advocated a false sense of humility, which functioned like an inner audio-loop incessantly reminding us how unworthy we were—how "worthless," in fact. As a result, many of us have been content to remain a dull red, a pale green, a faded blue. Each of us is far more vibrant and beautiful than that, as any faithful reading of the gospel makes clear. And until we see it for ourselves, we continue to cheat the world out of the Christ-light we have been created to radiate. To be humble requires we become our most authentic selves rather than attempt to be someone we are not, even if that someone is Jesus of Nazareth. The Christian vocation is not to mimic Christ but rather to allow Christ to recapitulate in each of us what he did in his public ministry, that is, to mediate the very presence and love of God in the world as only we are uniquely able.

Ultimately the contemplative disciple arrives at a kind of active-passivity, in which being and acting in the world become extensions of one another. We die to self, that Christ might rise in us. The contemplative disciple does not seek to apply Christ's teachings to their life but to actively surrender their whole self that Christ might see, listen, speak, bless, and love through them, to use Johnston's imagery. This is why the Church understands the communion of saints as mediating or magnifying Christ in the world rather than competing with him in some way. Saints are exemplary mediators and magnifiers of Christ's light in the world—shining examples of the fruits of deification. They do not replace Christ any more than a hand or foot replaces the body of which it is a part, or a rainbow replaces the light that is its very source. This is why Paul can say in the first chapter of his Epistle to the Colossians:

> I am now rejoicing in my sufferings for your sake, and in my flesh I am completing what is lacking in Christ's afflictions for the sake of his body, that is, the church. I became its servant according to God's commission that was given to me for you, to make the word of God fully known, the mystery that has been hidden throughout the ages and generations but has now been revealed to his saints. (Col 1:24-26)

Vocation, then, is best understood in view of the communion of saints through whom the mystery hidden for ages is ever more fully revealed in the context of community. Whatever gifts I embody are not private possessions but intended for service to others. The eye on the body is not an eye for its own sake but intended to bring light to the entire body. Recall Matthew 6:22-23: "The eye is the lamp of the body. So, if your eye is healthy, your whole body will be full of light; but if your eye is unhealthy, your whole body will be full of darkness." To be an *alter Christus* in the world means something different for each of us. If you are an eye, you must see faithfully. If you are an ear, you must listen compassionately. If you are a mouth, you must speak truthfully. Even where there is disagreement or competing interpretations about the meaning of Christian faith, the Body of Christ needs all of its members serving to their fullest capacity if the mystery of Christ is to be ever more fully revealed. One's deepest identity is discovered in communion of relationship, and the particular manner in which one becomes another Christ in the world is always in relation to the universal Body of Christ. That is to say, one's personal identity in Christ is fundamentally relational.

To discover one's true self, then, is to discover one's vocation. It is to move beyond the illusion of the egoic "me" into a greater awareness that in Christ, "I AM." I am the hand, foot, eye, ear *of Christ.* To realize this is to realize myself as an *alter Christus* because one cannot realize oneself as hand, foot, eye, or ear *of Christ* without at once realizing "I AM" Christ. My deepest "I" does not refer to my identity as "hand" or "foot" or "eye" but to the Body of which these members are a part. Or, put otherwise, Christ can look upon his hand and say "It is I." Christ can look upon his foot and say, "It is I." My deepest "I" is always "Christ," not merely the member of the body that I manifest.

To die to oneself, therefore, is to die to the false self; a death we will no doubt experience as real to the extent we have come to identify the false self as the "I" of our existence. This, however, is a death that does not terminate in annihilation, but in resurrection. Freed from the illusion of separation that constitutes the identity of the false self, one's unique identity is raised up and re-membered in the risen Christ (Col 3:1-11). We are remembered as hand, foot, eye, ear of Christ. In this way we return to the primal awareness of the mythical Eden: We are not fully someone until we are someone-in-relation.

Understood this way, the contemplative vocation to become an *alter Christus* is the vocation to die to the false self in order to become more authentically who you already are. We should not, then, erroneously conflate the false self with the body and the true self with spirit. Resurrection faith cannot ultimately admit of a dualism between body and soul. The body is a symbol and extension of the true self, not its enemy. One's body is not a prison of the soul or merely a shell that one inhabits temporarily until released by death. Rather the body participates in one's ultimate identity as an incarnation of God's love. And it is this love, particularly the love of the incarnate Christ, that manifests the unity of the whole person. This is expressed poignantly in Colossians, where again we see a theology of dress employed to express an inner truth: "Above all, clothe yourselves with love, which binds everything together in perfect harmony" (Col 3:14).

The contemplative disciple is one who is clothed with love. That is, one whose progress in the spiritual life is measured by their ability to embody compassion for others, especially those who, by society's estimation, are least deserving (cf. 1 Cor 12:22-26). One meditates, then, not in order to produce a successful meditation but in order to be transformed into an ever more compassionate person. We pray not that we might become mystics but that we might become ever more authentic Christians who embody the love of Christ in the world.

John of the Cross takes up the analogy of a smudgy window to make the connection between deification and contemplative discipleship. A smudgy window, he says, is less able to transmit the sunlight shining through it. The more cleaned and polished the window, the more identical it appears with the rays of sunshine. While the nature of the window is distinct from the sun's ray, a clean window better participates in the ray of sunlight that passes through it. As one progresses in the spiritual life it is as if the window all but disappears, allowing the Christ light to shine through it without hindrance.[15] We should notice in this metaphor the sun does not change in the process, nor does the intensity of light that shines forth from it. God is always and everywhere doing what God does: shining upon us with infinite love. What changes as we progress spiritually is the window, that is, ourselves—our ability to let the divine light shine through us with ever-greater clarity.

This interior progression is reflected in the final monologue of John the Baptist in the Fourth Gospel: "He must grow greater, I must grow less" (John 3:30). Like the Baptist, the contemplative disciple is one who strives to stop striving, who actively becomes passive, who "grows less" in order that the light of Christ may shine through them with greater transparency. This is what it means to realize or live into the reality of one's deification. It is not mystical experience we are after but radical interior transformation, so that others may experience Christ more fully in us. Thus, mystics are not necessarily those who themselves have an experience of Christ within but *through whom* others experience the immediacy of Christ because they have been inwardly transfigured through deifying grace.

Drawing on Genesis 1:26, some church fathers found it helpful to distinguish between being in the image of God and being in the likeness of God. To be human is to be in the image of God, but to conform to God's likeness (whereby we become indistinguishable from the light of God shining through us) requires prayer, asceticism, and the practice of virtue. In this way, one's interior reality (*image of God*) is reflected in one's outward participation in Christ's identity and mission in the world (*likeness of God*). The more our divine likeness reflects our divine image, the more we become what Jesus was for those to whom he ministered: the presence and love of God in the world. This is what it means to embody prayer—to live into oneself as a deified member of Christ's body.

The Wayless Way

The manner in which the contemplative enters the solitude of the heart even in the midst of outward engagement is perhaps nowhere more deliberated than in the interpretation of Luke 10:38-42, the story of Mary and Martha.

> Now as they went on their way, [Jesus] entered a certain village, where a woman named Martha welcomed him into her home. She had a sister named Mary, who sat at the Lord's feet and listened to what he was saying. But Martha was distracted by her many tasks; so she came to him and asked, "Lord, do you not care that my sister has left me to do all the work by myself? Tell her then to help me." But the Lord answered her, "Martha, Martha, you are worried and distracted by many things; there is need of only one thing. Mary has chosen the better part, which will not be taken away from her."

A brief survey of various interpretations will prepare us for a closer look at Meister Eckhart's exegesis of the passage in which he upholds Martha as a paradigm of contemplative discipleship. Origen was among the first to interpret this passage as an allegory for the contemplative life. He upholds Mary as the archetype of the contemplative, spiritually advanced beyond her sister Martha who is still "distracted by many things (Lk. 10:41)."[16] This interpretation has traditionally been employed to extol the spiritual superiority of the cloistered life to a life of active engagement in the world. Other commentators, however, have given more nuanced views. Augustine, for example, sees Martha's activity not as inferior to that of Mary but as a necessary service that allows Mary to sit at the feet of Christ. "Martha has to set sail in order that Mary can remain quietly in port."[17]

Still more balanced views between the two sisters were developed by the twelfth-century Cistercian monks Bernard of Clairvaux and Aelred of Rievaulx. For Bernard, the home of Mary and Martha symbolizes the womb of the Virgin Mary, which received both the human Jesus and the divine Christ. He thus sees in the Virgin the perfect synthesis of both sisters. Aelred extends the allegory of the home to represent all Christian souls in whom both sisters (i.e., contemplation and action) are united. In the thirteenth century, Thomas Aquinas argued that verse 42 of Luke's narrative demonstrates the preeminence of the contemplative life but insists that it is better still to share the fruits of contemplation with others through preaching and teaching. Clearly, Aquinas is drawing comparisons between religious orders, not between monastics and contemplatives in the world. Still, as a Dominican, not a cloistered monk, it is easy to see a defense of the Order of Preachers behind his interpretation! Thus, he concludes, "For just as it is better to illumine than merely to shine, so it is better to give to others the things contemplated than simply to contemplate."[18]

These are just a sampling of interpretations of Luke 10:38-42 over the course of Christian centuries. But Meister Eckhart's interpretation in *Sermon 86* is perhaps most unexpected in its elevation of Martha's role over that of Mary. Underlying his reading of the story is the idea that the written word is vulnerable to misinterpretation because it does not always convey the correct inflection of the spoken word. Thus in verse 40 when Martha asks, "Lord, do you not care that my sister has left me to do all the work by myself?" Eckhart suggests that she is not being spiteful as other interpretations have implied: "Rather, she said it because of endearment; that is what motivated her. We might call it affection or playful chiding."[19] Later, when Martha further insists, "Lord, tell her to help me," Eckhart observes, "This last remark was said with tender regard, but this could not be gathered from the words themselves."[20] Arguing in this way he highlights two central features of his spirituality: the first is his concern that meditation can too easily become an end in itself rather than a means to an end; the second is his understanding of detachment as the highest virtue of the spiritual life. I will address each in turn.

First, Eckhart opens his sermon by describing three motivations that led Mary to sit at Jesus' feet: the goodness of her soul, a deep longing for something she could not yet identify, and the "consolation and delight" that flowed from listening to the words of Christ. Fearing that "Mary was sitting [at the feet of Jesus] more for enjoyment than spiritual profit," Martha's "tender regard" was rooted in her concern that Mary would remain "stuck in the pleasant feeling of sitting at Christ's feet and progress no further." In other words, Eckhart was cautioning that a person can become so attached to the delightful feelings of spiritual consolation in prayer that they meditate because it feels good rather than for God alone. Thus, one's spiritual "practice" can itself become an obstacle to knowing God. In another of his sermons he makes this point forcefully and colorfully:

> Indeed, if a [person] thinks [they] will get more of God by meditation, by devotion, by ecstasies or by special infusion of grace than by the fireside or in the stable, that is nothing but taking God, wrapping a cloak around His head and shoving Him under a bench. For whoever seeks God in a special way gets the way and misses God, who lies hidden in it. But whoever seeks God without any special way gets Him as He is in Himself, and that man lives with the Son, and he is life itself.[21]

The "special way" Eckhart refers to here is any approach to prayer that confuses spiritual feelings, experiences, or particular methods with attaining God. As we have seen, for the Christian contemplative there is nothing to attain. Through the incarnation God has already rendered a divine-human union that need only be realized in any given moment. So, it seems if a lack of monastic structure and communal accountability present some of the greatest obstacles for living as contemplatives in the world, by contrast the rigidity of structure and overt monastic trappings may present the greatest obstacles for professed religious who would more easily be tempted to over-identify with them.[22] The Cistercian way, the Benedictine way, the Ignatian way, the Carmelite way can be as much a help as a hindrance to one's spiritual progress. If we become attached to any spiritual way, method, or discipline that stifles the movement and freedom of the Spirit within us, Eckhart cautions we will be left only with the method ("the way") but miss God "who lies hidden in it."

In contrast to Mary, who is perilously close to this kind of attachment, Eckhart holds out Martha whose service is also motivated by three things: her advanced age and life experience, a maturity that enabled her to serve with perfect love, and, finally, the dignity of her guest, who was Christ. With these in mind, Eckhart concludes that Martha had matured beyond the need for spiritual consolations. She was not attached to any spiritual way but remained fluid and flexible in her ability to carry out her service in complete serenity as love demanded in any given situation. Martha's perfect embodiment of action and contemplation is signified by the fact that Jesus names her twice when he addresses her concern in verse 41. The first "Martha" refers to "her perfection in temporal works." The second "Martha" indicates that "she lacked nothing of all that is necessary for eternal happiness."[23] Martha, in other words, has grown beyond seeking God in a "special way" and thus "gets Him as he is in himself." To live nimbly moment to moment as the Spirit calls and love demands is to live in perfect union with God. Here again is contemplative discipleship.

The "dear guest" whom Martha served is the same Christ we each serve in one another. This is the significance of deification for contemplative discipleship. The contours of Christ's body are fluid and expansive, at once fully identified with the historical Jesus and also a corporate reality in which we participate. This participation constitutes our deepest identity even as it transcends our individuality. Thus, deification in Christ is at once a union with all members of Christ's body who together form a unified humanity. As Henri de Lubac observed, "If Christ is the sacrament of God, the Church is for us the sacrament of Christ; she represents him, in the full and ancient meaning of the term, she really makes him present. She not only carries on his work, but she is his very continuation."[24]

If the Church is the *incarnatio continua*, then the ministry of the church must be the *labor continuus*—the continuation of Christ's work in the world, not our work on behalf of Christ. As the Mystical Body of Christ, the church is most authentically an instrument for the work of the Spirit in the world. Understood properly, the faith-versus-works debate fought for so long between Protestant and Roman Catholic Christians collapses in on itself. It is not I who work but Christ who works in me. It is not I who serve but Christ who serves in me.[25] And again, it is not I who love but Christ who loves in me. Eckhart likewise concludes his sermon insisting it is impossible "to achieve freedom from works." He assures us Mary herself would eventually realize the same. He explains, it was only after Christ was resurrected and she received the Holy Spirit that "she really for the first time began to serve."[26]

We turn then to a second feature of Eckhart's spirituality that underlies his interpretation of Martha. It comes in part from his treatise on detachment. He writes, "I find no other virtue better than a pure detachment from all things; because all other virtues have some regard for created things, but detachment is free from all created things. That is why our Lord said to Martha: 'One thing is necessary' (Lk. 10:32), which is as much to say: 'Martha, whoever wants to be free of care and to be pure must have one thing, and that is detachment.' "[27] Eckhart goes on to elevate the virtue of detachment above that of love, humility, even mercy. He employs a number of rich images to explain what a state of detachment looks like. It is the immovability of a mountain against a "little breath of wind." It is the hinges of a door that remain still even as the planks of the door swing open and shut. It is the receptivity of a blank writing tablet, because any tablet already filled with words, no matter how sublime, must be erased if one is ever to write on it again. Immobility, stillness, emptiness. These are the virtues of detachment that Martha embodies, allowing her to live in total freedom: to love as love is.

This is what Eckhart calls in *Sermon 86* the "wayless way," by which he really means the total absence of a way (or method) because there is nowhere to go and nothing to achieve. Martha embodies this wayless way, indicated by the fact that she no longer has need to sit at the feet of Christ. She is simply present to Christ in everything she does. Or, better, she knows Christ, her "dear guest," is present to her. Thus, she is free to do what love demands in the moment, which is to serve her guest rather than simply sit at his feet. This, Eckhart says, is to live "without Why," to live no longer in need of anything. It is the way of pure detachment. She lives only in the present moment, in mystical union with God, desiring nothing but what is given in the moment, free of the need for spiritual techniques, methods, disciplines, or practices. There is nothing to strive for, nothing to desire, not any goal to be met.

By contrast, Mary's contemplation of Jesus' words indicates that she still possesses desire. Namely, she desires the bliss that comes from sitting at the Master's feet. This may well be a pure desire, but it is desire nonetheless. And because of this she is still not purely detached and thus not entirely free. To interject an insight from Maximus the Confessor: even the smallest string tied to the leg of a sparrow will prevent her from taking flight.[28] As Mary sits on the ground, Martha has taken flight. For her, and those who are truly detached, Eckhart says,

> Here God's ground is my ground and my ground is God's Ground. Here I live from my own as God lives from His own. . . . Out of this inmost ground, all your works should be wrought without a Why. I say truly, as long as you do works for the sake of heaven or God or eternal bliss from without, you are at fault. It may pass muster, but it is not the best.[29]

Notice the manner in which Eckhart's language blurs the distinction between divine and human: "God's ground is my ground and my ground is God's Ground." It is the same blur inherent in Paul's theology of the Body of Christ and in Jesus' own teaching: "I am the vine, you are the branches." Mary, however, still seeks Jesus outside of herself, desiring "eternal bliss" that she believes is beyond herself. Martha has no such desire or need for anything external because she "lives from [her] own as God lives from his own." Somewhat provocatively he argues in his treatise on detachment that a purely detached heart like that of Martha does not even know how to pray.

> What is the prayer of the heart that has detachment? And to answer it I say that purity in detachment does not know how to pray, because if someone prays he asks God to get something for him, or he asks God to take something away from him. But a heart in detachment asks for nothing, nor has it anything of which it would gladly be free. So it is free of all prayer, and its prayer is nothing else than for uniformity with God.[30]

So it is, if we want to fulfill the vocation to "pray always," even prayer must drop away. As long as there is an "I" praying to God, there is necessarily an "I" who believes themselves to be outside of God and therefore in need of something from God. And thus, like Mary, the "I" is still stuck in longing or desiring, failing to realize there is really nothing to long for or desire. If we imagine Eckhart's pure state of detachment is the destination at the end of a spiritual journey, the desire we feel along the way compels us onward even as it reminds us we have still not arrived. But when we do arrive at a state of pure detachment we realize that "God's ground is my ground and my ground is God's ground." There is no longer desire and thus no longer a need to pray *for* anything. Like Martha, we are simply living in uniformity with God's will as every moment demands. One has, in a sense, *become* prayer. This is what it means to become another Christ in the world.

Holy Transgression: Discipleship and the Incarnation

For contemplatives who are on the journey to becoming the very embodiment of prayer, or what we have been calling the *incarnatio continua,* there is no greater exemplar than Christ himself. Christ, who said, "I am the Way" (John 14:6), is for us the wayless Way, the path that is a person, the method that is a relationship. Jesus, let us not forget, was a layperson who lived the vast majority of his life as a member of the working class in relative anonymity (cf. Mark 6:1-6). Even before stepping onto the stage of world history he was no less God incarnate. Thus, if Christian tradition is correct in affirming that everything about the life and person of Jesus is revelatory, these thirty years cannot be dismissed as an insignificant precursor to his public ministry. Aside from the brief account of the twelve-year-old Jesus in the temple (Luke 2:41-51), the whole of Jesus' life prior to his public baptism is summed up in one line of Luke's gospel: "And Jesus increased in wisdom and in years, and in divine and human favor" (Luke 2:52). As Jean Sulivan once wrote, "I can't get Galilee out of my head. To think he remained silent for thirty years. Such a silence."[31] Indeed, the virtual silence around those thirty years speaks eloquently of the contemplative in the world who, like Christ himself, is to be found hiding in plain sight.

Amid our marketplaces and crowded streets, our subways and skyscrapers, it is the vocation of the contemplative to embody a "single great prayer" in order that they might season every hour with the salt of faith and shine on every person the light of love: that in every situation they may knead the leaven of hope, and in every place sow the seeds of joy. For the contemplative in the world, spiritual maturity is not measured by ever-extended periods of meditation but by an ever-expanding heart of compassion. There is no need or desire for attention-grabbing spiritual feats, mystical fanfare, or grandiose epiphanies. There is only the sacrament of the present moment—the hidden, imperceptible, but endless ways in which they are present to God and God to them. The demands of daily life become a school of holiness where the contemplative is led to the patient realization that they are extensions of the very Christ who walked the ancient streets of Jerusalem and who even now walks in our midst as neighbor, friend, stranger, and enemy.

Even throughout his brief years of public ministry, Jesus did not fraternize with spiritual elites, gurus, or learned scribes; rather, he plunged himself into the heart of the ordinary. Routinely, he drew his teachings and parables from the natural world, familiar to those around him, and used the most mundane images to shock his listeners into seeing the new world that was breaking upon them. In this new world—*the kingdom of God*, as he called it—the very idea of holiness and what it meant to be holy was radically challenged and transformed. No longer was holiness to be identified with something "set apart," as the original Semitic root (*qdš*) implies. Rather, the in-breaking of the kingdom was just that, the realm of God breaking into the realm of humanity.

It is this transgression that makes possible Eckhart's mysticism in which God is the "ground" of one's being. But if this is true of any individual, so must it be true of every individual. To realize Christ in oneself is to realize Christ in everyone. This interior realization brings with it the vocation to blur, transgress, and ultimately tear down whatever boundaries prevent one from "living without a Why." That is, from doing what is most loving, most compassionate, most liberating so that all who have been made to believe themselves an outsider may come to know that in God there is no outside.

The gospels are replete with narratives that center around the theme of transgression. Through his actions, parables, and sermons Jesus transgressed religious, social, ethnic, and legal boundaries of his day and inspired others to do the same. This takes on many different forms. Jesus broke with centuries of kosher law by declaring all foods clean (Mark 7:14-31); he dined with "tax collectors and prostitutes" to the scandal of many (Matt 9:10-13); he conversed with Samaritan women (John 4:1-42) and physically touched those whom his society would regard as unclean: women who were menstruating (Luke 8:43-48), those suffering from skin diseases (Mark 1:40-45), corpses (Luke 8:40-42, 49-56), and Gentiles (Mark 6:53-56). In solidarity with an accused adulteress he challenged the moral hypocrisy of those who would stone her (John 8:1-11). He overtly dismissed the observance of religious fasts (Mark 2:18-22) and was accused of openly breaking the sabbath on multiple occasions (Mark 2:23-28; 3:1-6). In an act of prophetic defiance that many scholars believe ultimately led to his execution, he expelled the money changers from the temple for thwarting its divine purpose to be "a house of prayer for all people" (Mark 11:15-19; cf. Isa 56:7).

Jesus embodied a holy transgression. His actions and teachings consistently emphasized the spirit of the law over the letter. He insisted that no religious observance was of greater importance than the practice of compassion and indiscriminate love for all (Matt 5:43-48; Luke 6:27-38; 10:29-37). Among those called to manifest his kingdom in the world, all divisions and boundaries of exclusion must give way to a fundamental unity in Christ:

> As many of you as were baptized into Christ have clothed yourselves with Christ. There is no longer Jew or Greek, there is no longer slave or free, there is no longer male and female; for all of you are one in Christ Jesus. And if you belong to Christ, then you are Abraham's offspring, heirs according to the promise. (Gal 3:27-29; cf. Col 3:11)

This is the spiritual unity born of the Gospel. Boundaries transgressed, broken, and torn down give witness to a kingdom that respects no borders, knows no ethnicity, defies social status and transcends gender. There is but an endless diversity sustained in the unity of Christ. Throughout the ministry of Jesus, anyone made to believe they were outsiders were healed, raised up, restored to society, and empowered to become witnesses of the Gospel—often to the very communities from which they were outcast (cf. Mark 5:20; John 4:28-30, 39). Repeatedly, the gospel narratives insist that healing, liberation, and reconciliation are never for one's personal benefit alone, but for the betterment of the community they are called to serve (cf. Luke 4:38-39).

Contemplative discipleship thus begins as an encounter with Christ that is as communal as it is personal. It begins with the end of my world and the in-breaking of the kingdom. It begins with a death to myself, and the rising of Christ within. And thus, contemplative discipleship is thoroughly cruciform, patterned on the paschal mystery of Christ's dying and rising. It begins and ends in paradox. In order to live fully in Christ, I must lose my life for the sake of the Gospel:

> Jesus called the crowd with his disciples, and said to them, "If any want to become my followers, let them deny themselves and take up their cross and follow me. For those who want to save their life will lose it, and those who lose their life for my sake, and for the sake of the gospel, will save it. For what will it profit them to gain the whole world and forfeit their life? (Mark 8:34-36)

In this we are summoned to let go of all that binds us from living fully in the Spirit, in order that we might be evermore transformed into the risen Body of Christ. We too are empowered to rise above the letter of the law, that its spirit may shine through us. We are called now, as were the first disciples, to take up our cross and to lay down our life, that Christ might continue the work of holy transgression in our own day and time.

There are a number of rather stylized passages in the Synoptic Gospels in which Jesus summons his first disciples who, at the time, are fishing with nets. On hearing the Master's call, they immediately drop what they are doing and follow after him (i.e., Mark 1:16-20; Matt 4:18-22, Luke 5:1-11):[32]

> As Jesus passed along the Sea of Galilee, he saw Simon and his brother Andrew casting a net into the sea—for they were fishermen. And Jesus said to them, "Follow me and I will make you fish for people." And immediately they left their nets and fol-

> lowed him. As he went a little farther, he saw James son of Zebedee and his brother John, who were in their boat mending the nets. Immediately he called them; and they left their father Zebedee in the boat with the hired men, and followed him. (Mark 1:16-20)

The fishing nets left behind by the first disciples serve as a poignant metaphor for the contemplative whose vocation it is to see all and serve all as Christ. "Whatsoever you do to the least of my sisters and brothers, you do to me" (Matt 25:40). The call to discipleship always requires us to leave behind all that ensnares us—the false self, attachments, illusions of separation from God. If we are to be "fishers of people" it is incumbent on each of us to examine how far our nets extend. Jesus demanded that his Judean contemporaries see God at work in Samaritans and Gentiles, in tax collectors, prostitutes, and adulterers. These were counted among the most morally repugnant people in Jesus' day, the antithesis of a righteous Israelite who had given their lives to God. This begs the questions: in whom do you see God today? In whom do you see Christ? Or, more important, in whom do you *not* see God?

Are you able to see with Martha that the "dear guest" you serve is Christ? How far and wide do you cast the net of "we"? Does your net extend to your family, your tribe, your people, your nation, your species? Who lies outside of the boundaries of your net? Where do you draw the line between "me and you," "us and them," "we and they"? Consider this question and reflect long on its implications, because wherever we mark the boundaries of our nets we mark the boundaries of our compassion.

The trajectory of Christian history has evidenced an ever-expanding net of inclusivity: from a small Jewish sect to the inclusion of ever widening circles of Gentiles; from the exclusion of women to an ever expanding inclusion of women in church leadership and ministry; from sectarianism and mutual excommunications to ecumenical and interreligious dialogue; from a blanket condemnation of the LGBT community to the increasing recognition of marriage equality in ever greater denominations; from Christian-based anti-Semitism and deep-seated racism to increasing solidarity with those who have been oppressed and marginalized throughout history; from myopic forms of Christian anthropocentrism to expanding engagement in Christian environmental activism.

Not unlike Jesus' own day, advances toward compassionate inclusivity are still met with resistance, persecution, and hostility too often from within the church itself. To be sure, the expansion of human consciousness is never a linear progression but marked with setbacks and failures that so often reflect our unspoken anxieties. Weighed down by fear, the expansive nature of authentic spirituality becomes stifled by religious legalism or biblical literalism that turns our fishing nets into personal safety nets, arming us with the false certitude that our little net contains all that can be caught from the fathomless ocean depths. Indeed, fear wrapped in a veneer of religion is capable of perpetrating terrible injustices. One's spiritual safety and well-being becomes idolized and religion is reduced to a security blanket, indeed an opiate.

The result is a repudiation of the Spirit of freedom and an enslavement to the letter of the law lest one incur the wrath of a vengeful God through an inadvertent misstep. Yet, Christ never commissioned his disciples to "go and be safe" but to "go and do likewise." Mature faith requires questioning, and discipleship demands risk. It is not *failure* but the *failure to risk* that incurs the Master's rebuke in the parable of the Pounds (cf. Luke 19:11-27). This is why Jesus insisted, "The sabbath was made for humans, not humans for the sabbath" (Mark 2:27).

Fear-driven religion thrives in the narrow demarcation of boundaries where one can feel assured about who is inside and outside the net of salvation. Fear-based faith is intellectually myopic and spiritually stingy, concerned more about being right than about embodying compassion. Such disciples of fear are so anxious about their spiritual well-being that they can hardly allow themselves to ponder the corporate nature of salvation. So deeply bound are we in the sinews of Christ's Body as to make it impossible for anyone to be saved until we are all saved.

But such spiritual anxiety rooted in an "us and them" mentality is nothing new. These are precisely the kinds of fear-based boundaries that Jesus' ministry transgressed in his own day. So too, amid advances and setbacks, the vocation of the contemplative is rooted in an interior commitment to an increasing expansion of their own consciousness in ever greater fidelity to the Gospel call to love. The other side of holy transgression is solidarity with those whom our boundaries of judgment, fear, and condemnation have excluded or set apart.

Luke's version of the call of the first disciples elucidates this point perhaps better than any other. Jesus instructed Peter to put his nets out to sea even after having been unsuccessful all day. As a result, he caught so many fish his nets began to tear (Luke 5:4-6). At first Peter and his companions, fearful and awestruck, begged Jesus to leave them alone. But instead he reassured them with a promise to make them "fishers of people." With that, "They brought their boats to shore [and] left everything and followed him" (Luke 5:11).

There is wisdom here. No matter how broad or wide our net, no matter how far it is cast or how abundant the catch, a net is still a net and the fish beyond its reach remain infinitely more abundant than those that lie within. As the nets of our exclusion begin to tear under the expanding consciousness of God as "ground" of our being, we begin to touch on the transgressive nature of Jesus' own ministry. With Christ, we are compelled to tear down any boundary that threatens to separate anyone from the ocean of God's love (cf. Rom 8:35-39). If the contemplative is to become a disciple of Christ, it is not enough that we merely widen our nets. We must abandon them altogether.

The transgressive nature of Christian holiness and contemplative discipleship is patterned in the incarnation itself. As we saw in chapter 2, the original transgression of Adam and Eve has been ameliorated by the unthinkable scandal of the Word-Made-Flesh, that divine transgression of the very boundaries between heaven and earth, divinity and humanity, life and death. This is the great reversal of human sinfulness by divine love, of human arrogance by divine humility, and of human disobedience by the divine obedience of Christ (Phil 2:8).

This great reversal is expressed in the overall structure of Mark's gospel, which frames, perhaps better than any other, the public ministry of Jesus as an act of divine transgression. Two parallel events, which serve as literary bookends, herald the first and last moments of Jesus' public ministry. At his baptism, and again at his death, Mark describes the Spirit of God having been unleashed into the world through a divine act of "tearing." The unmistakable repetition of Mark's reference to the *tearing* of the heavens in 1:10 and the *tearing* of the temple veil in 15:38 provides a linguistic thread that inextricably links these two moments in the gospel. It is an unexpected—indeed almost violent—image by which Mark describes the in-breaking of God into the world (cf. Isa 64:1). Having transgressed the boundaries between heaven and earth, the sacred and the profane, holiness can never again be set apart from a world now penetrated by the glory of God.

It is no coincidence that a Gentile centurion keeping guard at the cross is the first to proclaim what the reader has known from the outset: Jesus is the Son of God (cf. Mark 1:1 and 15:39). Mark wants his readers to understand that the divine presence now ushering forth from the temple is to be poured out on all nations. So Stephen Motyer rightly observed, "The veil is rent asunder, the glory of God hidden behind it begins to radiate out into the world and as an initial reflection of this unveiling, a human being (and a Gentile at that!) acclaims Jesus' divine sonship for the first time in the Gospel."[33] When compared side-by-side, Mark's literary parallel is unmistakable:

A **Mark 1:1** Evangelist declares Jesus "Son of God"

  B **Mark 1:10** The heavens are "torn apart": The Spirit descends

  B' **Mark 15:38** The temple veil is "torn in two": The Spirit is unleashed

A' **Mark 15:39** Centurion declares Jesus "Son of God"

This kind of parallelism is called an INCLUSIO or "inclusion" by which Mark is signaling that everything in between (i.e., Jesus' entire public ministry!) is to be understood in light of these two events. Notice the CHIASTIC pattern A-B-B'-A', where there is a correspondence between A, A' and B, B'. Jesus is declared "Son of God" at the very beginning and the end of the gospel (A and A'). This is closely connected with the "tearing" of the heavens in Mark 1:10 and the temple veil in Mark 15:38 (B and B').

However, biblical scholarship has been divided as to which of two possible veils Mark was referring: the inner veil that separated the Holy of Holies from the remainder of the temple, or the outer veil that hung between the forecourt and the temple proper.[34] Because the Holy of Holies was reserved for the *Shekinah*, the glory of the divine presence abiding in the temple, it is tempting to interpret Mark's reference to the inner veil.[35] However, a description of the outer veil by the first-century Jewish historian Flavius Josephus furthers the connection between the tearing of the veil at the death of Jesus and the tearing of the sky at his baptism. Roughly eighty-one feet in height, the outer veil was a dramatic representation of the heavens and was adorned with embroidered stars and constellations. Josephus describes it this way:

> It was . . . embroidered with blue, and fine linen, and scarlet, and purple: and of a contexture that was truly wonderful. Nor was this mixture of colours without its mystical interpretation: *it typified the universe*. . . . This curtain had also embroidered upon it *all that was mystical in the heavens*.[36]

If this is indeed the veil Mark intended, we can see in its tearing a microcosm of the heavens rent by the Spirit at Jesus' baptism. Thus, the parallel would be clear. First, the heavens are torn asunder at Jesus' baptism as he enters the world stage to begin his public ministry. And finally, in the moment of his death, there is a parallel tearing of the microcosm of the heavens in the form of the outer veil which "typified the universe."

The rending of sky and veil frames the incarnation as a singular transgressive act of a God who refuses to respect the boundaries we establish to keep the divine tucked away in a far-off heaven, much less set apart in the sacred temples of our own making. In Christ, God can never again be claimed by any one people in any one place—not even by Christians. God does not belong to us. We belong to God. The boundaries between the sacred and profane are forever transgressed not by humans but by God himself, fulfilling the prophecy of Isaiah 56:7, "My house shall be called a house of prayer for all peoples." So it is, in Christ, the God of Israel is revealed to every people and nation:

> [M]y own eyes have seen the salvation
> which you have prepared in the sight of every people:
> a light to reveal you to the nations
> and the glory of your people Israel.
> (Luke 2:29-32, Canticle of Simeon, *The Liturgy of the Hours*)

Despite the holy transgressions Jesus carried out in his revelation of the kingdom, in the Gospel of Mark it is not until his death on the cross that he is fully realized to be "Son of God":

> Then Jesus gave a loud cry and breathed his last. And the curtain of the temple was torn in two, from top to bottom. Now when the centurion, who stood facing him, saw that in this way he breathed his last, he said, "Truly this man was God's Son!" (Mark 15:37-39)

It is all the more fitting that a Gentile centurion is the first to proclaim Jesus "Messiah" as evidence of the power of the Spirit now unleashed into the world. For, "No one can say 'Jesus is Lord' except by the Holy Spirit" (1 Cor 12:3). As Joel Marcus observes, for a centurion the title "Son of God" is reserved for the emperor alone. Only a profound reversal of his worldview could allow a centurion to see in an executed criminal the true Son of God.[37] Might we then see in Mark's centurion, the making of the first gentile disciple, who came to believe not through Christ's life and teachings, but through his silence and death on the cross? No less today, a crucified Messiah so contravenes the world's image of divine omnipotence as to render the human intellect bankrupt before the scandal of the cross (1 Cor 1:23). Indeed, the God whom we encounter in the folly of the cross cannot be comprehended by the intellect but only apprehended in love.

Crazy in Love

Reflecting on von Balthasar's theology of Christ's crucifixion and descent into hell, Raymond Gawronski offers a disturbing reflection on the incomprehensibility of God expressed in the paradox of the cross. Christ's death becomes God's "loudest and clearest statement to the world." One can discern from his reflection three successive silences of the Word: The silence of the Eternal Word, the silence of the Word-Made-Flesh, and the "great silence" of Holy Saturday, "where the dead Christ has become the silent word of the Father":

> When the Word takes on flesh, the Word enters the realm of silence, for flesh is silence. The movement from the fullness of the Father to the emptying of the bleeding, screaming figure on the Cross is the movement from Word into silence. . . . Thus, the words culminate in the cry from the Cross and the becoming mute . . . of the corpse, the Holy Saturday mystery. In death, the Word becomes an un-word; a not-word. The descent into Hell is a passage in "pure wordlessness." The silence of Holy Saturday, the "great silence," is the final expression of God, where the dead Christ has become the silent word of the Father. As Jesus' silence, reflecting the silent word of God, the super-word, is sometimes more important than his speech, so also His descent into the silence of Hell becomes the Father's loudest and clearest statement to the world.[38]

It is here, in the cross, we encounter—as ultimately we must—the church's APOPHATIC theology. Also called APOPHASIS or "negative theology," this is the theology of the "great silence"; the theology of Holy Saturday where our words descend with Christ to become "un-words," "not-words" and "pure wordlessness." Many have come to think of apophasis as the opposite of CATAPHATIC theology, also called CATAPHASIS or "positive theology." This is the theology of verbosity, prolixity, or wordiness, which Gawronski, attributes to the inspiration of the Holy Spirit: "It is the Holy Spirit, expected to be 'the unknown beyond of the Word,' who begins to explain, to show what has come to pass, first through the Apostles and evangelists, then in an ever increasing volume of words, through the Church's theological reflection."[39]

Thus, if apophatic theology is the theology of silence before the ineffable mystery of God, cataphatic theology is anything and everything we might think of as speech about God: words, descriptions, music, poetry, art, doctrine, dogma, scripture, ritual, symbol, and so on. Without exception, every image, projection, thought, concept or idea one has of God falls into the category of cataphatic theology. As it is, however, these two fundamental approaches to theology are not independent categories much less opposed to one another.

How then, are they related? In his close reading of the Christian mystical tradition, Denys Turner observes that we arrive at the great silence of apophatic theology not when we *choose* to be silent before the mystery of God, but when our intellects are ultimately *reduced* to silence after all of our attempts to speak about God in every imaginable way have failed. Denys argues for a theology that is an "excess of babble," a mixing of metaphors, an incessant speaking about God, until we are driven to the embarrassing discovery of "the inadequacy of it all." That is, until our language "collapses under its own weight" and speech is transformed into silent awe.[40]

Is it possible that Mark's description of the two temple veils encapsulates something of the theological tension between the cataphatic and the apophatic? If the temple is an archetype of Christ himself (cf. John 2:19-21), might the tearing of the outer veil and the still-intact veil of the Holy of Holies suggest what

Thomas Aquinas would later insist about the mystery of the incarnation: "In the end, we know God as unknown."[41] That is to say, the very God who is fully revealed in the crucified Christ, whose divine presence (*Shekinah*) now breaks upon the world remains ineffable Mystery nonetheless. So, Oliver Clément:

> In Jesus . . . the mystery is at the same time disclosed and veiled. Because the inaccessible God reveals himself in the crucified, he is by that very fact a hidden and incomprehensible God, who upsets our definitions and expectations. The true "apophatic" approach (*apophasis* means the "leap" towards the mystery) does not rest solely, as is often thought, in negative theology. That has only the purpose of opening us to an encounter, a revelation, and it is this very revelation, in which glory is inseparable from *kenosis*, which is strictly unthinkable. The *apophasis* therefore lies in the antinomy, the sharp distinction in character between the Depth and the cross, the inaccessible God and the Man of Sorrows, the almost "crazy" manifestations of God's love for humanity and a humble and unobtrusive plea for our own love.[42]

Clément's point is as insightful as it is moving. The cross so disturbs our notion of an all-powerful God that we are unable to comprehend the very God that Jesus reveals. How is divine power, glory, and beauty revealed in the horror and utter defeat of the cross? This enigma opens the way to a relationship with the divine beyond images, ideas, thoughts, or anything we would call an "experience." It propels us toward the realization that any God we might imagine can only be just that—*an imaginary God*. It pushes us across the threshold from cataphasis to apophasis, that is, from the belief we might say something comprehensible about God to the silence of bewilderment and awe. The cross is the threshold through which we become lost in the very Christ in whom we are already found: "Whoever does not take up the cross and follow me is not worthy of me. Those who find their life will lose it, and those who lose their life for my sake will find it" (Matt 10:38-39).

Contemplative discipleship is ultimately a participation in the same *kenosis* or "self-emptying" of Christ in the incarnation—even unto "death on a cross" (Phil 2:8). As the Word descended into the heart of the cosmos, into human flesh itself, so too does the prayer of the contemplative descend from head to heart, from knowing to unknowing, from words into flesh, from saying prayers to becoming prayer. Or again, the descent of the Word in the incarnation renders so intimate a union between Lover and beloved as to transcend all words, transforming our prayer into flesh and our flesh into the *incarnatio continua*. It is not enough, then, that God should embrace us once in the days of antiquity. The love of God in Christ is a continual embrace—even now through a deified humanity. In the end, Contemplating Christ inevitably confronts us with a crucified God who will not tolerate confinement in the pages of history or the sacred precincts of our mind, but who tears beyond the veil of what we know, to enter our very flesh as One who is "crazy" in love and who begs to be loved in return.

Appendix

Mum's the Word: The Origins of Christian Mysticism[1]

In order to cut through the manifold interpretations of mysticism, we might look at the word itself and what it came to signify specifically within Christianity.[2] The English word "mysticism" comes from the classical Greek *mustikós*, which referred to something hidden or secret. As Louis Bouyer points out, the pre-Christian origins of the word referred strictly to the secret rituals of Greek mystery religions whose members were forbidden to disclose the form of their rites to the uninitiated.[3] The root of the word, *mu-*, is believed to be onomatopoeic. That is, a word that imitates the sound it describes, such as tick-tock, drip-drop, and meow. Pronouncing the word *mu-* requires one to press their lips together, implying silence and the keeping of secrets.[4] The familiar word "mum," also meaning silent, mute, or tight-lipped, functions similarly in English—as in "mum's the word."

Because of the early association of *mustikós* with ancient Greek mystery religions, it had been long assumed that mysticism was a pagan import into Christianity and had no real place in Christian faith. But Bouyer debunks that misconception by demonstrating the word *mustikós* and related terms had become so generalized and commonplace in the Greco-Roman world as to have lost all direct association with pagan mystery religions. In other words, since the time of Plato the term is used loosely across a broad literary spectrum to refer to virtually any kind of problem or enigma to be solved. It is this more general use that Paul adopts in Philippians 4:12, "I know what it is to have little, and I know what it is to have plenty. In any and all circumstances I have learned the *secret* [*memuēmai*] of being well-fed and of going hungry, of having plenty and of being in need." Clearly, Paul's use of the term "secret" has no relation to mystery cults or pagan religious rites. He uses it here poetically in reference to the wisdom that comes from experience. He has figured out the value of living through times of plenty and scarcity. Such uses of the term demonstrate how commonplace the word had become.[5]

It was this generalized use of the term that made its way into Christianity. But once adopted, *mustikós* took on its own meaning quite distinct from its original pre-Christian use. At no point does it represent the keeping of secret rituals; instead, it takes on three interrelated references that are uniquely Christian. Bouyer identifies these three categories in order of prominence: the biblical, the liturgical, and the spiritual. I will take each in turn.

For Christians, *mustikós* primarily referred to the hidden or secret meaning of the Scriptures—that which lies beneath the literal or surface meaning of the text. Shadowy intimations from ages past were now understood to have been fully revealed in the Christ-event. That which was known only in part was now believed to have been revealed in full. For example, in Colossians 1:25-26 we read:

> I [Paul] became [the church's] servant according to God's commission that was given to me for you, to make the word of God fully known, the mystery [*mustērion*] that has been hidden throughout the ages and generations but has now been revealed to his saints.

Discerning this hidden or mystical meaning of Scripture often entailed the use of allegory whereby characters and events in the Old

Testament would take on new meaning when read in light of the incarnation. For Christians, the allegorical meaning became synonymous with the mystical meaning of Scripture. For example, in the First Letter of Peter the great flood of Noah's time becomes an allegory for the purifying waters of Christian baptism (1 Pet 3:20-22). The literal story of the flood in Genesis 6–9 is now understood to conceal the deeper *mystical* meaning of Christian baptism revealed in Christ. In other words, Christ becomes the interpretive lens through whom the secret or hidden meaning of the Old Testament is revealed in the New. One could only break open this hidden sense of Scripture through faith in Christ. Thus, Christians perceived in the Scriptures two inseparable senses: the literal or surface sense and the allegorical or mystical sense. Each completed the other:

> There are, then, basically only two senses of Scripture recognized everywhere in the ancient tradition: the one, which consists in the history or the letter; the other, which is more generally named spiritual, or allegorical, or mystical. *The letter signifies one thing, mystic discourse another.*[6]

By the early third century the great theologian Origen of Alexandria already understood biblical interpretation not as an intellectual exercise but as an act of mystical contemplation, called *theoria*, by which one was brought into union with Christ.[7] It is here we already begin to see the connection between the mystical (*mustikós*) and contemplation (*theoria*). In other words, Origen's frequent use of the term *theoria* refers to a contemplative approach to Scripture that goes beyond mere intellectual knowledge to a kind of mystical participation in the One whom we come to know hidden in the Scriptures—namely, Christ.[8] Thus for Origen, to contemplate the mysteries of Scripture is more than just to arrive at a literal interpretation of the surface meaning. It is to plumb the depths of the allegorical meaning that leads to a mystical participation in the life of Christ hidden in the text. In this sense, contemplation was inseparable from biblical interpretation.

This manner of interpretation also informed the way Christians explained the mystical meaning of the sacraments—especially the Eucharist. The Christ hidden in the words of Scripture is the same Christ hidden in the bread and wine of the Eucharist. Put otherwise, just as the surface words of Scripture reveal Christ hidden in them, so too does the outward appearance of bread and wine reveal the hidden presence of Christ in the Eucharist.[9] Thus, there was an intimate link between breaking open the Scriptures and breaking open the bread in the Eucharist. This intimate connection is exemplified in Luke's narrative of the disciples on the road to Emmaus (Luke 24:13-35). First, "beginning with Moses and all the prophets, [Jesus] interpreted to them the things about himself in all the scriptures" (v. 27). Later Luke narrates,

> When [Jesus] was at the table with them, he took bread, blessed and broke it, and gave it to them. Then their eyes were opened, and they recognized him; and he vanished from their sight. They said to each other, "Were not our hearts burning within us while he was talking to us on the road, while he was opening the scriptures to us?"

Here Luke exemplifies what would later become an explicitly Christian understanding of the mystical: that hidden or secret presence of the divine that lies behind outward appearances. Christ becomes the lens through which the Christian is able to penetrate that outward appearance into the secret, hidden or "mystical" reality it conceals. Or again, Christ is the key who opens the door to the mysteries of Christian faith that otherwise remain beyond our sight. Through this christological lens, the story of a flood purifying the earth reveals the deeper truth about the waters of baptism purifying the individual believer baptized in Christ. Similarly, the outward appearance of bread and wine reveals the mystical presence of Christ in our midst.

Thus, the Christian liturgy provided the second context for the use of *mustikós*. Initiation into the Christian life and ongoing participation in the community was celebrated through the sacramental mysteries (*musteria*) of the church, primarily baptism and the Eucharist. To share in the sacraments was a mystical sharing in the life of Christ hidden and transmitted through them. As de Lubac points out, in the liturgy Word and Sacrament are united, since the liturgy consists not only in sacramental rituals but in the reading of biblical texts that were often chosen precisely because of their mystical content.[10]

The liturgy then becomes central to the Christian mystical life. It reveals in Word and Sacrament the same Christ we contemplate in the daily course of life. Christ hidden in creation, Christ hidden in society, Christ hidden in our own hearts. This then brings us to Bouyer's observations about the third common use of the term *mustikós*, which referred to the hidden presence of Christ in our daily lives. This idea is echoed in Colossians 3:1-3:

> So if you have been raised with Christ, seek the things that are above, where Christ is, seated at the right hand of God. Set your minds on things that are above, not on things that are on earth, for you have died, and your life is hidden with Christ in God.

In the early sixth century, the writings of a theologian known to us only as Pseudo-Dionysius still refer to *mustikós* in light of the biblical, liturgical, and spiritual dimensions of Christian life in which it had always been understood.[11] In the intervening centuries, however, these three dimensions gradually became unmoored from one another, allowing the last—Christ hidden in the spiritual life of the Christian—to become isolated from the mysteries of Word and Sacrament. As a result, by the Middle Ages the church saw a preponderance of spiritual literature emphasizing personal interior encounters with God. Louth observes at this point in church history, "The meaning of the mystical has now been completely transformed: it refers primarily to access to divine power on behalf of the individual . . . manifest in evident signs of divine presence."[12] In other words, mysticism was no longer centered on the hidden presence of Christ revealed in Scripture, liturgy, and daily life of all Christians but on spiritual elites who claimed to have had direct or immediate experiences of God. This had spiritual as well as political implications. If an individual could potentially access God apart from Scripture and the liturgy, the church and its power to mediate the divine could easily be sidelined. Women especially found themselves at odds with church authorities because in theory their claims of access to the divine threatened to rival the power of an all-male hierarchy. In fact, however, this rarely happened—at least not overtly. Regardless, from then onward this potential threat was enough to create a fissure of mistrust between the church as institution and the mystical, which now became focused on individual persons. Many of these visionaries would be challenged, scrutinized, even persecuted by the church only to have their life and work endorsed posthumously.[13] However, these individuals were not yet called "mystics."

It was not until the seventeenth century that the English word "mysticism" made its way into Christianity and not until the nineteenth century that it became widely studied as a distinctive theological subject in the English-speaking world.[14] Earlier saints and visionaries such as John of the Cross, Catherine of Sienna, and Julian of Norwich whom we have since categorized as "mystics" would not have understood themselves as such. As Bernard McGinn rightly notes, "No mystics (at least before the present century) believed in or practiced 'mysticism.' They believed in and practiced Christianity (or Judaism, or Islam, or Hinduism), that is, religions that contained mystical elements as parts of a wider historical whole."[15] It is this sense of the mystical as the deepest dimension of Christian faith that underlies my reflections on the Christian contemplative life throughout this book.

To summarize then, the idea that there is such a thing as a "Christian mystic" is relatively modern. As we have seen, it is the result of shifts that took place gradually up through the Middle Ages by which the adjective "mystical" (*mūstikos*) was unmoored from its original reference to Christ hidden in the scriptural, sacramental, and spiritual life of the church. In its place, the noun "mystic" increasingly referred to an individual, who was believed to have had a direct encounter with God. What was once the core of the faith was relegated to the sidelines. What was once the possession of the universal church became the sole possession of individuals who were held with both suspicion and fascination. That is, the emphasis on the church as a mystical entity itself shifted to an emphasis on individuals whose claims to divine access set them apart as spiritually elite members of the church as an institution. These individuals often found themselves in conflict with the church because their claims to divine access threatened to circumvent the church's role to mediate the divine.

As a result, there developed and still remains a significant body of Christian literature emphasizing ecstatic mystical experiences, visions, or spiritual insights as we see famously in the *Shewings* of Julian of Norwich, *The Interior Castle* by Theresa of Ávila, and the various poems and treatises by John of the Cross, among others. By the modern era this literary genre would be gathered under the rubrics of "mystical literature," further solidifying the notion that there is a separate "mystical tradition" in Christianity. The study of mysticism has since become a distinctive branch of theology in its own right. Andrew Louth refers to this development as the modern invention of mysticism or more specifically of "Christian mystical tradition."[16]

Without dismissing the authenticity of this historical development or the spiritual insights that come from what is now called "mystical literature," whatever notions about mysticism are conjured by the modern Christian, we should be aware they are largely informed by a relatively recent development in church history. In other words the starting point for the study of Christian mysticism is not the *Shewings* of St. Julian or the *Dark Night* of St. John as might be assumed, but in something more fundamental to which all of our so-called Christian mystical literature is heir: the incarnation. Thus, to say, "The incarnation has made mystics of us all," should not be too hastily conflated with this more recent individualized view of the mystic or the extraordinary experiences frequently associated with mystical literature. I am interested, rather, in the scriptural witness that inevitably gave rise to the Christian doctrine of the incarnation, and how that doctrine continues to inform the interior life of Christians. Thus, when I speak of the Christian contemplative life throughout this book, I presume the more ancient and integrated understanding of the mystical as referring to Christ hidden in the Scriptures, sacraments, and the daily life of the Christian.

Glossary

Alter Christus (plural, Alteri Christi): Latin meaning, "another Christ" or plural "other Christs." The term traditionally referred to the identity of the priest functioning in the person of Christ in the liturgy. More broadly, and as intended throughout this book, the term refers to the deified person who has been made 'another Christ' through the incarnation.

Apatheia: A Greek term that literally means "without passion." While easily confused with the English word "apathy," in Christian contemplative spirituality *apatheia* does not refer to indifference or a lack of concern, but to a kind of interior equanimity or peace of mind, undisturbed by one's emotions or passions, which opens the way for one to love more freely and without conditions.

Apophatic (Apophasis): Literally means, to "say away from." In Christian theology, apophasis emphasizes the absolute unknowability of God, and thus the utter failure of language to say anything ultimate of God. Also called, "negative theology," "the *via negativa*," or "the way of negation," apophasis is often mistakenly believed to be the opposite of Cataphasis (the abundance of speech about God). But in fact, the two are rooted in one another. One does not 'choose' to be silent before the unknowability of God; rather one speaks about God profusely (cataphasis) until one is led to the silence of mental exhaustion (apophasis). See, Cataphatic, Cataphasis.

Asceticism, Ascesis: Borrowed from the athletic world of the Greeks, the word "*askēsis*" means "practice." Like the physical training of an athlete, asceticism refers to rigorous spiritual training with the goal of attaining Apatheia, or interior equanimity. Asceticism, or ascesis, is traditionally associated with practices of self-denial, fasting, and long hours of prayer by which one is gradually freed from the influences of their passions or "demons" in order to love others with greater freedom and authenticity.

BIBLE: The Christian Scriptures consisting of the Old and New Testaments.

CATAPHATIC, CATAPHASIS: Literally means, "to say with." In Christian theology cataphasis refers to any attempt to say something about God, whether in speech, music, art, symbol, ritual, and so on. Also called, "positive theology," the "*via positiva*," or "the way of affirmation," cataphasis is often mistakenly believed to be the opposite of APOPHASIS (the denial of speech about God). But, in fact, the two are rooted in one another. Authentic cataphatic theology is marked by a profusion of language about God in every conceivable way, only to lead to the realization that God transcends all of manner of conceptions, thoughts, ideas and images. See: APOPHATIC, APOPHASIS.

CANONICAL: An adjective that describes those texts which have been officially included in an authoritative body of religious literature. For Christians, all the books of the Bible are considered "canonical." One may speak of the whole Bible as the Christian "canon" of Scripture.

CHIASTIC: An adjective describing a literary structure, common throughout biblical literature, which in its simplest form takes the pattern A-B-B'-A'. The pairs A/A' and B/B' correspond to one another. For example, "The sabbath [A]/ was made for humans [B]/ not humans [B']/ for the sabbath [A']." Chiastic structures or "chiasms" were used to emphasize linguistic or thematic connections through the use of repetition of main ideas.

CONTEMPLATION: Typically refers to a manner of prayer marked by silence, interior rumination, and meditation. Less of a method or technique, Christian contemplation is a way of being in the world by which opens one to a deepening awareness of union with God and all.

CHRIST-EVENT: The totality of the life, teachings, passion, death, and resurrection of Jesus of Nazareth, professed by Christians as the Christ (Messiah).

DEEP INCARNATION: The theological insight that the incarnation in Jesus assumes a cosmic embodiment not limited to human beings but that extends into the very core of the material universe and all biological life.

DEIFICATION: Literally, "to be made God." Rooted in Scripture and developed in the writings of the early Church, deification refers to the manner by which humanity comes to participate in the divine nature through the divine-human union of the incarnation. Often referred to as a "process" by which one is brought into union with God through grace, deification is best understood as a pure gift, a corollary of the incarnation, which contemplative practice may bring us into deeper awareness, but is not itself a cause. In other words, God alone, through the incarnation of Christ and the grace of the Spirit is the cause of deification, which cannot otherwise be rendered by any human effort.

DIVINIZATION: Literally, "to be made divine," this term is used synonymously with DEIFICATION and THEOSIS.

EGO: One's adopted identity in the world that can be taken up for constructive or destructive purposes. Like the clothing we wear or the roles we play in society, the ego is not an aspect of our eternal existence and will be shed in death. When under the influence of the TRUE SELF one's egoic identity can mediate collaboration, compassion and liberation. However, when one over-identifies with the ego, mistaking it for one's true identity over-against other people, it can become a tool of the FALSE SELF, and as such becomes a force for competition, oppression, and injustice.

ENLIGHTENMENT: Spanning from roughly the late seventeenth through eighteenth centuries, the Enlightenment was a European social and cultural movement that emphasized rationalism and individualism over religious doctrine. While the history and leading figures of the Enlightenment varied among European countries, it was marked by an emphasis on science over religious tradition and brought about innovations in education and politics.

EXEGESIS (noun. EXEGETE): Literally means, "to draw meaning from." In biblical studies, it implies the careful and methodological interpretation of a scriptural passage in order to arrive at the most accurate or authentic interpretation possible. Spiritual exegesis offers interpretations of a biblical text that look to explain its mystical or theological meaning beyond its mere historical meaning.

FALSE SELF: Often confused with the EGO in Christian spirituality, it is rather a non-entity, a "false" identity that does not actually exist. The False Self is symptomatic of the interior void that is experienced as a result of humanity's illusory separation from God. It is called "false" precisely because it does not exist.

HESYCHASTIC (HESYCHASM, HESYCHAST): Refers to inner tranquility, quiet, or stillness of one who lives in continual remembrance of God—as through the JESUS PRAYER, or contemplative practice in general. The term Hesychasm is used to refer to this overall practice and a Hesychast is one who practices this form of prayer or who possess such a state of interior stillness.

HISTORICAL CRITICISM: A contextual method of interpreting the Bible developed primarily in the Renaissance and especially in the Enlightenment. Historical Criticism emphasizes a scholarly and scientific approach to understanding the Bible that seeks to recover, as closely as possible, the original meaning of a biblical text in light of its historical origins.

INCARNATION: A central doctrine of Christian faith which affirms that in Jesus of Nazareth, God has fully communicated the divine self to humanity and as a consequence has raised humanity to a full participation in the life of the Trinity.

INCLUSIO: A passage in Scripture whereby the opening word or phrase is repeated in the closing word or phrase, much like a pair of bookends. An *inclusio* often indicates to the reader that the material in between is to be understood in the context of the "bookends."

INFANCY NARRATIVE: The New Testament narratives about the birth of Jesus found in Matthew 1–2 and Luke 1–2.

JESUS PRAYER: A brief meditative prayer repeated in the mind and heart and on the lips consisting of the repetition of the name of Jesus. The traditional formula is "Lord Jesus Christ, Son of God, have mercy on me a sinner." However, this is often abbreviated in any number of ways, "Lord Jesus Christ, Son of God, have mercy," or "Lord Jesus Christ," or even simply "Jesus." Early Christian tradition understood the Jesus Prayer as a fulfillment of the exhortation in 1 Thessalonians 5:17 to "Pray without ceasing."

KENOSIS: The self-emptying of Christ in the incarnation. As proclaimed in Philippians 2:7, Christ pours himself out into the world, not clinging to his divinity but taking the form of the servant of all—even to his death on the cross (see Phil 2:5-11).

LXX: A Greek translation of the Hebrew Old Testament, completed by the year 132 BCE, undertaken by Jewish rabbis to make the Hebrew Scriptures available to Greek-speaking Jews who were living outside

Israel and thus no longer understood the original Hebrew Scriptures. It is this Greek version of the Old Testament, called the Septuagint, that was adopted by the first Christians, and most often cited by them. The Septuagint is abbreviated by the Roman numeral for 70 (LXX) because one legend ascribes its origin to 70 Jewish scribes who independently arrived at identical translations. The tradition developed in order to defend the accuracy and authenticity of the translation as having been divinely inspired.

MYSTICISM: Generally refers to the pursuit or attainment of experiential union with God, usually through contemplative practice, asceticism, and self-emptying. In the context of this book, mysticism is understood as a corollary of the incarnation, meaning that mystical union between God and humanity is achieved by God in the incarnation. Christian mysticism then, is not a means by which to achieve union with the divine, but a way of life by which we gradually awaken to the reality of the union that already exists with God, through Christ, in the Spirit.

PATRISTIC: From the Latin word, meaning "Father," this is an adjective referring to the writings of the early Church Fathers from roughly the end of the Apostolic Age (c. AD 100) to the eighth century. The Patristic theologians were formative in the establishment of foundational Christian dogmas such as, the canonical books of the New Testament, the divinity of Christ, and the Trinity.

PERICHORESIS: A term derived from Greek *Peri* ("*around*") and "*chorein*" (to "go forward" or "contain"). The Latin word for the same concept is "*Circumincession*." Thus, the terms imply a kind of "mutual interpenetration." The idea typically refers to the dynamic relationship of the Persons of the Trinity—Father, Son, and Spirit—each mutually penetrating one another in an eternal dance of self-giving and self-emptying. Alternatively, the term has a more static notion that conveys the nature of the trinitarian relationships as more of a mutual "indwelling" or subsistence in one another.

PHILOKALIA: From the Greek meaning, "love of the beautiful" (or "love of the good"), the *Philokalia* is an eighteenth century compilation of primarily Eastern Orthodox texts on the contemplative life, spanning from the fourth to the fifteenth centuries. It emphasizes the practice of the Jesus Prayer.

TELOS: From the Greek word meaning "end," in theology *telos* refers to the ultimate aim or goal, as in, "the *telos* of Christian faith is union with God."

THEOPHANIC: An adjective derived from the noun "theophany," which is a visible appearance or manifestation of God. A theophanic universe is one in which God is manifested everywhere.

THEOSIS: Synonymous with DEIFICATION and DIVINIZATION.

TRINITY: The central dogma of Christian faith that models the Divine as One God in Three Persons: Father, Son, and Holy Spirit. Each Person of the Trinity is fully divine and neither can be conflated with the other. It is the Second Person of the Trinity that is incarnate in Jesus Christ.

Notes

Chapter One—pages 1–34

1. Olivier Clément, *The Roots of Christian Mysticism*, trans. Theodore Berkeley and Jeremy Hummerstone (Hyde Park, NY: New City Press, 1995), 100.

2. Cf. R. R. Reno, "Origen," in *Christian Theologies of Scripture: A Comparative Introduction*, ed. Justin S. Holcomb, 21–38 (New York: New York University Press, 2006), 28, observes, "For . . . the larger patristic tradition, interpretation is preparatory. The primary function of exegesis is to get us moving in the right direction. It cannot bring us to the destination the way a syllogism can bring us to a conclusion. The end or goal of exegesis is to dispose the reader in such a way that he or she can 'see' Christ."

3. Thomas Merton, *Bread in the Wilderness* (Collegeville, MN: Liturgical Press, 1953), 51.

4. Eugene H. Peterson, *Eat This Book: A Conversation in the Art of Spiritual Reading* (Grand Rapids, MI: Eerdmans, 2006), 113.

5. Raimon Panikkar, *Christophany: The Fullness of Man*, trans. Alfred DiLascia (New York: Orbis Books, 2009), 128, 179.

6. Symeon the New Theologian, in *The Enlightened Heart: An Anthology of Sacred Poetry*, ed. Stephen Mitchell (New York: HarperCollins, 1989), 38–39.

7. Adam Cooper, *Naturally Human, Supernaturally God: Deification in Pre-Conciliar Catholicism* (Minneapolis, MN: Fortress Press, 2014), 41, observes, "Incarnation and deification are two sides of a single soteriological coin, structural corollaries one of the other."

8. Athanasius, *De Incarnatione* 54, in *Nicene and Post-Nicene Fathers: A Select Library of the Christian Church*, 2nd series, ed. Philip Schaff and Henry Wace (Peabody, MA: Hendrickson, 1995), 4:65.

9. Andrew Louth, "The Place of *Theosis* in Orthodox Theology," in *Partakers of the Divine Nature: The History and Development of Deification in the Christian Traditions*, ed. Michael J. Christensen and Jeffery A. Wittung (Grand Rapids, MI: Baker Academics, 2007), 34. Cf. Daniel A. Keating, "Deification in the Greek Fathers," in *Called to Be the Children of God: The Catholic Theology of Human Deification*, ed. David Meconi and Carl E. Olson (San Francisco: Ignatius Press, 2016), 43–44.

10. Michael Casey, *Fully Human, Fully Divine: An Interactive Christology* (Liguori, MO: Liguori, 2004), 10.

11. Anthony J. Kelly, "'The Body of Christ: Amen!' The Expanding Incarnation," *Theological Studies* 71 (2010): 729–816, at 800.

12. Vladimir Lossky, *Orthodox Theology: An Introduction*, trans. Ian and Ihita Kesarcodi-Watson (Crestwood, NY: St. Vladimir's Seminary Press, 1978), 36.

13. Kelly, "The Body of Christ," 801–2.

14. Ibid., 801.

15. Henri de Lubac, *Catholicism: Christ and the Common Destiny of Man*, trans. Lancelot C. Sheppard, and Elizabeth Englund (San Francisco: Ignatius Press, [1947] 1988), 76. Cf. Adam G. Cooper, *Naturally Human, Supernaturally God: Deification in Pre-Conciliar Catholicism* (Minneapolis: Fortress Press, 2014), 177.

16. Oliver Davies, "Lost Heaven," in *Transformation Theology: Church in the World*, ed. Oliver Davies, Paul D. Janz, and Clemens Sedmak (New York: T&T Clark, 2007), 11.

17. For example, St. Augustine, *Confessions*, XII.18, trans. Henry Chadwick (New York: Oxford University Press, 1991), 286–87, noted, "These matters you set out most wisely with us, my God, through your book, your solid firmament, so that we may discern everything by a wonderful contemplation, even though for the present only by signs and times and days and years."

18. Pope John Paul II, "Message to Pontifical Academy of Sciences on Evolution," *Origins* 26 (Nov. 14, 1996): 349–52.

19. For a summary of patristic citations on deification, see Panikkar, *Christophany*, 16.

20. So, for example, even one of the central architects of Trinitarian theology, Gregory of Nyssa, *Homily VI*, in *Homilies on the Song of Songs: Writings from the Greco-Roman World*, vol. 13, trans. Richard A. Norris (Atlanta, GA: Society of Biblical Literature, 2012), 195, speaks of God "whose existence is known only in incomprehension of what it is, in whose case every conceptual trait is an obstacle to its discovery for those who seek it." Similarly, Augustine, *Sermons III* [Sermon 52:16] *on the New Testament*, in *The Works of Saint Augustine: A Translation for the 21st Century*, trans. Edmund Hill (Brooklyn, NY: New City Press, 1991), 57, "So what are we to say, brothers, about God? For if you have fully grasped what you want to say, it isn't God. If you have been able to comprehend it, you have comprehended something else instead of God. If you think you have been able to comprehend, your thoughts have deceived you. So he isn't this, if this is what you have understood; but if he is this, then you haven't understood it. So what is it you want to say, seeing you haven't been able to understand it?"

21. Denys Turner, *The Darkness of God: Negativity in Christian Mysticism* (Cambridge, NY: Cambridge University Press, 1995), 21–22.

22. The Episcopal Church, *The Book of Common Prayer and Administration of the Sacraments and Other Rites and Ceremonies of the Church* (New York: Seabury Press, 1979), 358. The original Greek word *anthropos* is best translated in modern English as "human." The Greek word for "man," *aner*, appears nowhere in the Nicene Creed.

23. Augustine, *The Trinity*, *The Fathers of the Church: A New Translation*, v. 45, trans. Stephen McKenna (Washington, DC: Catholic University of America Press, 2002), 187–88.

24. Panikkar, *Christophany*, 17.

25. Paul M. Collins, *Partaking in Divine Nature: Deification and Communion* (New York: T & T Clark, 2010), 42.

26. Cf. Stephen Thomas, *Deification in the Eastern Orthodox Tradition: A Biblical Perspective* (Piscaraway, NJ: Gorgias Press, 2008), 94–101.

27. See Meconi and Olson, eds., *Called to Be the Children of God*, 42.

28. Norman Russell, *The Doctrine of Deification in the Greek Patristic Tradition* (Oxford: Oxford University Press, 2004), 99.

29. Thomas, *Deification in the Eastern Orthodox Tradition*, 11.

30. Russell, *The Doctrine of Deification*, 101.

31. Clement of Alexandria, *Paedagogus* 1.6 in *Fathers of the Second Century: Hermas, Tatian, Athenagoras, Theophilus, and Clement of Alexandria*,

ANF, vol. 2, ed. A. Cleveland Cox (Grand Rapids, MI: Eerdmans, 1979), 215. Cf. Keating, "Deification in the Greek Fathers," 43.

32. Thomas, *Deification in the Eastern Orthodox Tradition*, 17–18.

33. See Carl Mosser, "The Earliest Patristic Interpretations of Psalm 82, Jewish Antecedents, and the Origin of Christian Deification," *Journal of Theological Studies* 56, no. 1 (2005): 30–74, at 58–59. Cf. Collins, *Partaking in Divine Nature*, 33–34; Thomas, *Deification in the Eastern Orthodox Tradition*, 11–13.

34. Stephen Finlan, "Second Peter's Notion of Divine Participation," in *Theōsis: Deification in Christian Theology*, ed. Peter Finlan and Vladimir Kharlamov (Eugene, OR: Pickwick Publications, 2006), 46, 47.

35. Augustine, *Sermons,* III/4 [Sermon 133.8], in *The Works of St. Augustine: A Translation for the 21st Century*, trans. Edmund Hill (Brooklyn, NY: New City Press, 1992), 338. For an excellent and concise summary of Augustine's underappreciated theology of deification, see David Vincent Meconi, "No Longer a Christian but Christ: Saint Augustine on Becoming Divine," in Meconi and Olson, *Called to Be the Children of God* (San Francisco: Ignatius Press, 2006), 82–166.

36. Acts 9:1-22; 22:1-16; 26:9-23; 1 Cor 9:1; 15:3-11; Gal 1:13-24; Phil 3:2-11; 1 Tim 1:12-17.

37. Augustine, Tractate 28, on John 7:1-13, in *The Fathers of the Church, Volume 88, Tractates on the Gospel of John 28–54*, trans. and ed. John W. Rettig (Washington, DC: The Catholic University of America Press, 2010), 3–4.

38. See also Rom 12:4-5; 1 Cor 6:15-17; 10:16-17; Eph 1:22-23; 4:4-16, 25; 5:22-32; Col 1:18, 24; 2:16-19; 3:15.

39. Kelly, "The Body of Christ," 806.

40. See Emile Mersch, *The Whole Christ: The Historical Development of the Doctrine of the Mystical Body in Scripture and Tradition*, trans. John R. Kelly (Milwaukee, WI: Bruce, 1938), 518.

41. See Denis Edwards, *Jesus and the Cosmos* (Mahwah, NJ: Paulist Press, 1991), 35, who notes, "According to Aquinas, creation is fundamentally and essentially a relationship. Creatures do not have within themselves the reason for their own existence. They are contingent beings—creatures who need not exist, who cannot account for their own being."

42. See Douglas Burton-Christie, *Word in the Desert: Scripture and the Quest for Holiness in Early Christian Monasticism* (New York: Oxford University Press, 1993), 156.

43. Raymond Gawronski, SJ, *Word and Silence: Hans Urs von Balthasar and the Spiritual Encounter Between East and West* (Grand Rapids, MI: Eerdmans, 1995), 102.

44. Henri de Lubac, *Medieval Exegesis: The Four Senses of Scripture*, vol. 1, trans. Mark Sebanc (Grand Rapids, MI: Eerdmans, 1998 [1959]), 237, speaks beautifully to this: "Jesus Christ brings about the unity of Scripture, because he is the endpoint and fullness of Scripture. Everything in it is related to him. In the end, he is its sole object. . . . Scripture leads us to him, and when we reach this end, we no longer have to look for anything beyond it. Cornerstone that he is, he joins together the two Testaments, just as he joins together the two peoples. He is the Head of the body of the Scriptures, just as he is the Head of the body of His Church. He is the Head of all sacred understanding, just as he is the head of all the elect. He is the whole content of Scripture, just as he contains all of it in him."

Chapter Two—pages 35–64

1. Serge Boulgakov, *Du Verbe incarné* (Paris: Aubier, 1943), 97–98, trans. Andrew Louth, "The Place of *Theosis* in Orthodox Theology," in *Partakers of the Divine Nature: The History and Development of Deification in the Christian Traditions*, ed. Michael J. Christensen and Jeffery A. Wittung (Grand Rapids, MI: Baker Academics, 2007), 35. Cf. Paul M. Collins, *Partaking in Divine Nature: Deification and Communion* (New York: T & T Clark, 2010), 84.

2. See Hans Urs von Balthasar, *Heart of the World*, trans. Erasmo Leiva (San Francisco: Ignatius Press, 1979), 43.

3. Olivier Clément, *The Roots of Christian Mysticism* (Hyde Park, NY: New City Press, 1995), 9. Cf. Joel Marcus, *The Way of the Lord: Christological Exegesis of the Old Testament in the Gospel of Mark* (Louisville, KY: Westminster/John Knox Press, 1992), 92, who writes, "[Christ] . . . is not just the invisible essence behind the changing appearances of the cosmos but a holy warrior whose triumph means the liberation of the captive universe. The [Kingdom] of God in which the Son participates is more than God's invisible control over the course of events in an unchanging world; it is God's active movement *into* the world, the way of the Lord, which is at the same time the way of Jesus."

4. English translation from the Latin, *Conditor Alme Siderum*, *Anon*, 7th century.

5. See Hans Urs von Balthasar, *The Grain of Wheat: Aphorisms*, trans. Erasmo Leiva-Merikakis (San Francisco: Ignatius Press, [1953] 1995), 46, who observed, "Atheism can be like salt for religion. It is negative theology posited in the most absolute way. Most of the time, psychologically speaking, atheism represents a disappointment with the narrowness and limitations of a certain concept of God, and impatience stretching into anonymity." Cf. Clément, *The Roots of Christian Mysticism*, 30.

6. See Benedicta Ward, ed. and trans., *The Sayings of the Desert Fathers*, rev. ed. (Kalamazoo, MI: Cistercian Publications, 1984).

7. Jonathan Edwards, *The Works of President Edwards*, vol. 6 (New York: Burt Franklin, [1817] 1968), 458.

8. This insight about the nature of myths is often attributed to the fourth-century Roman historian Gaius Sallustius Crispus.

9. Eden, which means "delight," is referred to as the Lord's Garden or the Garden of God throughout Israel's prophetic tradition, cf. Isa 51:3; Ezek 31:8-9; Joel 2:3.

10. Cf. Gen 2:7, "YHWH God formed the red 'earthling' [*'adam*] from the dust of the red earth [*'adamah*]." The reference to the color red signifies the elemental relationship between humanity and the clay of the earth from which *'adam* is formed. The wordplay in Hebrew is unmistakable, beautifully poetic, and clearly signifies that *'adam* is not a historical person but a mythical persona representing the whole of humanity. This wordplay, and thus the intention of the author, is lost when *'adam* is rendered in English translation simply as "man."

11. Cf. Gen 21–25 where the Hebrew now employs a different word for "man" (*ish*) in relation to "woman" (*ishah*).

12. Augustine of Hippo, *City of God* 14.13, in *Fathers of the Church: A New Translation*, 86 vols., trans. and ed. R. J. Deferrari (Washington, DC: Catholic University of America Press, 1947–), 14:382–83, "The conclusion is that the devil would not have begun by an open and obvious sin to tempt man into doing something that God had forbidden, had not man already begun to seek satisfaction in himself and consequently to take pleasure in the words 'you shall be as gods.' The promise of these words, however, would much more truly have to pass if, by obedience, Adam and Eve had kept close to the ultimate and true source of their being and had not, by pride, imagined that they were themselves the source of their being. . . . Whoever seeks to be more than he is becomes

less. Whenever he aspires to be self-sufficing, he retreats from the One who is truly sufficient for him."

13. Anselm Stolz, *The Doctrine of Spiritual Perfection*, trans. Aidan Williams (Eugene, OR: Wipf & Stock, [1938] 2013), 169.

14. Ibid., 170.

15. This citation appears in his July 27, 1869, entry. Ronald H. Limbaugh and Kirsten E. Lewis, eds., *The John Muir Papers*, 1858–1957 MICROFORM (Stockton, CA: University of the Pacific, 1980).

16. John Muir, *My First Summer in the Sierra*, Sierra Club Books [1988] (Boston: Houghton Mifflin, 1911), 110.

17. My translation. Cf. Vincent A. Pizzuto, *A Cosmic Leap of Faith: An Authorial, Structural, and Theological Investigation of the Cosmic Christology in Col 1:15-20* (Leuven, Belgium: Peeters Press, 2006), 205.

18. Jürgen Moltmann, *The Crucified God* (Minneapolis: Fortress Press), 205.

19. Panayiotis Nellas, *Deification in Christ: Orthodox Perspectives on the Nature of the Human Person*, trans. Norman Russell (New York: St. Vladimir's Seminary Press, 1987), 39, notes that the real meaning of deification is Christification: "It is no accident that in his Letter to the Colossians, where he hymns Christ as 'the image of the invisible God, the firstborn of all creation' (Col 1:15), St. Paul calls on 'every man' to become 'mature in Christ' (Col 1:28), and adds that the faithful 'have come to fullness of life in Him' (Col 2:10). . . . He is not advocating an external imitation or simple ethical improvement but a real Christification."

20. Raimon Panikkar, *Christophany: The Fullness of Man*, trans. Alfred DiLascia (New York: Orbis Books, 2009), 181.

21. Paul S. Fiddes, "The Quest for a Place Which Is 'Not-a-Place': The Hiddenness of God and the Presence of God," in *Silence and the Word: Negative Theology and the Incarnation*, ed. Oliver Davies and Denys Turner (Cambridge, MA: Harvard University Press, 2002), 45.

22. Hans Urs von Balthasar, *Homo Creatus Est. Skizzen zur Theologie V.* (Einsiedeln: Johannes Verlag, 1986), 51, trans. in Raymond Gawronski, *Word and Silence: Hans Urs von Balthasar and the Spiritual Encounter Between East and West* (Grand Rapids, MI: Eerdmans, 1995), 84–85.

23. Ibid., 85.

24. See Denis Edwards, *Jesus and the Cosmos* (Mahwah, NJ: Paulist Press, 1991), 35, who notes, "According to Aquinas, creation is fundamentally

and essentially a relationship. Creatures do not have within themselves the reason for their own existence. They are contingent beings—creatures who need not exist, who cannot account for their own being." Thus, it is impossible to reverse the vine and branch analogy."

25. Gregory of Nyssa, *Oratio Catechetica Magna*, trans. J. H. Srawley (London: Society for Promoting Christian Knowledge, 1917), 79–80.

26. Nikos Kazantzakis, *Report to Greco,* trans. P. A. Bien (New York: Simon and Schuster, 1965), 191–92.

27. Karl Rahner, *Hominisation: The Evolutionary Origin of Man as a Theological Problem* (New York: Herder and Herder, 1965); Karl Rahner, "Natural Science and Reasonable Faith," in *Theological Investigations*, vol. 21, trans. Hugh M. Riley (New York: Crossroad, 1988), 37. Cf. Edwards, *Jesus and the Cosmos*, 36–38.

Chapter Three—pages 65–92

1. Fragments of Christianity's earliest tradition about the resurrection can be seen in 1 Cor 15:3-4; Rom 1:3-4; and 1 Thess 1:9-10.

2. On this development, see Joseph A. Fitzmyer, *The Gospel According to Luke (I–X)*, Anchor Bible, vol. 28 (New York: Doubleday, 1981), 305–6.

3. For a helpful summary of these endings and their implications, see Joel Marcus, *Mark 1–8*, Anchor Bible, vol. 27A (New Haven, CT: Yale University Press, 2009), 1088–96.

4. See L. Ramaroson, "Le Coeur du troisième évangile: Lc 15," *Biblica* 60 (1979): 248–60. Cf. Joseph A. Fitzmyer, *The Gospel According to Luke X–XXIV*, vol. 28A (New York: Doubleday, 1985), 1071.

5. Arthur A. Just, ed., *Luke: Ancient Christian Commentary on Scripture*, New Testament vol. 3 (Downers Grove, IL: InterVarsity Press, 2003), 247.

6. Ambrose, *Exposition of the Gospel of Luke*, 7.213–14.10; Cf. Just, *Ancient Christian Commentary on the Scriptures: New Testament*, vol. 3, 248.

7. See Luke Timothy Johnson, *The Gospel of Luke*, Sacra Pagina, ed. Daniel J. Harrington, vol. 3 (Collegeville, MN: Liturgical Press, 1991), 241.

8. Just, *Ancient Christian Commentary on the Scriptures: New Testament*, vol. 3, 251.

9. See Fitzmyer, *Luke, X–XXIV*, vol. 28A, 1086.

10. T. W. Manson, *The Sayings of Jesus as Recorded in the Gospels According to St. Matthew and St. Luke Arranged with Introduction and Commentary* (London: SCM, 1971), 286.

11. Just, *Ancient Christian Commentary on the Scriptures: New Testament*, vol. 3, 247.

12. St. Ambrose, *Exposition of The Gospel of Luke* 7.213–14 in Just, *Ancient Christian Commentary on the Scriptures: New Testament*, vol. 3, 248.

13. Thomas Merton, *The Collected Poems of Thomas Merton* (New York: New Directions, [1946] 1980), 89. Anyone who has considered Merton's social commentary understands well that he harbored no sentimental associations about the nativity.

14. Cf. Raimon Pannikar, *Christophany: The Fullness of Man*, trans. Alfred DiLascia (New York: Orbis Books, 2009), 128ff.; also Niels Henrik Gregersen, ed., *Incarnation: On the Scope and Depth of Christology* (Minneapolis, MN: Fortress Press, 2015).

15. This is the most literal translation of Matt 1:1 and is clearly intended to echo the Greek version of the Old Testament known as the SEPTUAGINT (abbreviated LXX), which uses identical Greek wording to introduce the second creation story in Gen 2:4 (*biblos geneseos* = "the book of origins").

16. Panikkar, *Christophany*, 54.

17. D. H. Lawrence, "God Is Born," in *The Complete Poems of D. H. Lawrence*, ed. Vivian de Sola Pinto and Warren Roberts (New York: Viking Press, 1971), 682–83.

18. Denis Edwards, *Jesus and the Cosmos* (Mahwah, NJ: Paulist Press, 1991), 66.

19. Pseudo-Dionysius, *The Divine Names* in *Pseudo-Dionysius: The Complete Works*, trans. Colm Luibhéid and Paul Rorem, The Classics of Western Spirituality (New York: Paulist Press, 1987), 71.

20. St. Bonaventure, *The Soul's Journey into God* in *Bonaventure*, trans. Ewert H. Cousins, The Classics of Western Spirituality (New York: Paulist Press, 1978), 103.

21. See Richard Bauckham, "The Incarnation and the Cosmic Christ," in Gregersen, *Incarnation*, 33, who observes, "Jesus, as fully human, enjoys genetic continuity with the whole human race and shares all sorts of features of the common life of humanity." This being so, we must not fail to recognize that humans share genetic continuity with all living creatures. Thus, God shares genetic continuity with all living creatures.

22. Meister Eckhart, *Sermon One* in *Meister Eckhart Sermons and Treatises*, vol. 1, ed. and trans. M. O'C. Walshe (Boston, MA: Element, 1987), 1.

23. John of the Cross, *The Selected Words of John of the Cross*, vol. 2, trans. David Lewis (New York: Cosimo Classics, 2007), §284, 595.

24. My translation. See St. Ephrem, "Hymn to Mary 11.6," in *Sancti Ephraem Syri: Hymne et Sermones*, ed. Thomas Josephus Lamy (Mechliniæ: H. Dessain, 1882–1902), §570, 316.

25. Hans Urs von Balthasar, *Prayer*, trans. Graham Harrison (San Francisco: Ignatius Press, [1955] 1986), 28.

26. See Hans Urs von Balthasar, *Love Alone Is Credible*, trans. D. C. Schindler (San Francisco: Ignatius Press, [1963] 2004), 42.

27. See Steve Moyise, *Was the Birth of Jesus According to the Scriptures* (Eugene, OR: Cascade Books, 2013), 67, who demonstrates other such parallels between Matthew's portrait of Jesus and non-canonical Jewish texts such as Philo's *Antiquities of the Jews*. Cf. Charles H. Talbert, *Matthew*, Paideia Commentaries on the New Testament (Grand Rapids, MI: Baker Academics, 2010), 38.

28. Raymond E. Brown, *The Birth of the Messiah: A Commentary on the Infancy Narratives in the Gospels of Matthew and Luke*, updated ed. (New York: Doubleday, 1993). See also Moyise, *Was the Birth of Jesus According to the Scripture?*, 67.

29. Hans Urs von Balthasar, *The Grain of Wheat*, trans. Erasmo Leiva-Merikakis (San Francisco: Ignatius Press, [1953] 1995), 42.

Chapter Four—pages 93–135

1. Douglas Burton-Christie, *The Word in the Desert: Scripture and the Quest for Holiness in Early Christian Monasticism* (New York: Oxford University Press, 1993), 193. Cf. Peter Brown, *The Making of Late Antiquity* (Cambridge, MA: Harvard University Press, 1978), 90.

2. See Athanasius, *The Life of Antony*, trans. Robert C. Gregg (New York: Paulist Press, 1980), 38, §9.

3. Cf. Benedicta Ward, trans., *The Sayings of the Desert Fathers* (Kalamazoo, MI: Cistercian Publications, 1975), 122.

4. Peter Brown, *The Making of Late Antiquity* (Cambridge, MA: Harvard University Press, 1978), 90. See especially Burton-Christie, *The Word in the Desert*, 193, to whom I am indebted for these insights.

5. Ward, *Sayings*, 3.

6. Macarius, *Homily* 43:7 cited in John Anthony McGuckin, trans., *The Book of Mystical Chapters: Meditations on the Soul's Ascent from the Desert Fathers and Other Early Christian Contemplatives* (Boston, MA: Shambhala, 2003), 54, §83.

7. Ibid., 55–56, §86.

8. Hans Urs von Balthasar, *The Glory of the Lord: Theological Aesthetics*, vol. 1: *Seeing the Form*, trans. Erasmo Leiva-Merikakis, ed. Joseph Fessio and John Riches (San Francisco: Ignatius Press, 1982), 18.

9. William Wordsworth, *Poems, in Two Volumes* (London: Printed for Longman, Hurst, Rees, and Orme, 1807), 1:122.

10. Cf. Aidan Nichols, *The Word Has Been Abroad: A Guide through Balthasar's Aesthetics* (Washington, DC: The Catholic University of America Press, 1998), 1.

11. Phil Ochs, liner notes to *Pleasures of the Harbor* (A&M Records, 1967).

12. As was famously said by Albert Camus, *Notebooks, 1935-1942* (New York: Knopf, 1963), 51, "We must live to the point of tears."

13. John Keats, "Ode on a Grecian Urn," in *The English Romantics: Major Poetry and Critical Theory*, ed. John L. Mahoney (Lexington, MA: D. C. Heath and Company, [1807] 1978), 620.

14. Cf. Olivier Clément, *The Roots of Christian Mysticism* (Hyde Park, NY: New City Press, 1995), 273–74.

15. Maximus Confessor, *Question to Thalassius* 43 (PG 90:408), trans. in Clement, *Roots*, 49.

16. Evagrius Pontus, *On Prayer*, §125.

17. Clément, *The Roots of Christian Mysticism*, 273–74.

18. Andrew Louth, *The Origins of the Christian Mystical Tradition: From Plato to Denys*, 2nd ed. (Oxford: Oxford University Press, 2007), 96–97.

19. This translation is mine. On the correct translation of *Ioudaion* as "Judeans," see John H. Elliot, "Jesus the Israelite Was Neither a 'Jew' Nor a 'Christian': On Correcting Misleading Nomenclature," *Journal for the Study of the Historical Jesus* 5 (2007): 119–54, esp. 137–40.

20. Cf. Hans Urs von Balthasar, *Heart of the World* (San Francisco: Ignatius Press, [1944] 1979), 42–44.

21. Cf. 1 Peter 2:21-25.

22. John Wortley, ed. and trans., *The Anonymous Sayings of the Desert Fathers: A Select Edition and Complete English Translation* (New York: Cambridge University Press, 2013), 233, N.355/17.22.

23. R. T. France, *The Gospel of Matthew: The New International Commentary on the New Testament* (Grand Rapids, MI: Eerdmans, 2007), 493.

24. Cf. John R. Donahue, *The Gospel of Mark*, Sacra Pagina, vol. 3, ed. Daniel J. Harrington (Collegeville, MN: Liturgical Press, 2002), 171.

25. Burton-Christie, *The Word in the Desert*, 161.

26. Ibid., 195.

27. Ward, *Sayings*, 171, §31.

28. St. Nikodimos of the Holy Mountain and St. Makarios of Corinth, *The Philokalia*, vol. 1, trans. and ed. G. E. H. Palmer, Philip Sherrard, and Kallistos Ware (New York: Faber and Faber, 1979), 14–15.

29. Harvey D. Egan, *What Are They Saying about Mysticism* (New York: Paulist Press, 1982), 92, summarizes the thought of von Balthasar, on this subject: "The highest value for the Christian is not the experience of transcendence, but the radical fidelity to the demands of daily life." See also Anselm Stolz, *The Doctrine of Spiritual Perfection*, trans. Aidan Williams (Eugene, OR: Wipf & Stock, [1938] 2013), 42ff. who argues similarly.

30. See Burton-Christie, *The Word in the Desert*, 223.

31. Ibid., 222.

32. Ruth Burrows, *Before the Living God* (London: Sheed and Ward, 1975), 75.

33. Hans Urs von Balthasar, *The Grain of Wheat*, trans. Erasmo Leiva-Merikakis (San Francisco: Ignatius Press, [1953] 1995), 42.

34. Pseudo-Macarius, *The Fifty Spiritual Homilies and The Great Letter*, trans. George A. Maloney, Classics of Western Spirituality (New York: Paulist Press, 1992), 144.

Chapter Five—pages 136–74

1. Benedicta Ward, ed. and trans., *The Sayings of the Desert Fathers* (Kalamazoo, MI: Cistercian Publications, 1975), XXIV-XXV.

2. Francis de Sales, *An Introduction to the Devout Life*, trans. John K. Ryan, rev. ed. (New York: Doubleday, [1966] 1972), 97.

3. Francis of Assisi, *Mirror of Perfection*, Chapter 65 in *St. Francis of Assisi: Writings and Early Biographies: English Omnibus of Sources for the Life of St. Francis*, ed. and trans. Marion Alphonse Habig and John R. H. Moorman (London: Society for Promoting Christian Knowledge, 1979), 1191–92.

4. Evelyn Underhill, *Mysticism: A Study of the Nature and Development of Man's Spiritual Consciousness* (New York: E. P. Dutton and Company, 1912), 52–82, emphasized the idea that the life of contemplation was universally available to all who would undertake it. Moreover, her approach to the field of psychology anticipated the more popular integration of spirituality and psychology in modern contemplative literature.

5. Meister Eckhart, *Sermons and Treatises*, vol. 3, "The Talks of Instruction 6," trans. M O'C. Walshe (Boston: Element, 1987), 16. Cf. Ibid., *Sermons and Treatises*, vol. 1, "Sermon 69," trans. M O'C. Walshe (Boston: Element, 1987), 165–71.

6. Cf. Thomas Merton, *New Seeds of Contemplation* (New York: New Directions, 1961), 14. The parable of the Sower (Matt 13:1-15) provides a helpful analogy.

7. Origen, *On Prayer*, 12, *Patrologia Graeca* 11:452, in Olivier Clément, *The Roots of Christian Mysticism*, trans. Theodore Berkeley and Jeremy Hummerstone (Hyde Park, NY: New City Press, 1995), 212.

8. See, for example, Lev Gillet, *On the Invocation of the Name of Jesus* (Springfield, IL: Templegate, 1985); Martin Laird, *Into the Silent Land: A Guide to the Christian Practice of Contemplation* (New York: Oxford University Press, 2006); Irma Zaleski, *Living the Jesus Prayer* (Ontario: Novalis, 2011); Ignatius Brianchaninov, *On the Prayer of Jesus*, trans. Father Lazarus (Boston: New Seeds, 2005).

9. Basil of Caesarea, *On the Holy Spirit*, Chap. 12, Popular Patristic Series 42, trans. Stephen Hildebrand (Yonkers, NY: St. Vladimir's Seminary Press, 2011), 59.

10. Walter Burghardt, "Contemplation: A Long, Loving Look at the Real," *Church* 5 (Winter 1989): 15. Cf. William McNamara, *Wild and Robust: The Adventure of Christian Humanism* (Cambridge, MA: Cowley Publications, 2006).

11. See further, Georgios I. Mantzaridis, *The Deification of Man: St. Gregory Palamas and the Orthodox Tradition*, trans. Liadian Sherrard (Crestwood, NY: St. Vladimir's Seminary Press, 1984), 41–60; Andrew

Hofer, "Introduction: Becoming Icons of Christ," in *Divinization: Becoming Icons of Christ Through the Liturgy*, ed. Andrew Hofer (Chicago: Hillenbrand Books, 2015), 7–11.

12. Augustine, *Sermon 272* (PL 38:1247), in Anthony J. Kelly, "'The Body of Christ: Amen!': The Expanding Incarnation," *Theological Studies* 71 (2010): 729–816, at 800. Cf. Augustine, *The Works of Saint Augustine: A Translation for the 21st Century; Sermons 3:7, (230–272B) on the Liturgical Seasons*, Sermon 272, trans. Edmund Hill, John E. Rotelle, and Boniface Ramsey (Brooklyn, NY: New City Press, 1990), 300.

13. Aldous Huxley, *Grey Eminence* (New York: Harper and Brothers, 1941), 101. Cf. William Johnston, *The Still Point: Reflections on Zen and Christian Mysticism* (New York: Fordham University Press, 1970), 145.

14. Ibid., 147–48.

15. St. John of the Cross, *The Ascent of Mount Carmel*, in *The Collected Works of Saint John of the Cross*, rev. ed., ed. and trans. Kieran Kavanaugh and Otilio Rodriguez (Washington, DC: ICS Publications, 1991), 164–65, 5.6.

16. Origen, *Homilies on Luke: Fragments on Luke*, trans. Joseph T. Lienhard in *The Fathers of the Church*, v. 94 (Washington, DC: Catholic University of America Press, 1996), 192–93.

17. See Augustine of Hippo, "Sermon 103" and "Sermon 104," in *The Works of St. Augustine: A Translation for the 21st Century: Sermons III/4 (94a–147a) on the New Testament*, ed. John E. Rotrans, trans. Edmund Hill (Brooklyn, NY: New City Press, 1991), 76–87.

18. Thomas Aquinas, *Summa Theologiae*, v. 47: *The Pastoral and Religious Lives* (2a2ae, 183–9), trans. Jordan Aumann, (New York: McGraw-Hill, 1973), 205.

19. Bernard McGinn, ed., *Meister Eckhart: Teacher and Preacher*, The Classics of Western Spirituality (Mahwah, NJ: Paulist Press, 1986), 338.

20. Ibid., 339.

21. Eckhart, "Sermon 13(b)," vol. 1, trans. M O'C. Walshe, 117–18.

22. Though penned over fifty years ago, Thomas Merton's essay "The Inner Experience: Problems of the Contemplative Life" (VII), *Cistercian Studies* 19, no. 3 (1984): 267–82, offers a critique and comparison between the monastic life and contemplative life in the world that still resonates today.

23. McGinn, *Meister Eckhart*, 340.

24. Henri de Lubac, *Catholicism: Christ and the Common Destiny of Man* (San Francisco: Ignatius Press, 1988), 76. See further, Adam G. Cooper, *Naturally Human, Supernaturally God: Deification in Pre-Conciliar Catholicism* (Minneapolis: Fortress Press, 2014), 171–81.

25. Emile Mersch, *The Whole Christ: The Historical Development of the Doctrine of the Mystical Body in Scripture and Tradition*, trans. John R. Kelly (Milwaukee, WI: Bruce, 1938), 518.

26. McGinn, *Meister Eckhart*, 344.

27. Edmund Colledge and Bernard McGinn, trans., *Meister Eckhart: The Essential Sermons, Commentaries, Treatises, and Defense*, The Classics of Western Spirituality (Mahwah, NJ: Paulist Press, 1981), 285.

28. See John Anthony McCuckin, ed. and trans., *The Book of Mystical Chapters: Meditations on the Soul's Ascent from the Desert Fathers and Other Early Christian Contemplatives* (Boston: Shambhala, 2002), §79, 53.

29. Meister Eckhart, *Sermons and Treatises*, vol. 1, "Sermon 13(b)," trans. M O'C. Walshe (Boston: Element, 1987), 117.

30. Meister Eckhart, "On Detachment," in Colledge and McGinn, *Meister Eckhart*, 292.

31. Jean Sulivan, *Morning Light: The Spiritual Journal of Jean Sulivan* (New York: Paulist Press, 1988), 34.

32. John 21:1-8 also narrates a version of this story (most similar to Luke) but contextualizes it as a resurrection narrative rather than a call to discipleship. For his version of Jesus' calling of the disciples see John 1:35-51.

33. S. Motyer, "The Rending of the Veil: A Markan Pentecost," NTS 33 (1987): 155–57. Cf. Joel Marcus, *Mark 8–16: A New Translation with Introduction and Commentary*, Anchor Yale Bible, vol. 27A (New Haven, CT: Yale University Press, 2009), 1067.

34. Ibid., 1057, 1066–68.

35. For a concise and accessible summary of the debate about which veil Mark was referring to, see David Ulansey, "The Heavenly Veil Torn: Mark's Cosmic 'Inclusio,'" *Journal of Biblical Literature* 110, no. 1 (Spring 1991): 123–25.

36. Flavius Josephus, *Jewish War*, 5:212–14. Cf. Exod 26:21-36; 38:18-20; Lev 16:2; Mark 15:38. Emphasis is mine.

37. Marcus, *Mark 8–16*, 1057.

38. Raymond Gawronski, *Word and Silence: Hans Urs von Balthasar and the Spiritual Encounter between East and West* (Grand Rapids, MI: Eerdmans, 1995), 102–3.

39. Ibid., 103.

40. Denys Turner, "Apophaticism, Idolatry and the Claims of Reason," in *Silence and the Word: Negative Theology and Incarnation*, ed. Oliver Davies and Denys Turner (Cambridge, NY: Cambridge University Press, 2002), 17–20.

41. St. Thomas Aquinas, *Expositio in Boethii* De Trinitate, q. 1, a. 2, ad. 1, *"In finem nostrae cognitionis Deum tamquam ignotum cognoscimus."* See in English, *The Trinity and the Unicity of the Intellect*, q. 1., a. 2, ad. 1, trans. Rose Emmanuella Brennan (St. Louis, MO: B. Herder, 1946), 27–28. Cf. Pseudo-Dionysius, *Mystical Theology*, Chap. 1, *The Classics of Western Spirituality*, trans. Colm Luibheid, 4.1 (New York: Paulist Press, 1987), 135, whom Augustine was referencing.

42. Clément, *The Roots of Christian Mysticism*, 38.

Appendix—pages 175–82

1. See Henri DeLubac, *Theological Fragments* (San Francisco: Ignatius Press, 1989), 49, who observes that Christian mysticism is to be found in the New Testament and is not "a late graft on the trunk of the Christian tree."

2. See Andrew Louth, *The Origins of Christian Mystical Tradition: From Plato to Denys*, 2nd ed. (Oxford: University Press, 2007), 200–214, to whom I am indebted for his excellent summation of the evolution of mysticism in Christianity. See Bernard McGinn, *The Presence of God: A History of Western Mysticism*, vol. 1: *The Foundations of Mysticism: Origins to the Fifth Century* (New York: Crossroad, 1992), 62–83, where he discusses the extent to which Christianity might be called "mystical," and 265–343, where McGinn summarizes modern approaches to mysticism in the Western church under the helpful categories of "The Theological," "The Philosophical," and "The Comparativist and Psychological." See also Harvey D. Eagan, *What Are They Saying about Mysticism* (New York: Paulist Press, 1982), which is a short and accessible volume on approaches to mysticism today.

3. Louis Bouyer, "Mysticism: An Essay on the History of the World," in *Understanding Mysticism*, ed. Richard Woods (New York: Image Books, 1980), 43.

4. Louth, *The Origins of the Christian Mystical Tradition*, 204–5.

5. Bouyer, "Mysticism," 44.

6. Henri de Lubac, *Medieval Exegesis: The Four Senses of Scripture*, vol. 2, trans. E. M. Macierowski (Grand Rapids, MI: Eerdmans [1959] 2000), 25.

7. Bouyer, "Mysticism," 50–51.

8. Louth, *The Origins of the Christian Mystical Tradition*, 214.

9. De Lubac, *Medieval Exegesis*, vol. 2, 26–27.

10. Ibid., 23.

11. Bouyer, "Mysticism," 52–53.

12. Louth, *The Origins of the Christian Mystical Tradition*, 211.

13. Ibid., 210–11. See Rom 1:1 and Gal 1:11-12 among others, however, which give evidence of a similar tension between the established church in Jerusalem (i.e., Peter and the apostles) and the "Apostle" Paul who never knew Jesus in the course of his lifetime (1 Cor 15:8). Thus, Paul himself claims to have had extraordinary experiences of grace and to have been called to be an Apostle in a personal encounter with the Risen Lord. This it seems was ultimately recognized by the original apostles (Gal 2:6-10), the authorities of the nascent church. While it would be anachronistic to call Paul a "mystic," the pattern of a direct revelation from God circumventing the channels of church authority is as old as Christianity itself.

14. McGinn, *Foundations*, 1:266–67.

15. Ibid., xvi. Cf. Friedrich Hügel, *The Mystical Element of Religion: As Studied in Saint Catherine of Genoa and Her Friends* (New York: E.P. Dutton), 1908.

16. Louth, *The Origins of the Christian Mystical Tradition*, 212.

Index

admirabile commercium: 13
alter Christus: 31, 34, 151–52, 183
Ambrose of Milan: 72, 76
asceticism: 5, 28, 46, 93–135
Athanasius of Alexandria: 13, 95, 115
Augustine of Hippo: 20, 25–27, 84, 146–47, 155
awakening: 12, 40, 139

baptism: 24, 47, 69, 94–95, 177–79
Basil of Caesarea: 145
Bauckham, Richard: 85n21
beauty: xvi, 39–45, 95, 105–119
Body of Christ: 11, 16, 25, 28–31, 32, 74, 111, 146, 158
Boulgakov, Serge: 37n1
Bouyer, Louis: 175, 176, 179
Brianchaninov, Ignatius: 143n8
Brown, Peter: 95n1, 96n4
Brown, Raymond E.: 90n28
Burghardt, Walter: 145
Burrows, Ruth: 127, 128
Burton-Christie, Douglas: 126

Casey, Michael: 14n10
Christ-event: 15, 29, 54, 176
Christophany: 21
Clement of Alexandria: 24
Clément, Olivier: 5, 24, 113, 173
Collins, Paul M.: 22
contemplation: xiv, 10, 40, 56, 112, 115, 134, 142, 145, 177, 184
Cooper, Adam: 13n7, 17n15, 158n24
Cosmic Christ: 16, 17, 58

Davies, Oliver: 17, 18,
deification: xv, xvi, 13–14, 16, 19–22; (and 2 Pet 1:4) 22–26; (and Acts 9:4) 26–28; (and 1 Cor 12:12–27) 28–31; (and John 15:5) 31–32; 85, 146, 150, 153, 184
de Lubac, Henri: 17, 158, 179
de Sales, Francis: 138
demons: 90–93; (and baptism) 94–95; (and Desert Mothers and Fathers) 96–97, 115; (and “renegades”) 98–100; (and “parasites”) 100–103; (and Christ) 116–19; (and exorcism) 119–22
Dionysius, Pseudo-: 19, 40, 42, 83, 132, 179

divinization: xv, 13, 21, 30, 32, 37, 114, 185
Donahue, John R.: 158n24

Eckhart, Meister: xvi, 85, 87, 141–42, 154, 155–60
Edwards, Denis: 83
Edwards, Jonathan: 41
Egan, Harvey: 159n29
ego: xv, 45–46, 48–49, 62, 77, 88, 90, 185
Elliot, John H.: 117n19
embodiment: 19, 79, 123, 124, 138, 161
Eucharist: 146, 147, 178–79
Evagrius Pontus: 113
exegesis: 66, 185

false self: 28, 44–61, 88, 90, 91, 103, 152, 185
Fiddes, Paul: 55
Finlan, Stephen: 25
Fitzmyer, Joseph A.: 196
Francis of Assisi: 138

Gillet, Lev: 143n8
Gawronski, Raymond, SJ: 171, 172
Gregory of Nazianzus: 84
Gregory of Nyssa: 57–58

Harrington, Daniel: 72n7, 158n24
Hofer, Andrew: 146n11
Hügel, Friedrich: 180n15
Huxley, Aldous: 148

imago Dei: 8
incarnatio continua: 12, 26, 29, 139, 158, 161, 174
incarnation: xiii, xv, 7, 10–18, 25, 26, 29, 31, 32, 34, 37, 53–58, 64, 65–92, 112, 115, 118, 152, 161, 167, 170, 173, 174, 181

John of the Cross: 86, 153, 180, 181
John Paul II: 190
Johnson, Luke Timothy: 196
Josephus, Flavius: 169

Kazantzakis, Nikos: 58–59
Keats, John: 108
Kelly, Anthony J.: 15, 16, 30
kenosis: 38, 84, 115, 173, 174, 186
kingdom of God: 57, 77, 104–5, 162

Laird, Martin: 143n8
liturgy: 141, 145–46, 178–80
Lossky, Vladimir: 15
Louth, Andrew: 115, 179, 181

Macarius of Egypt: 96–97, 126, 132, 133, 135
Manson, T. W.: 74
Mantzaridis, Georgios I.: 146 n11
Maximus Confessor: 159
McGinn, Bernard: 180
Mersch, Emile: 192, 203
Merton, Thomas: 65, 78, 142
Mindfulness: 8
Moyise, Steve: 89n27
Mosser, Carl: 192

Motyer, Stephen: 168
Muir, John: 52, 53
mysticism: xv, 3, 7–21, 115, 148–49, 175–82, 187
myth: xv–xvi, 36, 39, 42, 43–45, 51–52, 70, 73, 152

Nellas, Panayiotis: 195
Nichols, Aidan: 107n10
Nicene Creed: 19, 20

Ochs, Phil: 107
Origen of Alexandria: 142, 154, 177
other Christs: xvi, 14, 108, 137, 146, 147

Panikkar, Raimon: 12, 21, 25, 55, 81
Peterson, Eugene H.: 10
Pseudo-Dionysius: 19, 83, 179

Rahner, Karl: 61
Russell, Norman: 23n28, 24n30

Stolz, Anselm: 47
Sulivan, Jean: 161
Symeon the New Theologian: 12–13, 17, 32, 98

telos: 14, 126, 187
theology of dress: 47, 48, 74, 152
theosis: 13, 185, 187
Thomas Aquinas: 44, 155, 173
Trinity: 19–21, 81, 84, 145, 186, 187
Turner, Denys: 19, 172

Ulansey, David: 169n35
Underhill, Evelyn: 138n4

von Balthasar, Hans Urs: 56, 86, 92, 107, 108, 131, 171

Ward, Benedicta: 137, 143
Wordsworth, William: 107
Wortley, John: 157n22

Zaleski, Irma: 143n8